My
Bauhaus
Mein
Bauhaus

My Bauhaus

100 Architects on the 100th Anniversary of a Myth

Mein Bauhaus

100 Architekten zum 100. Geburtstag eines Mythos

Sandra Hofmeister (Ed. / Hg.)

Edition **DETAIL**

My Bauhaus
Mein Bauhaus

A School of Life
On the relevance of the Bauhaus
for architecture today
Sandra Hofmeister

Schule des Lebens
Zur Relevanz des Bauhaus für die
Architektur von heute
Sandra Hofmeister

The history of the Bauhaus is full of hopes and ideals. Together, they consolidate the idea that architecture and design can transform society and improve or even remake the world. The curriculum at the experimental, state-run Bauhaus school was designed to unite life, craft and art – it was not limited to individual disciplines. Not only did the comprehensive educational programme include subjects such as composition, construction and craft techniques, but also dietary guidelines and morning gymnastics.

The Bauhaus was a school of life. And architecture played a key role, right from the start. In its founding manifesto of 1919, the first Bauhaus director, Walter Gropius, stated: "The ultimate aim of creative activity is building." Despite all the changes and reorientation that the Bauhaus underwent during its nearly 14 years of existence, its primary aim was always to bring together the various disciplines and workshops as a kind of test laboratory for the building of the future. With Hannes Meyer and Ludwig Mies van der Rohe as its later directors, the institution was headed by three avant-garde architects until its closure in 1933.

There are many different stories, anecdotes and fates that have written the 100-year history of the Bauhaus and which continue to shape its reception. The Bauhaus has long since become a myth. Its forward-looking goals and principles live on

Die Geschichte des Bauhaus besteht aus Hoffnungen und Idealen. In ihnen verdichtet sich die Idee, dass Architektur und Gestaltung die Gesellschaft verändern und die Welt verbessern oder gar neu erschaffen können. Entsprechend war die Lehre an der staatlichen Schule darauf ausgerichtet, Leben, Handwerk und Kunst zusammenzuführen – das Experiment Bauhaus beschränkte sich nicht auf einzelne Disziplinen. Deshalb wurde nicht nur in Komposition, Konstruktion oder handwerklichen Techniken unterrichtet, die umfassende Ausbildung bezog auch Ernährungsregeln und morgendliche Turnübungen mit ein.

Das Bauhaus war eine Schule des Lebens. Der Architektur kam dabei von Anfang an eine Schlüsselrolle zu. Im Gründungsmanifest von 1919 hält der erste Bauhaus-Direktor Walter Gropius fest: „Das Endziel der bildnerischen Tätigkeit ist der Bau." Trotz aller Veränderungen und Neuausrichtungen, die das Bauhaus in seiner knapp 14-jährigen Geschichte erfuhr, blieb sein erstes Ziel stets die Zusammenführung der unterschiedlichen Bereiche und Werkstätten in einer Art Versuchslabor für den Bau der Zukunft. Mit Hannes Meyer und Ludwig Mies van der Rohe als weiteren Direktoren wurde die Institution bis zu ihrer Schließung im Jahr 1933 von drei Architekten der Avantgarde geleitet.

Es gibt viele einzelne Geschichten, Anekdoten und Schicksale, welche die 100-jährige Geschichte des Bauhaus geschrieben haben und seine Rezeption auch weiterhin fortschreiben.

everywhere in scattered fragments. Teachers and students from
Weimar, Dessau and Berlin brought the Bauhaus philosophy
to Palestine and the United States, to Russia and Turkey. Today,
the Bauhaus is part of the historical cultural heritage in many
countries. It has inspired regional phenomena such as "White
Modernism" in Tel Aviv and high-rise architecture in Chicago. Its
avant-garde experiment became an international model and, in
some areas, the influence of the Bauhaus can still be felt today.
The concept of teaching through workshops at German universities, the close relationships between industry, craft and architecture, and the practice of modular construction, are approaches
and models that reflect the fundamental concepts of the Bauhaus.
Attitudes characteristic of the Bauhaus are also evident in the
understanding of architecture as a team effort, in participatory
building processes and in the joy of experimentation. Nevertheless,
especially in architecture, the idea of the Bauhaus is usually over-
taken by reality – especially when social values are exchanged for
profits and returns as a building project's true aim.
        Anyone who ponders the importance of the Bauhaus for archi-
tecture today will soon realize that how the Bauhaus itself is
understood is quite contradictory. The term "Bauhaus" is associated
with a wide range of concepts, yet very narrowly defined.

Das Bauhaus ist längst zu einem Mythos geworden, seine Ideale und
hoffnungsvollen Ziele leben allenthalben in einzelnen Fragmenten
weiter. Lehrer und Schüler aus Weimar, Dessau oder Berlin haben
die Bauhaus-Idee nach Palästina und in die USA, nach Russland und
in die Türkei getragen. Heute zählt das Bauhaus in vielen Ländern
zum historischen Kulturerbe, es hat regionale Phänomene wie die
Weiße Moderne in Tel Aviv oder die Hochhausarchitektur in Chicago
beflügelt. Aus einem Experiment der Avantgarde wurde ein internationales Leitbild, in manchen Bereichen ist der Einfluss des Bauhaus
bis heute präsent. Das Werkstatt-Unterrichtskonzept an deutschen
Hochschulen, die enge Verquickung von Industrie, Handwerk und
Architektur oder die Praxis des modularen Bauens sind Methoden
und Ideale, in denen sich Grundgedanken des Bauhaus wiederfin-
den. Ebenso zeigen sich im Verständnis von Architektur als Team-
leistung, in partizipatorischen Prozessen am Bau oder in der Freude
am Experimentieren Haltungen, die am Bauhaus Usus waren. Trotz-
dem wird die Idee des Bauhaus gerade in der Architektur meistens
von der Realität überholt – besonders dann, wenn gesellschaftliche
Ideale gegen Profit und Rendite als Ziele von Bauvorhaben ausge-
tauscht werden.
        Wer sich nach der Bedeutung des Bauhaus für die Architektur
von heute fragt, wird schnell erkennen, dass das Verständnis der
Bauhaus-Idee sehr widersprüchlich ausfällt. Der Begriff „Bauhaus"
wird nicht selten mit beliebigen Konzepten in Verbindung gebracht

Sometimes the Bauhaus is cited as a commitment to flat roofs or as an architectural form; sometimes it is used as a label to sell real estate or to describe a furnishing style. But such flourishes have nothing to do with the notion of the Bauhaus as a school of life.

The 100th anniversary of the Bauhaus has prompted architects from all over the world to consider its significance in everyday life. What do they associate with the Bauhaus? Are its principles relevant to their work? What personal experiences do they have that relate to the Bauhaus? Is the Bauhaus a reference for their designs, processes or identity? This book brings together 100 voices of architects from several continents and many countries, including Brazil, China, India and Germany. Some of the personal experiences related in these brief texts are family stories that relate directly to the historical Bauhaus. Some architects are critical of the Bauhaus, while others are committed to its concrete ideas. Ultimately, the contributions in this book do more than reflect current views of the Bauhaus. They also reveal much about the architectural understanding of their authors. To mark the 100th anniversary of the Bauhaus, we compiled these contributions into a kind of dedication album. This resulting book sheds light on the relevance of the Bauhaus for architecture today.

und in seiner Bedeutung dramatisch verkürzt. Mal wird das Bauhaus als Bekenntnis zum Flachdach oder als architektonische Form zitiert, mal bezeichnet es ein Verkaufslabel für Immobilen oder einen Einrichtungsstil. Mit der Bauhaus-Idee als Schule des Lebens haben diese Blüten nichts zu tun.

Der 100-jährige Geburtstag des Bauhaus gibt Anlass dazu, Architekten aus aller Welt nach seiner Bedeutung im Alltag zu fragen. Was assoziieren sie mit dem Bauhaus? Ist seine Idee relevant für ihre Arbeit? Inwiefern haben sie persönliche Erfahrungen gemacht, die sich mit dem Bauhaus in Verbindung bringen lassen? Ist das Bauhaus überhaupt eine Bezugsgröße für ihre Entwürfe, für Prozesse oder ihr Selbstverständnis? Dieses Buch fasst 100 Stimmen von Architekten aus mehreren Kontinenten und vielen Ländern zusammen, darunter China und Brasilien, Indien und Deutschland. Manche persönlichen Erfahrungen, die in den Kurzbeiträgen dargelegt werden, sind Familiengeschichten, die mit dem historischen Bauhaus zu tun haben. Manche Architekten positionieren sich kritisch dem Bauhaus gegenüber, andere bekennen sich zu konkreten Ideen. Letztlich geben die Beiträge in der Gesamtschau nicht nur ein aktuelles Stimmungsbild zum Bauhaus ab. Sie verraten darüber hinaus viel über das Architekturverständnis ihrer Autoren. Zum 100. Geburtstag des Bauhaus haben wir diese Beiträge in einer Art Poesiealbum zusammengefasst. So entstand ein Buch, das einen Blick auf die Relevanz des Bauhaus für die Architektur von heute wirft.

100
Voices
100
Stimmen

Challenges of change

I admire the Bauhaus for its ability to formulate a strong, coherent narrative about the arts. It has proven to have a long-lasting effect that will impact architects and designers for generations. The ability to come up with a new approach radically transforming the perception of architecture and design, but also confronting the prevailing norms and traditions of society was truly remarkable. Ensuring innovation and development, finding new ways and methods, only happens if people continuously question prevailing ideas and standards. I'm driven by curiosity and see potential in the challenges of change, as I believe stagnation is our worst enemy. I embrace new technology and am constantly searching for new tools and materials to make sure we do things better, wiser and more sustainably. The equation of architecture, art and design with the aim of creating high-quality buildings as a kind of Gesamtkunstwerk has been a great source of inspiration for me. For me, the art forms are entwined and complement each other. I find great inspiration in art and nature for the architecture I do. One example is the depicted master plan. When I encountered an artist's work that had resembling characteristics, I realized that using similar geometric forms for the proposed buildings would fit the outline of the site perfectly with their combination of soft curves.

Herausforderungen des Wandels

Ich bewundere das Bauhaus für seine Fähigkeit, ein starkes, stimmiges Narrativ der Künste zu formulieren. Es hat erwiesenermaßen eine Langzeitwirkung entfaltet, die Architekten und Designer auf Generationen hin beeinflussen wird. Diese Fähigkeit, einen Ansatz zu entwickeln, der die Wahrnehmung von Architektur und Gestaltung radikal verändern, aber auch den herrschenden gesellschaftlichen Normen und Traditionen entgegentreten sollte, war absolut bemerkenswert. Innovation und Entwicklung, neue Arbeitsweisen und Methoden entstehen nur, wenn Menschen kontinuierlich gängige Vorstellungen und Maßstäbe in Frage stellen. Mein Antrieb ist meine Neugier: Ich sehe die Herausforderungen des Wandels als Potenzial, weil Stagnation meiner Ansicht nach unser schlimmster Feind ist. Ich begrüße neue Technologien und suche ständig nach neuen Werkzeugen und Materialien, um sicherzustellen, dass wir besser, klüger und nachhaltiger vorgehen. Die Gleichsetzung von Architektur, Kunst und Gestaltung mit dem Ziel hochwertiger Bauten als einer Art Gesamtkunstwerk ist für mich eine große Inspirationsquelle. Alle Kunstformen sind in meinen Augen miteinander verflochten und ergänzen einander. Für die Architektur, die ich schaffe, lasse ich mich sehr von Kunst und Natur inspirieren. Ein Beispiel dafür ist der hier abgebildete Masterplan. Als ich auf das Werk eines Künstlers stieß, der mit gleichartigen Strukturen arbeitete, wurde mir klar, dass die Verwendung ähnlicher geometrischer Formen für die vorgesehenen Gebäude perfekt zur Gliederung des Geländes mit seiner Mischung aus sanft geschwungenen Linien passen würde.

Kim Herforth Nielsen

Freedom in the air

The image of Russian soldiers drinking in the basement bar of the Bauhaus in Dessau is more likely to evoke black and white archive photographs; maybe taken a few years after the famous images of a Nazi signage desecrating the great typography which had embodied both the building and its short heroic spirit in the late 1920s.

However, on this occasion it was the summer of 1992. The coup d'état that imprisoned Gorbachev for a long weekend cut the chain of command from Moscow to the Russian military beside the Bauhaus. So why not go drinking in the modern palace next door?

Although it was well past its glory days, the Bauhaus remained a powerful magnet during those strange years after the fall of the Berlin wall. Buried in deepest East Germany, the Bauhaus now attracted a motley crew of students, artists and performers to see and participate in the greatest shift in the European centre of gravity in a generation. We were all between 18 and 30. We came from Germany, east and west, Britain, France, Finland, USA, Canada, Russia, Turkey and a Swiss cabinet maker and punk chef – if my memory serves me correctly. We were there for all sorts of reasons: urban renewal projects in Dessau Nord, experimental theatre, architecture courses which did not appear to have either students or teachers, and others who had simply floated in on currents of European politics. When not in the Bauhaus café, we worked/drank in a bar/artist collective in Dessau Nord. We made open-air cinemas in vacant plots destined for Plattenbau that would now never come. We swam naked in the lake near the Masters' Houses which were not at all masterful but just about recognizable under their GDR pitched roofs and rabbit hutch annexes.

We moved into the empty 19th-century townhouses of Dessau Nord, abandoned in haste for the west in case the wall should be re-erected – nobody was really sure of anything. We performed theatre, dance and music in abandoned factories and in the Bauhaus theatre, opening the rear wall into the refectory as Gropius had designed it. We made furniture in the neighbouring workshop out of the debris of Communism. We felt a momentary freedom, set apart from east or west. Despite the tumultuous 60 years that separated us from the real Bauhaus, those black and white walls and curtains of steel and glass still felt like a sanctuary for that freedom where soldiers without generals could drink a beer alongside everyone else and believe in the future, just before it became an official part of the past.

Die Idee der Freiheit

Die ruhmreichen Tage des Bauhaus waren im Sommer 1992 längst Geschichte. Dennoch übte das Gebäude in dieser seltsamen Zeit nach dem Fall der Mauer noch immer eine starke Faszination aus. Im hinterletzten Winkel Ostdeutschlands gelegen, hatte das Bauhaus eine buntgemischte Schar von Studenten, Künstlern und Kreativen angezogen, um die damalige, seit einer Generation wohl größte Verschiebung des politischen Gleichgewichts im Herzen Europas mitzuerleben und mitzugestalten. Wir waren alle zwischen 18 und 30 Jahre alt und kamen aus Deutschland, Ost und West, Großbritannien, Frankreich, Finnland, den USA, Kanada, Russland, der Türkei – und wenn ich mich recht entsinne, waren sogar ein Schweizer Schreiner und ein kochender Punk dabei. Wir waren aus den verschiedensten Gründen hier: von Stadterneuerungsprojekten in Dessau-Nord bis zu experimentellem Theater oder Architekturveranstaltungen ohne Studenten und Dozenten. Wir zeigten Open-Air-Filme auf unbebauten Grundstücken. Wir badeten nackt im See gleich in der Nähe der Meisterhäuser, die mit ihren DDR-Giebeldächern und den angebauten Kaninchenställen gerade noch als solche erkennbar und kein bisschen meisterhaft waren. Wir quartierten uns ein in die Reihenhäuser aus dem 19. Jahrhundert in Dessau-Nord, die von den Menschen in großer Eile Richtung Westen verlassen worden waren. Wir veranstalteten Theater, Tanz und Musik in verlassenen Fabriken und auf der Bauhaus-Bühne, entfernten die Rückwand zur Mensa, so wie Gropius es ursprünglich entworfen hatte. Und aus den Trümmern des Kommunismus bauten wir Möbel in der Werkstatt nebenan.

Wir spürten und genossen diesen kurzen historischen Moment in offenem Terrain jenseits von Ost und West. Trotz der turbulenten 60 Jahre, die uns vom „echten" Bauhaus trennten, verkörperten diese schwarzweißen Wände der Häuser mit ihren Stahl- und Glasfassaden noch immer das Ideal von Freiheit – einer Freiheit, in der Soldaten ohne ihre Generäle zusammen mit allen anderen Menschen ein Bier trinken und an die Zukunft glauben konnten, kurz bevor sie zum offiziellen Teil der Vergangenheit erklärt wurde.

Tom Emerson

My friend LJ Ruel in a sunflower field, which we planted behind the Bauhaus, sitting on one of
the chairs we made (video still, above);
The Bauhaus entrance: woman from the stage design class, me and Joeff (below)
Mein Freund LJ Ruel im Sonnenblumenfeld, das wir hinter dem Bauhaus-Gebäude gepflanzt
haben, in einem unserer Stühle (Filmstill, oben);
Der Bauhaus-Eingang: Frau aus der Bühnenklasse, ich und Joeff (unten)

Bauhaus lessons

At the University of Applied Arts in Vienna, Friedrich Achleitner opened my eyes to Bauhaus design, the all-encompassing vision that touches everything, down to a font. Two years earlier, as an exchange student in Chicago planning to become a choreographer, I stumbled into 860–880 Lake Shore Drive and discovered the world of Mies: openings instead of windows, blades instead of walls. This lesson on pure space sparked my imagination. I returned to Vienna with a new plan: to study architecture. Our first field trip at the Angewandte took us to Villa Tugendhat in Brno. The way Mies connected indoor and outdoor space, extending the architectural idea of the building to the entire site, was a revelation.

Thinking about the lasting impact that Mies has had on my own design practice, the underlying question remains: How can I do more, only to arrive at less? But how fortunate I am to practice in Los Angeles, where it is also possible to engage with the Bauhaus legacy through archival documents acquired by the Getty Research Institute. How surprising, to come upon Mies's letter announcing the closure of Dessau, along with the student and faculty communications leading up to it. How alarming, that 100 years later, apathy, conformism, intolerance and hatred still abound.

It's no surprise that the Bauhaus has yet another timely lesson for architects today: we cannot afford not to take a political stand.

Lernen vom Bauhaus

Als Studentin der Angewandten in Wien öffnete Friedrich Achleitner meine Augen für das Bauhaus-Design als allumfassende Vision, die bis hin zum Schriftsatz alles berührt. Zwei Jahre davor als Austauschstudentin in Chicago wollte ich eigentlich Choreografin werden, doch da stolperte ich in 860–880 Lake Shore Drive und entdeckte die Welt von Mies: Offene Flächen statt Fenster, freistehende Wandscheiben statt Wände. Die Idee vom befreiten Raum entfesselte meine Inspiration. Ich kehrte also mit einem neuen Plan nach Wien zurück und studierte Architektur. Unsere erste Studienreise an der Angewandten führte uns zur Villa Tugendhat nach Brünn. Wie Mies hier den Innenraum mit dem Außenraum verwoben hat und so die architektonische Leitidee auf das gesamte Grundstück transponierte, war eine nachhaltige Erfahrung für mich.

Mies blieb ein bestimmender Einfluß auf meine Praxis, und damit einhergehend stellt sich mir immer die Frage – what can I do more, only to arrive at less? Was für ein glücklicher Zufall, in Los Angeles zu leben, wo es möglich ist, das Bauhaus-Vermächtnis anhand von Originaldokumenten in der Sammlung des Getty Research Institute zu studieren. Wie überraschend, in diesem Zusammenhang den Brief von Mies mit der Ankündigung der Schließung von Dessau zu finden sowie die Korrespondenz zwischen Studenten und Fakultät im Vorfeld dazu. Wie alarmierend jedoch, dass uns hundert Jahre später noch immer Apathie, Konformismus, Intoleranz und Hass bestimmen. Auch deshalb hat die Lehre des Bauhaus bis heute in keiner Hinsicht an Relevanz verloren: Wir können es uns de facto nicht leisten, politisch nicht Position zu beziehen.

Andrea Lenardin

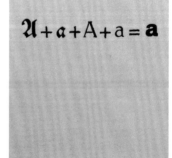

Franz Roh „warum 4 alphabete, wenn sie alle gleich ausgesprochen werden (großes lateinisches, kleines lateinisches, großes deutsches, kleines deutsches)", Max Burchartz, Internationale Ausstellung Kunst der Werbung, International Exhibition on Advertising Art, Essen, 30.5.-5.7.1931

Schließung des Dessauer Bauhauses.

Der Dessauer Gemeinderat stimmte dem nationalsozialistischen Antrag zu, das Bauhaus zum 1. Oktober zu schließen und allen Lehrern zu kündigen. Für den Antrag sprachen sich die 15 National-sozialisten, vier Bürgerliche und ein Magistratsmitglied aus. Dagegen stimmten fünf Stadtverordnete; die Sozialdemokraten enthielten sich der Stimme.

hochschule für gestaltung   **bauhaus dessau**

ihre zeichen	ihre nachricht vom	unsere zeichen	tag

24. 8. 1932

in der gemeinderatssitzung vom 22. 8. 1932 ist beschlossen worden, das bauhaus zum 30. 9. 1932 zu schließen.

ich werde versuchen, das haus an anderer stelle weiterzuführen; ob es gelingt, ist im augenblick noch nicht zu sagen. über den erfolg der bemühungen werde ich den studierenden bis gegen mitte september eine weitere nachricht zukommen lassen.

auch die für das ende der ferien vorgesehene arbeit in den werkstätten (ab 5. september), kann wegen der jetzt schon eingeleiteten auflösung des bauhauses nicht mehr stattfinden.

mies van der rohe.

postanschrift: bauhaus dessau

sammel-nr. 3136   bankkonto: städt. kreissparkasse dessau 2634   postscheck: magdeburg 13 701

Newspaper clipping announcing the closing the school, 22 August 1932 (above); memo from Mies van der Rohe, informing the Bauhaus community of the local concil's decision to close the school, 24 August 1932 (below)
Zeitungsausschnitt, „Schließung des Dessauer Bauhauses", 22. 8. 1932 (oben); Memo von Mies van der Rohe an die Gemeinschaft des Bauhaus zum Beschluss des Gemeinderats, das Bauhaus aufzulösen, 24.8.1932 (unten)

Rien ne se perd,
rien ne se crée...
 Being the son of an architect, I was introduced to the world of architecture at an early age. The smell of Ozalid ink, the wooden drawing tables, the models, the Prismacolor drawings and the ashtrays filled with cigarette butts stacked into pyramids, so tall that they defied the laws of gravity. My first impressions of architecture were seeing my father doodle sketches, watching one of his colleagues diligently draw details, and observing another scrambling to put everything to scale on large pages, all while an interior designer was playing with samples of colours.
 Eventually, I came to understand that my father did much more than doodle and colour; he also supervised construction sites!

His practice built functional projects that displayed a profound knowledge of construction. He would tell me that the whole process "is not so difficult, you know. The office's work is simply guided by one important principle: rien ne se perd, rien ne se crée." Nothing is lost, nothing is created.
 It was later, while I was studying architecture, that my grandfather told me his story. As a farmer with little financial or material means, he had built his farm with his arms, his legs, his back and his horses. He carefully planned out his task with a conscious awareness of the site constraints and tactfully assembled resources: wooden planks and beams came from the pine trees on the adjacent woodlot; the stones used for the foundations came from tilling the woods to create a

field. The barn was positioned to protect the main house from harsh winds, while sheltering the cows inside from the winter cold. His rigorous planning and rapid understanding of building techniques enabled him to make a building that was coherent and efficient, helping him to improve his productivity and quality of life.
 My grandfather's story resounded with my father's architectural approach according to "rien ne se perd, rien ne se crée". But I was starting to feel as though something was missing in their approach. They both highly valued pragmatic ideals based on a deep understanding of construction rules and efficiency, and saw aesthetics as being superfluous and subordinate to practicality. I quickly realized what would guide my

Rien ne se perd,
rien ne se crée ...
 Als Sohn eines Architekten kam ich schon früh mit der Welt der Architektur in Berührung. Der Geruch von Ozalid-Tinte, die hölzernen Reißbretter, die Modelle, die Prismacolor-Zeichnungen und die Aschenbecher voller Kippen, die so hoch zu Pyramiden gestapelt waren, dass sie den Gesetzen der Schwerkraft trotzten. Meine ersten Eindrücke von Architektur waren Bilder: Wie mein Vater flüchtige Skizzen hinwarf, wie einer seiner Kollegen sorgfältig die Details zeichnete und sich ein anderer darum riss, alles maßstabsgetreu auf große Seiten zu übertragen. Ich begriff schließlich, dass mein Vater viel mehr tat, als nur rumzukritzeln und irgendwas anzumalen. Er überwachte auch Baustellen! Das Ganze sei „gar nicht so schwierig", erklärte er mir. Die Arbeit im Büro stehe einfach unter dem Grundsatz: „Rien ne se perd, rien ne se crée." Also: Nichts

geht verloren, nichts wird geschaffen.
 Als ich später Architektur studierte, erzählte mir mein Großvater seine Geschichte. Als Bauer mit geringen materiellen Mitteln baute er sich seinen Hof selbst. Er hatte den Ehrgeiz, sich die Bautechniken der damaligen Zeit selbst beizubringen. Die Holzbohlen und -balken stammten aus dem benachbarten Kiefernwäldchen. Die Steine für das Fundament von gerodeten Feldern. Die Scheune schützte das Haupthaus vor rauen Winden und die Kühe vor der winterlichen Kälte.
 Die Geschichte meines Großvaters stand im Einklang mit dem architektonischen Ansatz meines Vaters und seinem Motto „rien ne se perd, rien ne se crée". Gleichwohl schien mir in ihrer Herangehensweise etwas zu fehlen. Beide schätzten pragmatische Ideale – so etwas wie Ästhetik war für sie vollkommen überflüssig. Mir wurde rasch klar, welchem Prinzip

meine eigene zukünftige Tätigkeit folgen würde: der Ausgewogenheit und Einheit von Technik und Ästhetik.
 Es faszinierte mich, Räume zu entwerfen, die Handwerk und Bautechnik miteinander verbanden, bei denen das Künstlerische und das Funktionale nahtlos ineinander übergingen – im Grunde also Räume, die mit Walter Gropius' Bauhaus-Manifest voll im Einklang stehen. Und so sehe ich eine Parallele zwischen meinen Kindheitserinnerungen, die zu einem tieferen Verständnis der Architektur führten, und den von Gropius formulierten Zielen, der die Architektur in der Kunst verankert sah, indem er „den Bau zu schmücken" als einstmals „vornehmste Aufgabe der bildenden Künste" ansah und von den Architekten verlangte, sie müssten „die vielgliedrige Gestalt des Baues in seiner Gesamtheit und in seinen Teilen wieder kennen und begreifen lernen".

Maxime-Alexis Frappier

own future practice: the challenge of balancing and integrating both the technical and the aesthetic.

I became fascinated with designing spaces that link craft and construction techniques, that seamlessly integrate artistic creations and practical solutions – essentially spaces that resonate with Walter Gropius's Bauhaus Manifesto. I see a parallel between how my childhood memories led me to a deeper understanding of architecture, and how Gropius explains that building is the goal of art, that "the ornamentation of the building was once the main purpose of the visual arts" and that "architects, painters and sculptors must learn a new way of seeing and understanding the composite character of the building, both as a totality and in terms of its parts."

Working across a range of scales, from a family farm to Hotel Monville and the Diane Dufresne Art Centre: art and craft at the service of functionality

Entwerfen mit unterschiedlichen Maßstäben, von einer Farm zum Hotel Monville und dem Diane Dufresne Art Centre: Kunst und Handwerk im Dienst der Funktionalität

Bygone bravery

The Bauhaus era was one of cultural upheaval and daring experimentation. Transdisciplinarity and technological progress created an atmosphere of almost magical energy. Although I have no formal connection with the way the Bauhaus worked, the romantic idealism and committed poetry of those years are important points of reference for me. The creators of this truly blessed era were enormously courageous, defying social convention and economic constraints with an almost unbelievable ease.

Today the Bauhaus lies far in the past. Our profession is completely absorbed by all-controlling consumerism, even though it should actually exercise technological disobedience and restore the appreciation of its own work. In any case, there isn't much to laugh about these days.

Mutige Zeiten

Die Bauhaus-Zeit war eine Ära kultureller Umbrüche und gewagter Experimente. Transdisziplinarität und technologischer Fortschritt schufen eine Atmosphäre von geradezu magischer Energie. Obwohl mich formal nichts mit der Arbeitsweise des Bauhaus verbindet, sind der romantische Idealismus und die engagierte Poesie jener Jahre doch wichtige Bezugspunkte für mich. Die Schöpfer dieser wahrhaft gesegneten Epoche waren enorm couragiert und setzten sich mit einer schier unglaublichen Leichtigkeit über gesellschaftliche Konventionen und ökonomische Zwänge hinweg.

Heute liegt das Bauhaus weit in der Vergangenheit. Unser Berufsstand geht völlig im alles beherrschenden Konsum auf, obwohl er eigentlich technologischen Ungehorsam üben und die Wertschätzung seiner eigenen Arbeit wiederherstellen sollte. Jedenfalls hat man heutzutage nicht mehr viel zu lachen.

Rudy Ricciotti

Beauty as the splendour of truth

The Bauhaus in my everyday life makes a claim for beauty as the "splendour of truth", as Plato said and St. Augustine repeated. The English poet John Keats captured this moment in the well-known lines of his poem, "Ode on a Grecian Urn," when he wrote, "Beauty is truth, truth beauty, – that is all / Ye know on earth, and all ye need to know."

The Bauhaus for me is a call for order. Reason is the first and the main instrument for an architect.

"The artist's brush should be dipped in reason," Johann Joachim Winckelmann wrote, a sentiment that Johann Wolfgang von Goethe shared.

For me, the Bauhaus means surrender, sobriety, austerity and essentiality. In his essay "What is a classic?" T.S. Eliot wrote, "There comes a time when a new simplicity, even a relative crudity, may be the only alternative." Now, to some extent, the sacrifice of some potentialities in order to realize others is a condition of artistic creation, as it is a condition of life in general. But without the constant application of the classical measure, we risk becoming provincial.

Schönheit als der Glanz des Wahren

Für mich gebührt dem Bauhaus der Anspruch auf die Schönheit als dem „Glanz des Wahren", wie Platon es einst ausdrückte und nach ihm der hl. Augustinus. Der englische Dichter John Keats beschrieb diesen erhabenen Moment in den bekannten Zeilen seines Gedichts „Ode auf eine griechische Urne": Schönes ist wahr, und Wahrheit schön – nur das / Ist unser irdisch Wissen, und mehr bedarfst du nicht.

Für mich ist das Bauhaus ein Aufruf zur Ordnung. Die Vernunft ist das erste und wichtigste Instrument eines Architekten. Oder, wie Johann Joachim Winckelmann es ausdrückte: „Der Pinsel, den der Künstler führet, soll in Verstand getunkt sein". Dieser Ansicht war auch Johann Wolfgang von Goethe.

Für mich bedeutet das Bauhaus Hingabe, Nüchternheit, Schmucklosigkeit und Wesentlichkeit. In seinem Essay „Was ist ein Klassiker?" schrieb T.S. Eliot: Es kommt eine Zeit, in welcher alsdann eine neue Einfalt, oder sogar gewisse Rohheit, als einziger Ausweg offenbleibt. Heute ist der Verzicht auf einige Möglichkeiten zur Realisierung anderer in gewisser Weise eine Grundbedingung künstlerischen Schaffens – und eine Grundbedingung des Lebens im Allgemeinen. Doch ohne die ständige Anwendung des klassischen Maßes laufen wir Gefahr, heillos provinziell zu werden.

Alberto Campo Baeza

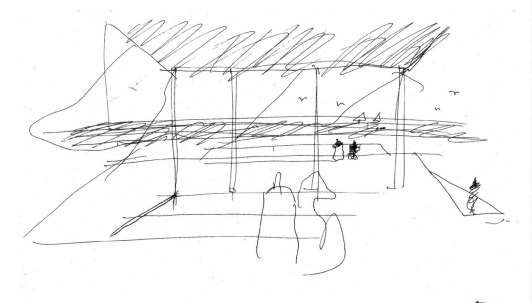

x 7 billion

Transforming society

What I fundamentally like about the Bauhaus is its claim to change society through design. I think that, today, many designers are not really aware of our social responsibility; on the contrary, many of us even reject it. But architecture has the power to change society. After all, we handle large budgets and valuable resources. We can limit ourselves to designing a building – but we can also build a community at the same time. We can design so that resources are exploited and just a few people become very rich. But we can also pursue an emancipatory approach that enables people to develop regional solutions with their existing potential – local materials, human labour and creativity. These, in turn, can strengthen smaller economic cycles, promote local identity and reduce our environmental impact. If I were to take a lead from the Bauhaus and reduce my inner architectural discourse to the essentials and focus on a universal strategy, then that would be: ×7 billion. I try to multiply every creative decision in my imagination with our current world population. I wonder what the world would look like if everyone would act, build and make decisions this way. Fair? Healthy? Sustainable? Liveable?

Die Gesellschaft verändern

Was ich am Bauhaus grundsätzlich mag, ist der Anspruch, per Gestaltung die Gesellschaft zu verändern. Ich finde, dass wir Gestalter uns derzeit unserer gesellschaftsprägenden Verantwortung nicht wirklich bewusst sind oder sie im Gegenteil sogar ablehnen. Doch Architektur hat die Macht, Gesellschaft mit zu verändern. Schließlich hantieren wir mit großen Budgets und wertvollen Ressourcen. Wir können uns darauf beschränken, ein Gebäude zu errichten – wir können aber auch zugleich eine Gemeinschaft aufbauen. Wir können so entwerfen, dass Ressourcen ausgebeutet und ein paar wenige sehr reich werden. Wir können jedoch auch einen emanzipatorischen Anspruch verfolgen, der Menschen befähigt, mit ihren vorhandenen Potenzialen – lokalen Materialien, menschlicher Arbeitskraft und Kreativität – regionale Lösungen zu entwickeln. Diese wiederum würden kleinere Wirtschaftskreisläufe stärken, lokale Identität fördern und die Umwelt entlasten. Wenn ich also nach Bauhaus-Manier meinen inneren Architekturdiskurs auf das Wesentliche reduzieren und auf eine Universalstrategie setzen würde, dann wäre es das: ×7 Milliarden. Ich versuche, jede gestalterische Entscheidung in meiner Vorstellung mit unserer derzeitigen Weltbevölkerung zu multiplizieren, und frage mich dabei, wie die Welt wohl aussehen würde, wenn jeder und jede so handeln, so bauen, so entscheiden würde. Fair? Gesund? Zukunftsfähig? Lebenswert?

Anna Heringer

A synthesis of spirit and matter I regard the Bauhaus as the most inspirational movement in contemporary architectural history, and I believe the Bauhaus spirit is even more relevant today, when the rapidly transforming built environment and related environmental depletion as well as socio-economic challenges call for radical rethinking. The Bauhaus was a creative laboratory where design came out of intense research, experimentation as well as self-discovery and set new standards. The designers involved boldly and courageously expanded the frontiers of their field of knowledge, while inspiring each other in an interdisciplinary community; recognizing and appreciating design as synthesis of spirit and matter, and design's potential of redefining everything we know and rethinking everything we see, make and use.

Housing, especially the affordability of housing, continues to be a pressing and growing concern globally. Through the 28 years of my practice, we continue to draw inspiration from the Bauhaus movement, as we undertake material research and innovation alongside investigations in non-material aspects of architecture like form, space, human scale and social behaviour. Beauty is the natural result of design decisions and negotiations that are part of the design process of synthesizing various concerns into unified solutions, by addressing real concerns through knowledge-based processes. The Full Fill Home prototype is an example of our work where we aim to deliver affordable homes, rapidly produced with minimum resources and maximum beauty.

Synthese aus Geist und Materie
Für mich ist das Bauhaus die inspirierendste Bewegung der zeitgenössischen Architekturgeschichte. Zu einer Zeit, in der sich die gebaute Umwelt derart rasant verändert und die damit einhergehende Ressourcenverknappung wie auch die sozioökonomischen Herausforderungen ein radikales Umdenken erfordern, scheint mir sein Spirit heute sogar noch relevanter und notwendiger denn je. Das Bauhaus war ein Kreativlabor, in dem Gestaltung aus dem Experiment, intensiver Forschungsarbeit und einem Spirit von Selbstfindung heraus geboren wurde und neue Maßstäbe setzte. Die mutig daran Beteiligten drangen in neue Wissensgebiete vor und inspirierten sich gegenseitig in einer interdisziplinären Gemeinschaft. Sie würdigten und wertschätzten Gestaltung als eine Synthese aus Geist und Materie und erkannten das ihr innewohnende Potenzial, alles uns Bekannte neu zu definieren, und alles, was wir sehen, herstellen und benutzen, neu zu überdenken.

Wohnraum, vor allem bezahlbarer Wohnraum, ist nach wie vor ein höchst akutes Problem weltweit. All meine mittlerweile 28 Berufsjahre hindurch hat uns das Bauhaus zu neuen Ideen inspiriert. Und wir betreiben noch immer Materialforschung, arbeiten an Innovationen und beschäftigen uns parallel auch mit nicht-materiellen Aspekten von Architektur wie Form, Raum, menschlichem Maß und sozialem Verhalten. Schönheit ist das natürliche Ergebnis von gestalterischen Entscheidungen und Verhandlungen. Sie sind integraler Bestandteil eines Entwurfsprozesses, der unterschiedliche Belange zu ganzheitlichen Lösungen zusammenführt, indem er reale Probleme mit wissensbasierter Erfahrung angeht. Der „Full Fill Home"-Prototyp ist ein Beispiel für unsere Arbeit, durch die wir mit minimalen Ressourcen und maximaler Schönheit schnell produzierte und erschwingliche Wohnungen liefern wollen.

Anupama Kundoo

Wassily

Illuminated by the summer sun that poured in through the window and hit it directly, the armchair would sit alone in the farthest corner of the room. On the walls, you could see refractions of light, like a kaleidoscope sprouting from its polished structure, while the smell of new leather filled the air. To the touch, its rigorous seams let you guess the limits and the geometric shapes, with which the different parts had joined together to give shape to the armchair – allowing me to sit in an unstable yet welcoming way.

People say that true memories are eternally engraved with emotions. I can't remember the place and the date, but I can remember the moment when, when I was little, I was dazzled by Marcel Breuer's marvellous Bauhaus creation, the "Wassily".

Wassily

Im Glanz der Sommersonne, die durchs Fenster strömte und direkt auf ihn fiel, stand der Sessel allein in der hintersten Ecke des Raumes. An den Wänden sah man wie durch ein Kaleidoskop die tanzenden Lichteffekte, während der Geruch von neuem Leder in der Luft lag. Bei Berührung des Sessels ließen einen die präzisen Nähte die Grenzen und geometrischen Formen ahnen, aus denen seine verschiedenen Teile zusammengefügt worden waren, um ihm Form zu geben – man saß in ihm zwar nicht sonderlich stabil, doch er wirkte einladend.

Erinnerungen, die mit starken Emotionen verbunden sind, prägen sich einem für immer ein, sagt man. An Ort und Tag habe ich keinerlei Erinnerung mehr, aber ich erinnere mich noch wie heute an den Augenblick als Kind, als ich völlig überwältigt war von Marcel Breuers wunderbarer Bauhaus-Kreation, dem Wassily Chair.

Anzilutti / Mendiondo / Garrido / Cairoli

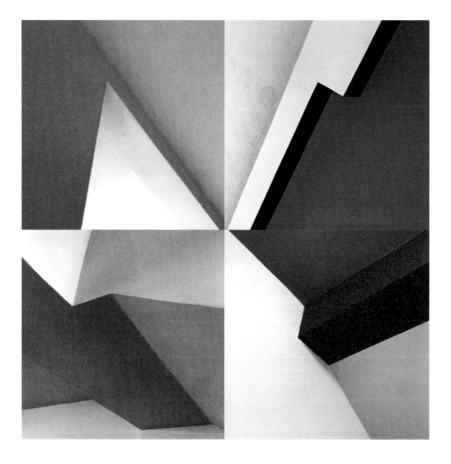

Pleasure

What if we wouldn't talk about all the merits and interpretations and appreciation and meanings and ideas and strategies and politics and craft and movement and history and future and people and groups and places and schools and so on – but just enjoy?

Maybe that was the very first thing that came to mind at the very first moment: pleasure.

Purer Genuß

Wie wär's, wenn wir über all die Verdienste und Interpretationen und Würdigungen und Bedeutungen und Ideen und Strategien und Politik und Handwerkskunst und Bewegung und Geschichte und Zukunft und Menschen und Gruppen und Orte und Schulen und so weiter nicht reden, sondern das Bauhaus einfach nur genießen würden?
Vielleicht war das der allererste Gedanke, der uns in den Sinn kam: Genuss.

Jan de Vylder, Inge Vinck, Jo Taillieu

Ambition and impact

With the Bauhaus, the potential for use and presentation united in a programme that corresponded, at least in the beginning, to an integrated approach to architectural thinking. But its almost purist ethos demanding equal amounts of functionality, good design, honest construction, natural materials and appropriate scale – as it was pursued through the reduced, not so robust Bauhaus architecture – did not endure, although its principles certainly remain valid today.

At the time, the erection of an iconographic building was more a question of appropriateness than a matter of mere distraction. The more precisely one grasped a building's substantive coherence, the more focused its ultimate expression would be.

We must assume that, during the course of its eventful history, the Bauhaus developed in a hostile environment, not only politically speaking. Its modern approach was naturally in competition with more traditional architectural content. Just as the settlement movement brought together a wide variety of political groups (such as "guild socialists", "patriots" and national socialists), the architectural styles within this movement were also heterogeneous, ranging from neo-classicism with heavily referential elements, to functional Bauhaus architecture. The spirit of the time thus reflected the pursuit of the speculatively possible – similar to today's "society of singularities" (Andreas Reckwitz) – as well as an uncompromising adherence to architectural concepts.

Anspruch und Wirksamkeit

Im Bauhaus bildeten Gebrauchs- und Darstellungspotenzial gemeinsam ein Programm und entsprachen damit, jedenfalls in der Anfangsphase, dem integralen architektonischen Denken. Allein der sich daraus entwickelnde, nahezu puristisch-ethische Anspruch mit seinen paritätischen Hauptforderungen wie Funktionalität, gute Gestaltung, konstruktive Ehrlichkeit, natürliche Materialität und maßstäbliche Angemessenheit ließ sich in der nötigen Konsequenz bei der Verfolgung dieser Ziele angesichts der feinen, an sich wenig robusten Bauhaus-Architektur auf Dauer nicht durchhalten, obwohl diese Grundsätze durchaus heute noch Gültigkeit haben sollten.

Die Errichtung eines ikonografischen Apparates war damals eher schon eine Frage der Angemessenheit als eine Frage der reinen Ablenkung. Je präziser man die inhaltliche Schlüssigkeit eines Gebäudes erfasste, desto fokussierter war letztlich dessen Ausdruck.

Man muss davon ausgehen, dass das Bauhaus sich in seiner wechselvollen Geschichte durchaus in – nicht nur politisch gesehen – feindlicher Umgebung entwickeln musste. In Konkurrenz zu seinem modernen Ansatz standen natürlich auch architektonische Inhalte traditioneller Art. So wie sich in der Siedlerbewegung unterschiedlichste politische Gruppen versammelten (von „gildensozialistisch" über „vaterländisch" bis nationalsozialistisch), waren analog auch die architektonischen Stilvorstellungen innerhalb der Bewegung heterogen und reichten von bedeutungsschwangerem Neoklassizismus bis hin zur leichtgliedrigen Bauhaus-Architektur. Damit befand man sich bereits im ethischen Bereich vom spekulativ Möglichen, wie dies heute in der „Gesellschaft der Singularitäten" vorherrscht (Reckwitz), bis hin zu einem dem architektonischen Gedanken verpflichteten Ansatz.

Adolf Krischanitz

Adolf Loos, Siedlung Heuberg, 1921–1924, Wien
Georg Muche, Haus am Horn, 1923, Weimar

For a society of shared values

The enduring mythology of the Bauhaus is primarily embodied by the ideas of two of its directors and the reverence in which they continue to be held. Walter Gropius and its third director, Mies van der Rohe, were leading protagonists in the ascendancy of the modern movement, and the impact and influence of their ideas on design and culture in general continue to resonate today.

Less heralded is the school's second director, Hannes Meyer, who took over from Gropius and changed the direction of the Bauhaus, setting out a more egalitarian ambition and overseeing a programme that emphasized collective practice and cooperative production. Meyer believed these to be fundamental to the creation of a society organized around common values rather than one that catered to individual desires, and as the key to integrating creative work with the immense potential of industrial production, moving away from the established idea of the architect or artist as the individual and authoritative creative force.

Meyer's image of the Co-op Zimmer shows an apparently spartan and rudimentary space with no defining formal characteristics. It seems to advocate a radically simple, almost monastic existence – introverted, earnest and highly economical. The gramophone in the corner is ambiguous in this context and hints at a different dimension, of culture and enjoyment as well as technological progress. Rather than a humble, monkish abode, it is more a vision of a private realm that is supplementary to the cultural and social richness of the city at large, a suggestion of a different dynamic where primacy is shifted from the private sphere to the public and collective life beyond.

With Assemble, we attempt to make projects in a collaborative way against a culture that is often keen to attribute achievements to a brilliant individual. We work at a point in time where public space and individual experience are increasingly privatized and mediated, looking to counter this through the production of adaptable spatial frameworks that support open and sociable environments enabling a diversity of use. And we try to make sense of the disconnection between modern consumer culture and the conditions in which much of what we consume is produced by pursuing a more direct relationship with the means of architectural and industrial production. The ideas that Hannes Meyer sought to promote resonate with the work and spirit of our practice, and they represent a critique of contemporary design culture as critical and relevant today as at any point since his stewardship of the school.

Für eine Gesellschaft gemeinsamer Werte

Der Mythos des Bauhaus verdankt sich vor allem den Ideen der beiden Direktoren Walter Gropius und Mies van der Rohe. Weniger bekannt ist der zweite Direktor der Schule, Hannes Meyer. Er vertrat ein stärker egalitär ausgerichtetes Programm, das kollektive Arbeit und genossenschaftliche Produktion in den Mittelpunkt stellte. Beides hielt er für grundlegende Säulen einer Gesellschaft, die sich mehr an gemeinsamen Werten orientiert als an den Wünschen Einzelner. Sie waren für ihn der Schlüssel zur Integration von kreativer Arbeit und industriellem Produktionspotenzial – womit er vom gängigen Bild des Architekten oder Künstlers als autonomem Schöpfergott abrückte.

Meyers Bild des „Co-op Zimmers" zeigt einen auf den ersten Blick spartanisch und rudimentär eingerichteten Raum ohne charakteristischen Merkmale – radikal einfach, introvertiert, ernsthaft und höchst asketisch. Das Grammophon in der Ecke ist in diesem Kontext jedoch mehrdeutig und verweist auf eine Lebenswelt des Vergnügens und des technischen Fortschritts. Statt einer bescheidenen Mönchszelle vermittelt der Raum die Vision eines privaten Bereichs als (durchaus ergänzendes) Gegenbild zur kulturellen und sozialen Überfülle der Stadt. Gerade so, als wollte es den Blick des Betrachters auf die unterschiedliche Dynamik zwischen Privatsphäre und dem sozialen, öffentlichen Leben draußen lenken.

Wir versuchen mit Assemble Studio, gemeinschaftliche Projekte gegen eine Kultur zu setzen, die Erfolge nur allzu gern der Genialität eines Einzelnen zuschreibt. Wir arbeiten in einer Zeit, wo der öffentliche Raum und die individuelle Erfahrung immer mehr privatisiert und medialisiert werden. Dieser Entwicklung möchten wir entgegenwirken durch das Schaffen flexibler räumlicher Kontexte, die offene und gemeinschaftsfördernde Umgebungen und eine Vielfalt an Nutzungsmöglichkeiten begünstigen. Und wir versuchen, die Abkopplung der heutigen Konsumkultur von ihren Produktionsbedingungen sinnfällig zu machen. Die von Hannes Meyer geförderten Vorstellungen decken sich mit der Arbeit und der Haltung unseres Studios. Wir verstehen sie als eine Kritik an der aktuellen Designkultur, die heute so wichtig und relevant ist wie seit seinem Direktorat.

James Binning

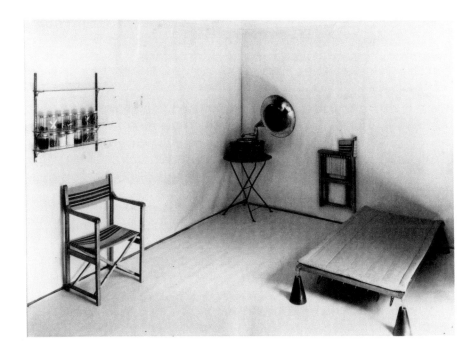

Hannes Meyer, Das Zimmer Co-op, 1926

Bow-Wow=Bau?

When we started our team, we tried to find a good name for ourselves. At the time, my parents had a sweet dog named Ume. Because of her, my father began calling all of our family members a new nickname, adding the Japanese word for the sound of a dog barking – wan – to the end. For example, the nickname "Tsuka-san" would be "Tsuka-wan". According to this family custom, we decided to name our team Atelier Wan in Japanese. After that, we translated Atelier Wan into English as Atelier Bow-Wow.

Dogs bark in the same manner no matter where they are in the world. But their human interpretation, the onomatopoeia for dog barking, reflects differences in culture. We, at Atelier Bow-Wow, are always interested in this kind of framing of society, architecture and space. Not to mention the fact that the word "Bow" reminds us of the German word Bau, as in building and the Bauhaus. We really like our name and how it reflects our interests.

Bow-Wow=Bau?

Als wir unser Büro gründeten, suchten wir nach einem passenden Namen für uns. Meine Eltern hatten damals einen Hund namens Ume. Und weil der kleine Kerl gar so süß war, verpasste mein Vater allen Familienmitgliedern einen neuen Spitznamen, indem er das japanische Wort für bellen – wan – an unsere Namen anhängte. „Tsuka-san" wurde so zu „Tsuka-wan". Nach diesem Familienbrauch beschlossen wir, unser Büro „Atelier Wan" zu nennen. Und als wir den Namen ins Englische übersetzten, kam dann eben „Atelier Bow-Wow" dabei heraus.

Hunde bellen überall auf der Welt auf die gleiche Weise, aber unsere lautmalerische Wiedergabe unterscheidet sich von Kultur zu Kultur. Wir von Atelier Bow-Wow interessieren uns genau für diese unterschiedlichen Bedeutungsrahmen einer Gesellschaft, ihrer Architektur, ihres Kulturraums – ganz abgesehen davon, dass uns das Wort „Bow" an das deutsche Wort „Bau" wie bei Bauhaus erinnert. Wir lieben diesen Namen wirklich sehr und die Art, wie er unsere Interessen widerspiegelt.

Momoyo Kaijima

Momonoura Village, architects: Kaijima & Sato Lab, University of Tsukuba, Atelier Bow-Wow, Satokura Architects, dot architects

Bauhaus for the 21st century?

These days, everyone is rushing to embrace the Bauhaus, and its 100th anniversary birthday has become the occasion for all kinds of activities. It all gives the impression that the process of its museumization, which has been occurring far too long anyway, is being intensified. The Bauhaus is being reduced to a historical phenomenon that is praised, admired and marvelled at – so that ultimately it is becoming domesticated. In banal terms, it is becoming part of the prevailing, mainly consumerist cultural machinery, part of the branding for cities or entire regions. From this perspective, the construction of two further Bauhaus museums in Weimar and Dessau seems dubious and more than superfluous.

It would be interesting to explore whether such a school for architecture and design could still provide interesting impulses for students today. Would it make sense to seek a Bauhaus for the 21st century? What spiritual basis would our society need for something like this to develop?

Which social drivers should be addressed by a school of this kind? Globalization, for instance? Growing social injustice and lack of differentiation? Demographic and ecological change? On the other hand, we should ask whether the Bauhaus is completely irrelevant today. All leftist experiments have so far

Bauhaus für das 21. Jahrhundert?

Jetzt stürzen sich alle auf das Bauhaus, und sein 100. Geburtstag wird zum Anlass für allerlei Aktivitäten. Der Eindruck, der sich dabei aufdrängt ist, dass der Prozess seiner ohnehin schon viel zu lange währenden Musealisierung dabei lediglich verstärkt wird. Das Bauhaus wird reduziert auf ein historisches Phänomen, gelobt, bewundert, angestaunt – um schlussendlich einfach nur domestiziert zu werden. Es wird, banal gesprochen, zu einem Teil der vorherrschenden, meist konsumistischen Kulturmaschinerie, des Branding von Städten oder ganzer Regionen. Aus dieser Perspektive betrachtet, erscheint auch der Bau von zwei weiteren Bauhaus-Museen in Weimar und Dessau als zweifelhaft und mehr als überflüssig.

Interessant wäre die Frage, ob eine solche Architektur- und Designschule heute noch interessante Impulse für die Ausbildung geben könnte. Wäre es sinnvoll, sich auf die Suche zu begeben nach einem Bauhaus für das 21. Jahrhundert? Welche geistige Grundlage bräuchte es in unserer Gesellschaft, damit so etwas entstehen kann?

Welche sozialen Triebkräfte sollte eine Schule dieser Art thematisieren? Etwa die Globalisierung? Die zunehmende soziale Ungerechtigkeit und mangelnde Differenzierung? Den demografischen und ökologischen Wandel? Umgekehrt sollte aber auch die Frage erlaubt sein, ob das Bauhaus heute nicht komplett

failed because capitalism seems to be stronger – perhaps
because it satisfies our most primitive human instincts. Shouldn't
it have been expected that the Bauhaus would ultimately fail as
an idealistic construct – not because it was shut down by the
Nazis, but because pure materialism is simply closer to human
nature, even if intellectuals don't want to admit it? The success of
Ikea shows that what remains of the Bauhaus legacy are mainly
its material elements. Or would a contemporary version of this
school be conceivable after all – one that is not based solely on
dealing proactively with the driving forces of the time, but instead
seeks a holistic approach to given facts, an objective expression
of the present? A school that counters our fragmented reality with
the image of a society that knows how to unite individual demands
with collective expression.

André Kempe, Oliver Thill

irrelevant ist. Alle linksorientierten Experimente sind bis dato
gescheitert, weil der Kapitalismus einfach der Stärkere zu sein
scheint – vielleicht gerade, weil er den primitivsten menschlichen
Trieben folgt. Und war das letztendliche Scheitern des Bauhaus
als idealistisches Konstrukt etwa nur folgerichtig – nicht weil
die Nazis es schließen ließen, sondern weil der reine Materialismus
einfach näher am Menschen ist, auch wenn es die Intellektuellen
nicht wahrhaben wollen? Der Erfolg von Ikea zeigt, dass als Vermächtnis des Bauhaus vor allem die materielle Komponente übrig
geblieben ist. Oder wäre doch eine zeitgenössische Variante
dieser Schule denkbar – eine, die nicht allein auf dem proaktiven
Umgang mit den Triebkräften der Zeit beruht, sondern stattdes-
sen in den objektiven Fakten das allgemeine Ganze sucht, einen
objektiven Ausdruck der Zeit? Eine Schule also, die unserer
fragmentierten Realität das Bild einer Gesellschaft entgegen-
setzt, die individuellen Anspruch mit kollektivem Ausdruck zu
verbinden weiß.

André Kempe, Oliver Thill

A sentimental relationship

Naturally, like nearly every architect today, I too am the progeny of the Bauhaus movement. I loved the Bauhaus, and then I fought against it, and then I loved it again. My intersections with it have been many and continuous, especially with the animistic side of its theories – meaning Paul Klee, Wassily Kandinsky and Oskar Schlemmer. On several occasions, I created projects with a direct reference to the Bauhaus, especially during the period of the Alchimia group in Milan. I am attaching an example of these. As you can see, my contact with the Bauhaus is anomalous, but very sentimental.

Eine sentimentale Beziehung

Wie fast alle Architekten stehe natürlich auch ich in der Nach-folge der Bauhaus-Bewegung. Es ist eine Art Hassliebe: Erst liebte ich das Bauhaus, dann bekämpfte ich es, um es erneut zu lieben. Die Überschneidungen mit seiner Theorie sind zahlreich und kontinuierlich, vor allem mit seiner animistischen Seite, sprich Paul Klee, Wassily Kandinsky und Oskar Schlemmer. Ich habe mehrfach und gerade zur Zeit der Alchimia-Gruppe in Mailand Projekte mit einem direkten Bezug zum Bauhaus geschaffen. Wie das beigefügte Foto zeigt, ist mein Verhältnis dazu schon fast nicht mehr normal, aber zugleich auch sehr sentimental.

Alessandro Mendini

Alessandro Mendini, Wassily chair by Marcel Breuer, 1978

The spirit of craft lives on

The Bauhaus represents the idea of craft, of building with a focus on the intrinsic qualities of materials, stripped of past ornamentation and representative features, driven by shape and use as a design philosophy.

The Bauhaus is the elaboration of a new way of doing things that seeks to depart from the past with the hope of uncovering something that exists but which has not yet been shaped or revealed, a break from traditional design constrained by habits and the past.

Is the spirit of the Bauhaus still alive today? It is in the will of architects who try to extract something new in architecture, mostly done through form. Paradoxically, the forms generated digitally often are not adapted to the body's scale or proportions, creating unmemorable or diffuse spaces, foreign to the body's geometry. There is today an uneasy relation between the poetics of materials and the building industry, which produces imitative materials always at a lower cost, seducing a potential client with images rather than craft and tactical experience.

For the Bauhaus to have survived as a movement and a reference is a sign that its approach is part of the process of creation.

Der Geist des Handwerks lebt

Das Bauhaus verkörpert die Idee von Handwerk – vom Bauen mit einem Gespür fürs Material und seine Eigenschaften, losgelöst von der rein dekorativen und repräsentativen Formensprache der Vergangenheit und angetrieben von einer auf Form und Funktion basierenden Entwurfsphilosophie.

Das Bauhaus steht für die Entwicklung einer neuen Vorgehensweise. Es versuchte, von der Vergangenheit abzurücken in der Hoffnung, etwas von dem freizulegen, das existiert, aber noch nicht geformt oder erschlossen wurde. Es suchte den Bruch mit dem traditionellen Entwurf, der den Zwängen von Konvention und Tradition unterlag.

Ist der Geist des Bauhaus heute noch lebendig? Er findet sich in der Entschlossenheit von Architekten, vor allem durch die Form etwas Neues aus der Architektur zu ziehen. Paradoxerweise sind die digital erzeugten Formen oft nicht auf das menschliche Maß zugeschnitten, was zu belanglosen, unklar definierten Räumen führt, die nicht mit der Geometrie des Körpers korrespondieren und harmonisieren. Heute herrscht eine ungute Beziehung zwischen der Poetik des Materials und der Bauindustrie, die Imitate zu immer niedrigeren Preisen produziert und einen potenziellen Bauherrn mit Bildern statt mit Haptik und Handwerk verführt.

Dass das Bauhaus als Bewegung und Bezugspunkt überlebt hat, ist ein Zeichen dafür, dass sein Ansatz Teil des kreativen Prozesses ist.

Paul Laurendeau

A family history
We encounter the Bauhaus nearly every day. This legacy of our family – through our grandparents Auböck and Aunt Kárász – is both exciting and challenging. The expectations that accompany this legacy remain high to this day. And the image of this alone runs the risk of becoming entrenched. The search for a lifestyle might be typical of every generation, but with the Bauhaus it became a radical decision for modern life. Who were these/my Bauhaus members, acting at the juncture between the lifestyle reform movement and exalted progressive thinking? Grandfather Carl Auböck came with his backpack from Vienna as a student of Johannes Itten. Mara Uckunowa-Auböck came to Weimar from Plovdiv via an art school in Munich. Aunt Judit Kárász rode her motorcycle from Szeged to Dessau, taking sociological photographs along the way.

The pretense of the Bauhaus students was: We want to do things ourselves. We will assemble our furniture and solder our lamps! They wanted to build their own world. Today, this vision of the world gives us food for thought. It still exerts a great attraction, precisely because it has become impossible to seriously represent it in its full consequence today. Yet it is precisely this attitude and the solidarity that went along with it that paradoxically opens current windows. Our work as landscape architects – especially in public spaces – is constantly associated with constellations that call into question a well-designed whole. They require a completely different approach that makes it possible to design and accompany processes with fragments. Beauty for everyone is a claim that our relatives would certainly have shared!

Eine Familiengeschichte
Wir begegnen dem Bauhaus fast täglich. Dieses Erbe unserer Familie – durch die Großeltern Auböck und Tante Kárász – ist spannend und herausfordernd zugleich. Bis zum heutigen Tag ist der damit verbundene vermeintliche Anspruch hoch. Allein schon das von außen herangetragene Bild läuft Gefahr, unter einen Glassturz zu geraten. Die Suche nach Lebensstil mag für jede Generation gelten, aber am Bauhaus war das eine radikale Entscheidung für das moderne Leben. Wer waren diese/meine Bauhäusler zwischen Lebensreform und exaltiertem Fortschrittsdenken? Großvater Carl Auböck reiste als Schüler von Johannes Itten mit dem Rucksack aus Wien an. Mara Uckunowa-Auböck kam von Plovdiv über eine Kunstschule in München nach Weimar. Tante Judit Kárász fuhr mit dem Motorrad von Szeged nach Dessau und machte unterwegs Sozio-Fotos.

Der Anspruch der Bauhaus-Schüler war: Wir wollen unsere Sachen selbst machen. Wir montieren unsere Möbel und löten unsere Lampen! Sie wollten ihre Welt selbst bauen. Dieser Entwurf von Welt stimmt heute nachdenklich. Er übt noch immer eine große Anziehung aus, gerade weil es unmöglich geworden ist, ihn in dieser Konsequenz heute ernsthaft zu vertreten. Dennoch ist es gerade diese Haltung und die damit verbundene Solidarität, die paradoxerweise aktuelle Fenster öffnet. Unsere Arbeit als Landschaftsarchitekten ist – vor allem im öffentlichen Raum – ständig mit Konstellationen verbunden, die ein durchgestaltetes Ganzes in Frage stellen. Sie erfordern einen ganz anderen Zugang, der es ermöglicht, mit Bruchstücken Prozesse zu entwerfen und zu begleiten. Schönheit für alle ist dabei ein Anspruch, den unsere Verwandten sicher geteilt hätten!

Maria Auböck, János Kárász

Judith Kárász, Rope, 1931

Processes and approaches
Since the beginning of our journey, our primary starting point has been to create a strong form out of a story, to maintain a simple and refined way of manufacturing with the use of authentic materials and colour palettes, and to multiply production with the right economy. Such has been our basic approach since Plywood, one of our first product series, came into existence. It is important for us that our products are structurally simple and transparent, and that our manufacturing techniques are coherent. On the other hand, we are architects with a passion for craft and a strong command of detail. Craftsmanship is one of the fundamental elements within our creative process. Ever since our school years, we have maintained an understanding of design where architecture, craftsmanship and art merge and inform one another. We give importance to the form creating a lasting value, even in a world of industrial production and fast consumption.

The Bauhaus was founded due to certain necessities of the post-war period, and the world has since seen many different periods and economic structures. These developments created new movements and influenced our way of living, which affects architecture. Nowadays, we are moving towards a period of lessening. Resources are scarce, leaving us with a need for rational behaviour and carrying out sustainable production with the right economic approach. We may therefore be able to state that the basic ideas of the Bauhaus are being put into practice again.

This is why the Bauhaus, being the strong movement it is, still influences the world of today in different ways, and will continue to do so. Even though we may not always be able to directly perceive the influence of the Bauhaus in products and architecture today, its presence may still be felt in contemporary processes and approaches.

Verfahren und Ansätze
Von Beginn an haben wir unsere Priorität als Designer darin gesehen, jeweils einer Geschichte eine starke Form zu geben, in der Fertigung schlicht, aber anspruchsvoll zu bleiben, mit authentischen Materialien und Farben zu arbeiten, und die Produktion auf ökonomisch sinnvolle Weise zu steigern. Das ist unser Grundansatz seit dem Entstehen von Plywood, einer unserer ersten Produktserien. Uns ist es wichtig, dass unsere Entwürfe klar strukturiert und unsere Fertigungstechniken stimmig sind.

Auf der anderen Seite sind wir Architekten mit einer Leidenschaft für das Handwerk und einer großen Liebe zum Detail. Handwerkliches Können ist ein fundamentales Element unseres Schaffensprozesses. Seit dem Studium vertreten wir eine Designauffassung, in der Architektur, Handwerk und Kunst miteinander verschmelzen und einander befruchten. Auch in einer Welt der industriellen Produktion und des schnellen Konsums möchten wir Formen schaffen, die von nachhaltigem Wert sind.

Das Bauhaus entstand aus dem Klima einer Nachkriegsepoche heraus. Seitdem hat die Welt verschiedene Epochen und Wirtschaftssysteme erlebt. Diese Entwicklungen haben neue Strömungen geschaffen und unsere Lebensweise verändert, was sich wiederum auf die Architektur ausgewirkt hat. Heute befinden wir uns in einer Phase des Rückgangs. Die Ressourcen sind knapp, wir müssen rational vorgehen und mit dem entsprechenden ökonomischen Ansatz nachhaltig produzieren. Die Grundsätze des Bauhaus, so könnte man sagen, kommen erneut zum Einsatz. Daher beeinflusst diese Bewegung die Welt von heute noch immer auf unterschiedlichste Weise – und wird es auch weiterhin tun. Auch wenn wir den Einfluss des Bauhaus in Design und Architektur heute vielleicht nicht immer wahrnehmen, ist seine Präsenz in den aktuellen Entwicklungen und Haltungen durchaus zu spüren.

Seyhan Özdemir, Sefer Çağlar

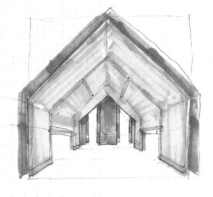

Mahzanom
TAPLE
2017
Autoban

ORHAY
2012
Autoban

Express yourself

The Bauhaus is a constant presence in my thoughts and observations. Primarily because it completely turned around concepts of art and technology, as well as ways of looking and seeing objects and paintings.

My first encounter with the Bauhaus was through a work by Kandinsky, followed by Paul Klee, Josef Albers and Marcel Breuer's furniture and designs of everyday objects. In each of these works I discovered how reinvention takes place with emphasis on form and function through another dimension of technology and attitude toward the industrialized world. Even today, all these objects of daily use bear the imprint of the Bauhaus through simplification, rediscovery and reinterpretation of use with grace as the only constant. Economy of time, economy of material and the reinterpretation of superficial things added on for embellishment were replaced by the form, simple yet graceful.

Contemporaries like Mondrian and Mies further broke new ground through their work. Mies's buildings made the space completely transparent and fluid as if it were contained by nothing, leading to self-discovery and raising questions: Is matter important or form? Is content important? The most valuable lesson I learned from this is that when you combine new ideas with new technology, it gives rise to a completely different kind of imagery, resulting in an experience that is unexpected. I think this especially influenced my career when I started the School of Architecture in Ahmedabad. It stirred up the courage in me to think in new ways, to have no boundaries and to connect with the natural forces of nature and material – giving every student the chance to rediscover himself/herself.

So for me, the Bauhaus is a place where you rediscover and express your innermost self.

Ausdruck des eigenen Ich

Das Bauhaus ist in meinen Gedanken und Betrachtungen stets präsent. Vor allem, weil es gültige Vorstellungen von Kunst und Technologie völlig auf den Kopf gestellt hat ebenso wie die Art und Weise, in der wir Objekte und Gemälde wahrnehmen.

Meine erste Begegnung mit dem Bauhaus war ein Werk von Kandinsky. Dann folgten Paul Klee, Josef Albers, Marcel Breuers Möbel und sein Gebrauchsdesign für den Alltag. In jedem dieser Werke entdeckte ich, wie sich in Form und Funktion eine Neuerfindung von Gewohntem vollzog und sich durch eine neue Dimension von Technik die Haltung gegenüber der industrialisierten Welt komplett veränderte. Selbst heute noch tragen all diese Dinge des täglichen Gebrauchs durch ihre einfache, neu entdeckte und interpretierte Funktion den Stempel des Bauhaus – ihre einzige Konstante ist die Anmut. Zeitökonomie, Materialökonomie und alles, was rein dekorativen Charakter hatte, wurde ersetzt durch einfache, aber elegante Formen.

Zeitgenossen wie Mondrian und Mies trieben die Entwicklung noch weiter voran. Die Bauten von Mies ließen den Raum vollkommen transparent und fließend erscheinen – so als kenne er keine Grenzen. Dies führte zur Entdeckung des eigenen Ich und zu neuen Fragen: Was ist wichtiger – Materie oder Form? Und welche Funktion hat eigentlich der Inhalt? Die wertvollste Lehre, die ich daraus gezogen habe, ist die: Wenn man neue Ideen mit neuer Technologie verknüpft, entsteht eine vollkommen andere Bildwelt, die einen das Unerwartete erfahren lässt. Dies hat meinen Werdegang entscheidend beeinflusst – besonders bei Gründung der Architekturschule in Ahmedabad. Es hat mir den Mut gegeben, die Dinge neu zu denken, Grenzen zu ignorieren und eine Verbindung zu den Kräften von Natur und Material herzustellen – und so jedem Studierenden die Möglichkeit zu geben, sich auch selber neu zu „erfinden".

Daher ist für mich das Bauhaus ein Ort, an dem man sein Innerstes neu entdecken und zum Ausdruck bringen kann.

Balkrishna Doshi

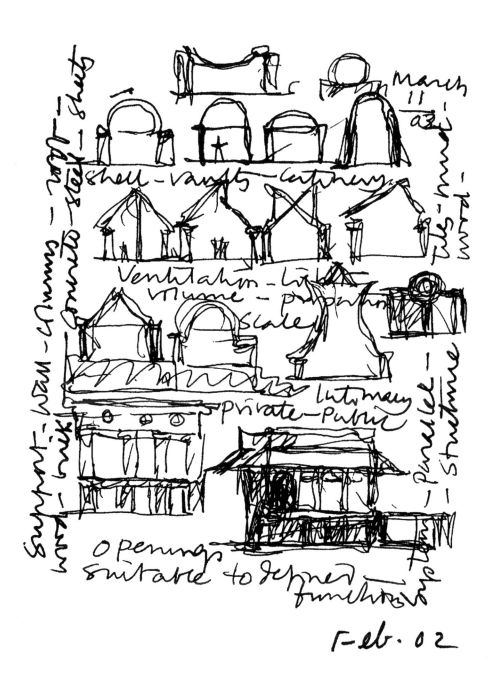

Fisher Body Plant 21, Detroit, 2018

Inspiration from unexpected places

In 1922, Walter or Ise Gropius photographed Albert Kahn's River Rouge Glass Plant at the Ford Motor Works. The image depicts a functionalist ideal: delicately faceted glass louvers and shed roofs, the bases of perfectly formed chimneys, a few workers in motion giving scale to the colossal building. They were an unintentional architecture, those silos and factories, which Gropius admired in the same way as artist Donald Judd, who, years later, would say that, "Dams, roads, bridges, tunnels, storage buildings and various other useful structures comprise the bulk of the best visible things made in this century." The European avant-garde admired these buildings. They observed and mined an American architecture of industry and agriculture that was matter-of-fact, pragmatic and powerful. A celebration of the ordinary.

Like Gropius, I went to Detroit this year to visit Ford and photographed Albert Kahn's Fisher Body Plant 21 from 1919. Like many of his factories it is now abandoned, a ruin: broken glass strewn across the streets. Perhaps its promise now is in imagining how it might be repurposed for a more optimistic future. My partner Regine and I have designed and built factories in Europe for years. In an inversion of this history, I find myself, an American architect raised in the agricultural/industrial state of Montana, curiously designing factories in the country that gave rise to the Bauhaus. We remind ourselves why the early modernists were so fascinated by those forms on the prairie.

Inspiration an unerwarteter Stelle

1922 fotografierten Walter oder Ise Gropius Albert Kahns Glasfabrik auf dem Gelände der Ford Motorenwerke in River Rouge. Das Bild zeigt ein funktionalistisches Ideal: fein facettierte Glaslamellen und Scheddächer, die Sockel perfekt geformter Schornsteine und ein paar Arbeiter, die einem eine Vorstellung vom Maßstab des riesigen Gebäudes geben. Diese Silos und Fabriken waren ein Stück unbeabsichtigte Architektur, die Gropius auf dieselbe Weise bewunderte wie der Künstler Donald Judd, der Jahre später sagen sollte: „Dämme, Straßen, Brücken, Tunnel, Speicher und andere nützliche Gebäude machen den Großteil der besten in diesem Land hergestellten sichtbaren Dinge aus." Die europäische Avantgarde war von diesen Bauten fasziniert. Sie schaute sehr genau hin und machte sich eine amerikanische Industrie- und Landwirtschaftsarchitektur zunutze, die nüchtern, pragmatisch und eindrucksvoll war. Eine Hommage an die Normalität.

Wie seinerzeit Gropius bin ich in diesem Jahr nach Detroit gereist, um mir die Ford-Fabrik selber anzusehen, und fotografierte Albert Kahns Fisher Karosseriewerk 21 von 1919. Wie viele seiner Fabriken steht sie mittlerweile leer, eine verlassene Ruine: Die Straßen waren mit Glasscherben übersät. Vielleicht besteht ihr heutiger Sinn einzig und allein darin sich vorzustellen, wie sie wohl für eine bessere Zukunft umgenutzt werden könnte. Meine Partnerin Regine und ich bauen seit Jahren Fabriken in Europa. In einer Umkehrung dieser Geschichte bin ich als ein im agrarisch-industriellen Bundesstaat Montana aufgewachsener amerikanischer Architekt kurioserweise damit konfrontiert, Fabriken in der Heimat des Bauhaus zu entwerfen. Unwillkürlich fällt uns ein, warum die frühen Modernisten von diesen industriellen Formen in der Prärie so fasziniert waren ...

Frank Barkow

Our Bauhaus

It's hard to make a choice among all the rich ideas that originated with the Bauhaus. And yet, the Dessau period and in particular Josef Albers's teaching is what has influenced our practice the most. His conceptual approach restores the essential character of the creative act. It develops the ability to invent (homo faber) and its double principle of economy – saving materials and working hours – remains an inspiration to us. It turns out that this is the path followed by Eladio Dieste in Uruguay and by Jean Prouvé in Paris, who have also had an important influential role in our work.

This centenary offers us the opportunity to reflect on today's architecture movements, some of which seem far too inclined to include superfluous elements, to mislead about the nature of the structure and to multiply envelope layers with excess. It is worth remembering the Bauhaus lesson of a century ago: that the aesthetic effect is not an end in itself, but the result of an intelligent implementation. Given the worsening state of the environment in particular, we should invoke the principles of Dessau and Josef Albers in order to uphold and promote the significance of a frugal, imaginative and masterful approach to architecture.

Unser Bauhaus

Es ist schwierig, aus der Fülle an Bauhaus-Ideen nur eine einzige auszuwählen. Und doch ist es die Dessauer Phase, insbesondere die Lehre von Josef Albers, die uns in unserer praktischen Arbeit am meisten beeinflusst hat. Sein Denkansatz gibt dem kreativen Akt seine fundamentale Bedeutung zurück und entwickelt den Erfindergeist (der Mensch als Homo Faber). Sein zweifaches Prinzip der Material- und Arbeitsökonomie ist für uns bis heute eine Inspirationsquelle. Ganz offensichtlich haben auch Eladio Dieste in Uruguay und Jean Prouvé in Paris diesen Pfad gewählt – und beide spielen in unserer Arbeit eine maßgebliche Rolle.

Dieses Jubiläum gibt uns Gelegenheit, über die Architekturbewegungen von heute nachzudenken, von denen einige einfach zu viele überflüssige Elemente einsetzen, sich um klare Strukturen drücken und ihre Entwürfe lagenweise in Hüllen packen. Daher lohnt es, an die Bauhaus-Lehre von vor hundert Jahren zu erinnern: Die ästhetische Wirkung ist nicht Selbstzweck, sondern das Ergebnis intelligenter Umsetzung. Der Zustand unserer Umwelt wird immer desolater. Angesichts dieser Entwicklung sollten wir uns an die Prinzipien von Dessau und Josef Albers halten und den Wert eines schlichten, fantasievollen und meisterhaften Architekturansatzes zu schätzen wissen und ihn fördern.

Sylvia Griño, Philippe Barthélémy

Pioneers of modernism

The Bauhaus movement has done much for architecture in the 20th and 21st centuries. Often referred to as "White Architecture", its actual quality lies in its holistic approach. Architecture, art, arts and crafts, stage design, furniture and product design, movement art and photography – to name but a few disciplines – were united in one school, one theory. Although it was not unique in the 20th century, given avant-garde trends such as the Hellerau Workshops, the Werkbund and Anthroposophy, the Bauhaus was based on a magnificent holistic design theory that also addressed the manufacturing process. It paved the way to modernism, the International Style, functionalism and many other schools and design approaches of the 20th century. That design could be not only decorative but functional and theoretically well-founded is not least due to the Bauhaus. Today we also recognize the political dimension of Bauhaus architecture. Perhaps it was because of us architects that the architectural debate was not continued in a similarly consistent, content-based manner, but mainly reduced to its purely creative, even aesthetic values – thus formally conserving it. But wouldn't the initiators of the Bauhaus come to completely different conclusions today? Wouldn't they take a different approach in terms of content and form? Based on similar ideas, but on completely new grounds? We should preserve the idea of the Bauhaus, instead of passing on its formal results as a mere trend.

Wegbereiter der Moderne

Die Bauhaus-Bewegung hat große Verdienste um die Architektur des 20. und 21. Jahrhunderts. Oft verkürzt auch „Weiße Architektur" genannt, liegt ihre eigentliche Qualität im ganzheitlichen Ansatz. Architektur, Kunst, Kunstgewerbe, Bühnenbild, Möbel- und Produktdesign, Bewegungskunst und Fotografie – um nur einige Disziplinen zu nennen – wurden in einer Schule, einer Theorie vereint. Obwohl nicht einzigartig im 20. Jahrhundert, betrachtet man avantgardistische Strömungen wie die Werkstätten Hellerau, den Werkbund, die Anthroposophie, lag dem Bauhaus eine großartige, ganzheitliche Gestaltungstheorie zugrunde, die sich auch mit dem Herstellungsprozess befasste. Sie bereitete den Weg zur Moderne, zum Internationalen Stil, zum Funktionalismus, sowie zu vielen weiteren Schulen und Gestaltungsrichtungen des 20. Jahrhunderts. Dass die Gestaltung den Weg aus dem Dekorativen zum Funktionalen und theoretisch Fundierten finden konnte, verdanken wir nicht zuletzt dem Bauhaus. Heute erkennen wir auch die politische Dimension der Bauhausarchitektur. Vielleicht lag es ja an uns Architekten selbst, dass die Architekturdebatte nicht in ähnlich konsequenter, inhaltlich fundierter Weise weitergeführt, sondern Architektur meist auf ihre rein gestalterischen, gar rein ästhetischen Werte reduziert – und damit formal konserviert wurde. Würden die Initiatoren des Bauhauses heute nicht zu völlig anderen Schlüssen kommen? Würden sie nicht eine andere inhaltliche und formale Herangehensweise wählen? Basierend auf ähnlichen Ideen, jedoch auf völlig neuen Grundlagen? Wir sollten die Idee des Bauhaus erhalten, statt seine formalen Ergebnisse als Mode weiterzutragen.

Stefan Behnisch

Building with vision
In the early 1970s, my high school landed like a UFO in the middle of our small town. The teachers on board were from the generation of '68, which had recently taken to the streets for the student revolution. Not only did the new school building impress us with its modernity, so did the teachers, with their surprising models for learning, thinking and interaction. Art was my favourite subject, and the teacher who accompanied me in this subject for years was "Master Strack". Through his open approach to teaching, for the first time I grasped that extra something, which develops from experimentation and research – when art and technology come together to realize a vision in construction. Isn't that architecture? And isn't it very close to the Bauhaus and its concept? This approach is what turns a learner into a questioning maker and designer, a developer and visionary who knows the pitfalls of the subject at hand, and who constantly elicits new spaces, aspects and possibilities from it. The ideas of the Bauhaus have often been poorly copied in theory and practice, and mistakenly referred to as "style". 100 years ago they were already far ahead of their time – and still are today. The strength of the Bauhaus comes from its ability to pose questions and clarify them in an interdisciplinary space.

Konstruktion mit Vision
Mein Gymnasium landete Anfang der 70er wie ein Ufo mitten in unserer Kleinstadt. An Bord ein Kollegium aus lauter 68ern, die gerade noch für die Studentenrevolution auf die Straße gegangen waren. Und nicht nur der Neubau beeindruckte uns schwer in seiner Modernität, auch die Lehrer überraschten uns mit erstaunlichen Modellen des Lernens, des Denkens und des gegenseitigen Umgangs. Kunst war mein Lieblingsfach, und der Lehrer, der mich über Jahre begleitete, war „Meister Strack": Durch seine offene Lehre begriff ich zum ersten Mal jenes Mehr, das sich aus Experiment und Forschung entwickelt – wenn Kunst und Technik zusammenfinden und sich daraus eine Vision in der Konstruktion realisiert. Ist das nicht Architektur? Ganz nah am Bauhaus und seinem Konzept? Es ist dieser Ansatz, der den Lernenden zum fragenden Konstrukteur und Gestalter macht, zum Entwickler und Visionär, der die Tücken der Materie kennt und ihr immer wieder neue Räume, Aspekte und Möglichkeiten entlockt. Die Ideen des Bauhaus wurden in Theorie und Praxis oft schlecht kopiert und fälschlicherweise als „Stil" bezeichnet. Sie waren schon vor 100 Jahren ihrer Zeit ganz weit voraus – und sind es noch immer. Ihre Kraft beziehen sie aus der Fähigkeit, Fragen zu stellen und im interdisziplinären Raum zu klären.

H.P. Ritz Ritzer

Homage by plaster cast

I taught at Anhalt University in Dessau for four years. During this time, we intensively dealt with the topic of space in the Master's programme. We used plaster casts of interiors to compare room characteristics from various origins and eras. In his 1952 article "Strutture e sequenze di spazi" Luigi Moretti analysed secular and sacral buildings using casts of their interiors. We referred to this study in our project, and also extended our models by making casts of their facades as well. Our aim was to sharpen the perception of space as the foundational moment of architecture, in order to create concrete spatial effects in a more targeted manner. We later documented some of our casts in the book Elementares zum Raum / A Primer to Space (2009). In 2008, my firm took part in a competition to replace one of the Masters' Houses in Dessau. We pursued the idea of reconstructing the destroyed building as an interior cast. The design was based on our own spatial experiments and intended to pay homage to the Bauhaus Masters.

Hommage per Abguss

Vier Jahre lang unterrichtete ich auch an der Hochschule Anhalt Dessau. Im Masterstudiengang setzten wir uns in dieser Zeit intensiv mit dem Thema Raum auseinander. So nutzten wir Innenraumabgüsse, um die Eigenschaften von Räumen unterschiedlicher Herkunft und aus verschiedenen Epochen miteinander zu vergleichen. Schon Luigi Moretti analysierte in seinem Artikel „Strutture e sequenze di spazi" von 1952 Profan- und Sakralbauten mithilfe von Abgüssen ihrer Innenräume. Darauf bezogen wir uns und erweiterten die Modelle um die Abgüsse der Fassaden. Es ging uns darum, die Wahrnehmung des Raumes als Grundmoment der Architektur zu schärfen, um so gezielter konkrete Raumwirkungen zu erzeugen. Einige unserer Abgüsse haben wir später in der Publikation „Elementares zum Raum / A Primer to Space" (2009) dokumentiert. 2008 nahm unser Büro am Wettbewerb für den Ersatz eines der Meisterhäuser in Dessau teil. Wir verfolgten die Idee, das zerstörte Gebäude als Innenraumabguss aufzubauen. Der Entwurf basierte auf unseren eigenen Raumexperimenten und sollte eine Hommage an die Meister des Bauhaus sein.

Roger Boltshauser

**Replacement Masters' Houses Bauhaus Dessau, competition model 2008, Roger Boltshauser
Ersatz Meisterhäuser Bauhaus Dessau, Wettbewerbsmodell 2008, Roger Boltshauser**

Ise Gropius, Meisterhäuser Dessau, Haus Gropius, 1925–26

Memoria and imprecision

For our competition entry to design the Masters' Houses in Dessau, one of our references was a photo album belonging to Ise Gropius. The private photographs they contain, taken by an amateur photographer, bear the traces of an almost mythical time. In their immediacy and intimacy, they have a very special presence of their own, a radiance that far surpasses official architectural history. The photos showed us that this competition was not primarily about a philological reconstruction, but about something much more subtle and profound – about memory and recollection. Memories thrive on inaccuracies and imprecision. In the search for an adequate approach to a past that can no longer be artificially regained, we wanted to work with this sense of imprecision. The atmospheric black-and-white images by Ise Gropius reminded us strongly of the series "Architecture" by Japanese photographer Hiroshi Sugimoto, in which blurred forms hover at the edge of recognizability. To what extent can a likeness be distorted, without rendering it unrecognizable? This was an important question for us in dealing with an architecture seen as the birthplace of modernity – but which is mainly passed on through images.

Memoria und Unschärfe

Zu unseren Wettbewerbsunterlagen für die Meisterhaussiedlung in Dessau gehörte auch ein Fotoalbum von Ise Gropius. Diese Privataufnahmen einer Amateurfotografin trugen die Spuren einer fast schon mythischen Zeit. In ihrer Unmittelbarkeit und Intimität entwickelten sie eine Präsenz von ganz eigener Strahlkraft – jenseits aller offiziellen Architekturgeschichte. Die Fotos zeigten uns, dass es in diesem Wettbewerb nicht primär um eine philologische Rekonstruktion ging, sondern um etwas viel Subtileres und Hintergründigeres – um Gedächtnis und Erinnerung. Erinnerungen leben nun mal von Unschärfe und Ungenauigkeiten. Auf der Suche nach einer adäquaten Haltung gegenüber einer Vergangenheit, die nicht mehr künstlich zurückgewonnen werden kann, wollten wir mit genau dieser Unschärfe arbeiten. Die atmosphärischen Schwarz-Weiß-Bilder von Ise Gropius erinnerten uns dabei sehr an Hiroshi Sugimotos Serie „Architecture", mit der sich der japanische Fotograf hart an der Grenze von Erkennbarkeit bewegt. Wie stark kann man ein Bild verfremden, ohne dass das Dargestellte unkenntlich wird? Diese Frage schien uns wichtig bei einer Architektur, die als Inkunabel der Moderne gilt – die aber hauptsächlich durch Bilder überliefert ist.

Piero Bruno, Donatella Fioretti, Jose Gutierrez Marquez

Once upon a time in Germany My father and I once built a house, when I was still a teen. For Germans, building houses and do-it-yourself seems to run in the blood. After all, you don't find the kind of hardware superstores you have in Germany anywhere else in the world. No wonder, then, that the Bauhaus originated here – and no, I don't mean the German DIY chain of the same name, but an entire architectural epoch – the epoch of modernism! What remains of the once ambitious German architecture, which 100 years ago saw itself as a Gesamtkunstwerk? At its heart were ideas and ideals – a connection between art and life, functionality and aesthetics, philosophy and technical progress… in the sense of a complete renewal: architecture as a possibility of conceiving new forms of living.

For me, the most important aspect of the Bauhaus remains the social utopia and the idea of a community that was the foundation of its true mission and vision. And this is a legacy we must continue to try to live up to – especially at a time when ideals are given far less importance than technical prowess and the market appeal of supposedly positive energy measures…

What can space mean? What role can architecture play in people's lives? How do we understand built space not only as matter and function, but also as emotional space, as a stage for human life and experiences?

I have been working intensely in Asia for nearly two decades – perhaps I am drawn to it because it is in a period of transformation, because it is not afraid to ask questions about the future, because there is a desire to create new models and prototypes for a better life – as was once the case in Germany, 100 years ago.

Es war einmal in Deutschland Ein Haus haben auch wir gebaut – mein Vater und ich, damals noch ein Teenager. Häuserbauen und Heimwerken liegt uns Deutschen wohl im Blut. Baumärkte gibt's ja auch nur in Deutschland. Kein Wunder eigentlich, dass hier das Bauhaus erfunden wurde – nein, ich meine nicht die gleichnamige Baumarktkette, sondern eine ganze Architekturepoche, ja, die Epoche der Moderne! Was ist uns geblieben von der einst so ambitionierten deutschen Architektur, die sich vor 100 Jahren einmal als Gesamtkunstwerk verstand? Im Zentrum standen Ideen und Ideale – eine Verbindung von Kunst und Leben, Funktionalität und Ästhetik, Philosophie und technischem Forschritt … auf dem Wege und ganz im Sinne einer Erneuerung: Architektur als Möglichkeit der Lebens(mit)gestaltung und -bestimmung.

Der für mich wichtigste Aspekt des Bauhaus bleibt die soziale Utopie und die Idee einer Gemeinschaft, die der eigentlichen Zielsetzung und Vision zugrunde lag. Und dies ist ein Erbe, dem wir auch weiterhin versuchen müssen, gerecht zu werden – gerade in einer Zeit, in der tatsächlichen Idealen viel weniger Bedeutung beigemessen wird als der technischen Effizienz und der Vermarktbarkeit vermeintlich positiver Energiebilanzen …

Was kann Raum bedeuten? Welche Rolle kann die Architektur im Leben der Menschen spielen? Wie verstehen wir gebauten Raum nicht nur als Materie und Funktion, sondern als Emotionsraum, als Schauplatz des Lebens und der Gefühle?

Seit fast zwei Jahrzehnten arbeite ich viel in Asien – vielleicht, weil dort eine Zeit des Aufbruchs herrscht. Weil Fragen an die Zukunft gestellt werden. Weil es eine Erwartung und ein Bedürfnis gibt, neue Modelle zu schaffen, Prototypen für ein besseres (zukünftiges) Leben – so wie das auch in Deutschland einmal der Fall war. Vor 100 Jahren …

Ole Scheeren

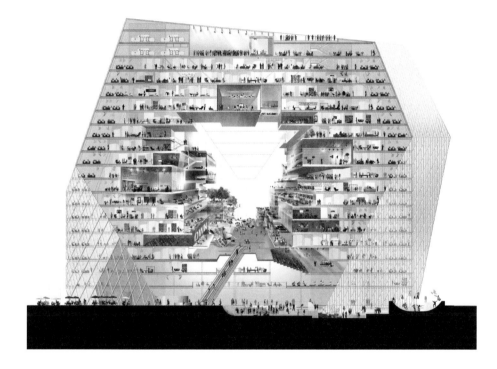

A primary inspiration

I was around 13 years old when I began noticing architecture. I lived a stone's throw away from Aalto's only building in Denmark – the Kunsten Museum of Modern Art in Aalborg. Often, I'd pass by simply to get a peek at it. My mother was a design enthusiast and introduced me to Jacobsen, Kjærholm and Wegner. Nearly all of my references at the time were Scandinavian.

When I was in high school, my older brother started studying architecture. He began talking enthusiastically about late German architects and thus I was introduced to Mies, Gropius and Meyer. He gave me my first Bauhaus book for my birthday when I turned 17. It was a popular, richly illustrated book by Taschen. I fell in love with the abstract graphics and the way they seemed to fit like a glove with the Bauhaus architecture. The idea of aesthetically unifying the entire built environment – from furniture to master plan was thrilling and new to me. Soon the Bauhaus spirit crept in under my skin and became part of my personal design vocabulary.

My favorite Bauhaus teacher is Paul Klee. Actually, his paintings are not totally aligned with the typical Bauhaus "look". Even so, Paul Klee remains my primary inspiration for both architecture and art. But mostly I admire the way he lived his life.

Eine zentrale Inspirationsquelle

Ich war ungefähr 13, als ich zum ersten Mal bewusst Architektur wahrnahm. Ich wohnte nur einen Steinwurf entfernt von Alvar Aaltos einzigem Gebäude in Dänemark, dem Kunsten – Museum of Modern Art in Aalborg. Häufig ging ich daran vorbei, um einfach nur einen Blick darauf zu erhaschen. Meine Mutter schwärmte für Design und machte mich mit Jacobsen, Kjærholm und Wegner bekannt. Fast alle meine Bezüge in dieser Zeit waren skandinavisch.

Als ich auf dem Gymnasium war, begann mein älterer Bruder, Architektur zu studieren. Er sprach begeistert von den deutschen Bauhaus-Architekten und machte mich mit Mies, Gropius und Meyer bekannt. Zu meinem 17. Geburtstag schenkte er mir mein erstes Bauhaus-Buch. Es war ein weit verbreitetes, reich bebildertes Taschenbuch, und ich verliebte mich auf der Stelle in die abstrakte grafische Gestaltung, die perfekt zur Bauhaus-Architektur zu passen schien. Die Vorstellung, die gesamte bebaute Umwelt – vom Möbel bis zum Masterplan – unter einem einzigen asketischen Konzept zu vereinen, war für mich aufregend, verlockend und neu. Bald schon ging mir der Geist des Bauhaus unter die Haut und wurde zu einem Teil meines persönlichen gestalterischen Vokabulars.

Mein Lieblingslehrer am Bauhaus ist Paul Klee. Seine Bilder entsprechen allerdings nicht ganz dem typischen Bauhaus-„Look". Dennoch ist Klee meine zentrale Inspirationsquelle für Architektur und Kunst, und ich bewundere grenzenlos die Art und Weise, wie er sein Leben lebte.

Mikkel Frost

Bauhaus 02

The fact that we initially wanted to call ourselves "Bau-Cooperative Himmelblau" reveals our enthusiasm for the Bauhaus programme, which championed the social integration of architecture, art and design. But as our own architectural development progressed, we increasingly began to doubt the works and buildings of the Bauhaus, with its Protestant, rational design details. In our dystopian times today, we clearly need a kind of Bauhaus 02 that can articulate a radical and positive expansion of the notion of architecture. If a Bauhaus 02 programme were to investigate not just new design and planning methods but also new construction methods, and if its theory would include a psychology of architectural development, it could become one of the most important architectural schools of the future. So let's get started!

Bauhaus 02

Dass wir uns am Anfang Bau-Cooperative Himmelblau nennen wollten, sollte die Begeisterung für das Lehrprogramm des Bauhaus zeigen, nämlich die Idee der sozialen Integration von Architektur, Kunst und Design. Allerdings wurden uns im Verlauf unserer fortschreitenden architektonischen Entwicklung die Werke und Gebäude der Bauhaus-Schule mit ihren protestantischen rationalen Details immer verdächtiger. Dass in unseren dystopischen Zeiten ein Bauhaus 02 wichtig wäre, das eine radikale und positive Erweiterung des Begriffs Architektur formuliert, ist evident. Wenn das Lehrprogramm des Bauhaus 02 neben neuen Entwurfs- und Planungsmethoden auch neue Baumethoden untersuchen und die Theorie auch eine Psychologie der Architekturentwicklung beinhalten würde, könnte es eine der wichtigsten Architekturschulen der Zukunft werden. Also los!

Wolf D. Prix

Apartment Complex Vienna 2, 1983

In defiance of the Bauhaus

My childhood memories are strongly influenced by the Bauhaus, its history and its ideals. My grandfather, Ludwig Hirschfeld-Mack, taught at the State Academy of Crafts and Architecture in Weimar. Colleagues like Arieh Sharon, Walter Gropius and Oskar Schlemmer literally walked in and out of my mother's house. And my parents studied at the Ulm School of Design, which was considered the extended arm of the Bauhaus. Artists like Max Bill, Johannes Itten and the architect Konrad Wachsmann were part of its community. Architecture, design and art were integrated into our family life, and the Bauhaus was always at the table. Whether breakfast or dinner, at every opportunity it offered topics of conversation and cause for countless discussions. But as fascinating as this period of my life was, I felt rather constricted by this constant sense of Bauhaus-above-all. Ultimately, it was the urge to escape this powerful influence that drove me to create something new architecturally. Although there are still many parallels to it in my work, especially in terms of project development, the pure functionality of the Bauhaus style was too rationalistic for my tastes. For me, the physiological and emotional levels are decisive components of every spatial experience and quality, which is why functionality is inconceivable without them. Our motto is that architecture is nothing more than applied physiology.

Dem Bauhaus zum Trotz

Meine Kindheitserinnerungen sind stark geprägt vom Bauhaus, seiner Geschichte und seinen Idealen. So unterrichtete mein Großvater, Ludwig Hirschfeld-Mack, an der Hochschule für Handwerk und Baukunst in Weimar. Kollegen wie Arieh Sharon, Walter Gropius und Oskar Schlemmer gingen bei meiner Mutter praktisch ein und aus. Und meine Eltern hatten an der Hochschule für Gestaltung in Ulm studiert, die als verlängerter Arm des Bauhaus galt. Zu ihrem Umfeld zählten Künstler wie Max Bill, Johannes Itten und der Architekt Konrad Wachsmann. Architektur, Design und Kunst gehörten bei uns zum Familienalltag, und das Bauhaus saß immer mit am Tisch. Ob Frühstück oder Abendessen, bei jeder Gelegenheit bot es Gesprächsstoff und Anlass für zahllose Diskussionen. Doch so faszinierend dieser Lebensabschnitt auch war, fühlte ich mich durch dieses ständige Bauhaus-über-Alles doch ganz schön eingeengt. Letztlich war es der Drang, mich diesem mächtigen Einfluss zu entziehen, der mich dazu trieb, architektonisch etwas Neues zu schaffen. Obwohl es vor allem in der Projektentwicklung bis heute viele Parallelen gibt, war mir persönlich die reine Funktionalität des Bauhaus-Stils einfach zu rationalistisch. Für mich sind die physiologischen und die emotionalen Ebenen entscheidende Komponenten jeder Raumerfahrung und -qualität, weshalb Funktionalität ohne sie undenkbar ist. Unser Motto lautet: Architektur ist nichts anderes als angewandte Physiologie!

Roman Delugan

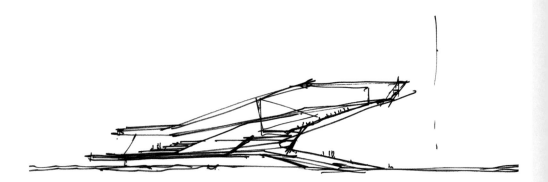

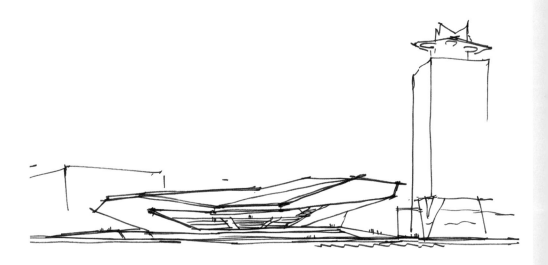

Dynamism and permanence

Bauhaus and Bauhaus! What makes an encounter with the Bauhaus and its heritage so special is the simultaneity of dynamism and permanence. The school's programme was to be radically experimental in form and content. Its history has been a constant source of new discoveries. Meanwhile, the Experimental House and the Director's Room in Weimar, the Bauhaus and Masters' Houses in Dessau and all the furniture and objects from both studios are living icons for architecture and design.

Dynamik und Permanenz

Bauhaus und Bauhaus! Die wunderbare Erfahrung mit dem Bauhaus, seinem Erbe, ist die Gleichzeitigkeit von Dynamik und Permanenz. Das Programm der Schule: in Form und Inhalt radikal experimentell. Ihre Geschichte: eine ständige Quelle neuer Entdeckungen. Versuchshaus und Direktorenzimmer in Weimar, Bauhaus und Meisterhäuser in Dessau und all die Möbel und Objekte aus beiden Ateliers: lebendige Ikonen für Architektur und Design.

Roger Diener

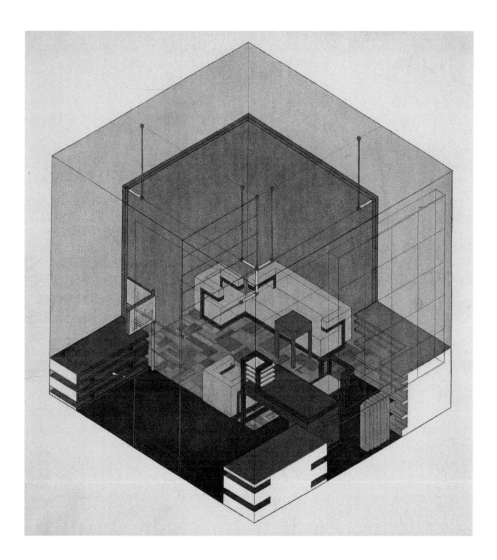

**Director's Office in Bauhaus Weimar, design: Walter Gropius 1923,
drawing: Herbert Bayer**
**Direktorenzimmer im Bauhaus Weimar, Isometrie, Entwurf: Walter Gropius 1923,
Zeichnung: Herbert Bayer**

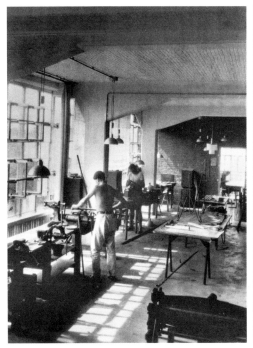 

Combining artistic process and craft – this guiding principle of the Bauhaus inspires our work and teaching. Left: Metal workshop at the Bauhaus in Dessau. Right: Überholz Interdisciplinary master's programme for timber construction at the University of Art and Design Linz (Director: Helmut Dietrich)
Zusammenführung von künstlerischem Prozess und handwerklichem Tun – diese Leitidee des Bauhaus inspiriert unsere Arbeit und unsere Lehre. Links: Metallwerkstatt im Bauhaus Dessau. Rechts: Überholz – Interdisziplinärer Universitätslehrgang für Holzbaukultur an der Kunstuniversität Linz (Leitung Helmut Dietrich)

Easier said than done

The significance of the Bauhaus and the fascination it holds rests on several very different levels. Its profound influence on all art forms, especially product design and architecture, is obvious. In just 15 years, the Bauhaus provided an entire century with valid forms and colours. The range of products, furniture and buildings that emerged from the Bauhaus, or were inspired by it, is wide and varied. Many of these objects have long since become part of how we perceive everyday life – synonymous with good form.

What makes the Bauhaus so unique is the incredible concentration of extraordinary artistic personalities who worked there as teachers or students. A central aspect of its curriculum was the departure from the purely academic approach that had been customary until then, and its combination of artistic process with craftsmanship. We owe the Bauhaus for showing us the immense creative potential that can be unleashed by such a connection. This, in turn, leads to the question: To what extent can we integrate this basic principle into today's architectural training and work processes? Ever since the Bauhaus, the creative process can no longer be regarded as an individual achievement – it requires the experience of many and the integration of everyone who is involved in development and production. What was once an avant-garde approach is now considered common sense in art and architecture. But that does not necessarily mean that its implementation has been equally successful.

Gelingt die Umsetzung?

Die Bedeutung und Faszination des Bauhaus liegt gleich auf mehreren, sehr unterschiedlichen Ebenen. Sein tiefgreifender Einfluss auf alle Kunstformen, insbesondere die Produktgestaltung und Architektur, ist unübersehbar. In nur 15 Jahren hat das Bauhaus einem ganzen Jahrhundert gültige Formen und Farben geschenkt. Die Palette seiner Produkte, der Möbel und Bauten, die ihm unmittelbar entstammen oder von ihm inspiriert wurden, ist groß und vielfältig. Viele dieser Objekte sind längst Teil unserer alltäglichen Wahrnehmung geworden – zu Synonymen für die gute Form.

Was das Bauhaus darüber hinaus noch so einzigartig macht, ist diese unglaubliche Konzentration von außergewöhnlichen Künstlerpersönlichkeiten, die hier als Lehrer tätig waren oder als Schüler ihre Ausbildung erfahren haben. Ein zentraler Aspekt seines Curriculums war die Abkehr von der rein akademischen Ausrichtung der bis dahin üblichen Ausbildung und die Zusammenführung des künstlerischen Prozesses mit dem handwerklichen Tun. Die Erfahrung, welch immenses kreatives Potenzial in einer solchen Verbindung steckt, verdanken wir dem Bauhaus. Das wiederum führt unmittelbar zu der Frage, inwieweit wir dieses Grundprinzip nicht in heutige Ausbildungen und Arbeitsprozesse integrieren können. Seit dem Bauhaus kann der kreative Prozess nicht mehr als Leistung eines Einzelnen angesehen werden – er bedingt die Erfahrung vieler und muss alle beteiligten Akteure in die Entwicklung und Herstellung integrieren. Dieser avantgardistische Ansatz gilt heute als Common Sense in Kunst und Architektur, was aber nicht unbedingt heißt, dass die Umsetzung ebenso gut gelingt.

Helmut Dietrich, Dominik Philipp, Patrick Stremler, Much Untertrifaller

Complexity and design

The Bauhaus welcomed all disciplines, regarding them as equal – this aspect is always present in my work as well. For me, the arts are never separate. They complement each other, engaging in a dynamic relationship. I feel that those who are committed to the design process must tap into multiple disciplines and related fields. After all, the complexity of the world is an enrichment and the engine of all creativity. Acknowledging this complexity also means going out and implementing new methods and procedures that can adapt to a wide variety of contexts. At our studio, for example, we use colour according to a specially developed autonomous logic that sometimes causes an intentional sense of irritation when experiencing the space. This effect raises questions about space and its structure and enables multiple interpretations. It's as if we would enter a kind of open narrative that affects us profoundly.

Komplexität und Gestaltung

Das Bauhaus hat sich gegenüber allen Disziplinen geöffnet und sie als gleichberechtigt angesehen – dieser Zusammenhang ist auch in meiner Arbeit immer präsent. Für mich sind die Künste niemals voneinander getrennt. Sie ergänzen sich gegenseitig und sind Teil einer wechselseitigen Dynamik. Ich glaube, dass sich Gestaltungsprozesse zu verschiedenen Disziplinen und benachbarten Bereichen hin öffnen müssen. Schließlich ist die Komplexität der Welt eine Bereicherung und der Motor aller Kreativität. Diese Komplexität anzuerkennen bedeutet auch, sich auf den Weg zu machen und neue Methoden und Verfahren umzusetzen, die sich den verschiedensten Kontexten anzupassen vermögen. In den Entwürfen unseres Büros folgt die Farbe einer eigens entwickelten autonomen Logik, die den Raumeindruck bisweilen bewusst irritiert. Dieser Effekt wirft Fragen auf zum Raum und seiner Struktur. Mehrere Deutungen sind möglich. Wir begeben uns sozusagen in eine offene Konstellation, die uns betroffen macht.

Dominique Coulon

Objectivity meets emotion

An approach that can handle all scales of design without ever being a "total look" is one way that the Bauhaus spirit could be described. This image of the French National Library (BnF) expresses the values present in this precursor of contemporary architecture and design as a kind of heir to the Bauhaus legacy.

The BnF presents a global order, designed down to the details of the lamp or the reading chair. With little ornamentation, apparent sobriety, a taste for a geometric rigor and structural truth within the architectural elements. At the same time, it creates environments that spark a synesthetic experience. Another striking parallel it has with the Bauhaus may be found in its recognition of the aesthetic value of raw and industrial materials. The overall logic of BnF creates an atmosphere, a cognitive field. Space mobilizes our senses, sight, hearing and touch, while simplifying and ordering functional and studied elements. Concrete, metal, wood and glass are authentic materials that create a landscape with depth, shadow and light. Wood, a single essence, as a divider element, chair, table or shelf, evokes the smell of paper – the warm side of a library. Concrete, raw and smooth, has the softness of marble, while the floor, covered with tightly woven carpet the colour of "African soil", softens the sounds and contributes to a sense of sheltered intimacy. Finally, metal – the ultimate industrial material – takes the form of a large woven mesh that hangs like curtains from the ceilings.

The Bauhaus has this ability to move design from the objectivity of the technique to the emotion of the material. It opened our eyes to the idea that an object can be at once simple, functional and aesthetic. Its aptitude for multidisciplinarity and the reconciliation between industrial know-how and modernist aesthetics, with innovation and generosity, is now more alive than ever.

Objektivität trifft auf Emotion

Ein Ansatz, der sich für alle Entwurfsmaßstäbe eignet, ohne je zum „total look" zu werden – das ist eine Möglichkeit, den Geist des Bauhaus zu beschreiben. Die französische Nationalbibliothek (BnF) bringt perfekt die Werte zum Ausdruck, für die jener Wegbereiter aller zeitgenössischen Architektur und allen modernen Designs steht.

Die BnF besitzt eine allumfassende Ordnung, die bis ins kleinste Detail einer Leuchte oder eines Lesesessels durchdacht ist. Mit minimaler Ornamentierung, offenkundiger Schlichtheit und einer Vorliebe für geometrische Strenge und strukturelle Wahrheit innerhalb der architektonischen Elemente. So entstehen Umgebungen, die ein synästhetisches Erlebnis auslösen. Eine weitere markante Parallele zum Bauhaus ist die ästhetische Wertschätzung von Industrie- und Rohmaterialien. Das Gesamtkonzept der BnF schafft eine Atmosphäre, ein kognitives Feld. Raum mobilisiert unsere Sinne, das Sehen, Hören und Fühlen, und vereinfacht und ordnet funktionale und wohldurchdachte Elemente. Die authentischen Materialien Beton, Metall, Holz und Glas generieren eine Landschaft mit Tiefe, Licht und Schatten. Das Holz bildet die Essenz, die als Raumteiler, Stuhl, Tisch oder Regal den Geruch von Papier heraufbeschwört – die warme Seite einer Bibliothek. Beton, roh und glatt zugleich, verbreitet die Weichheit von Marmor, während der Boden, bedeckt mit einem engmaschig gewebten Teppich in der Farbe „afrikanischer Erde", den Schall dämpft und ein Gefühl von geschützter Intimität vermittelt. Und Metall – das ultimative Industriematerial – nimmt die Form eines Netzgewebes an, das wie ein Vorhang von der Decke herabhängt.

Das Bauhaus besitzt diese Fähigkeit, das Design von der Objektivität der Technik zur Emotion des Materials zu verschieben. Es öffnete uns den Blick dafür, dass ein Objekt gleichzeitig einfach, funktional und ästhetisch sein kann. Seine Fähigkeit zur Multidisziplinarität und die innovative, großzügige Annäherung von industriellem Know-how und modernistischer Ästhetik ist heute lebendiger denn je.

Dominique Perrault

Bibliothèque nationale de France, Salle de lecture

A holistic approach

When the production machinery of architecture shifts into high gear and starts rolling, it is a fiercely efficient and powerful machinery – financially, logistically and technically. It is also the exact time when it is crucial to insist on a continuous hands-on approach that goes beyond concept and theory. To me, the holistic Bauhaus approach provides a source of inspiration.

Creating a Gesamtkunstwerk is no small feat. The idea that architecture – like all art forms – is a craft is true, but the craftsmanship is extremely technical, so complex. Attempting to reconnect with associated art forms is a way for me to disrupt and improve on an otherwise quite technical process.

I have always admired the Bauhaus movement for its ability to blur the lines between functionality and aesthetics. In the process of stripping architecture of ornamentation, it somehow united the two. Functionality became an aesthetic experience and the aesthetics were strictly functional.

While designing the Wadden Sea Centre on the west coast of Denmark, I had a rare opportunity to truly connect functional architecture with craftsmanship. The functionality and flow of the exhibition spaces, the building itself, its sculpturally thatched roof and the powerful bareness of the landscape all became one, in what I almost dare to consider a modern Gesamtkunstwerk.

Ein ganzheitlicher Ansatz

Wenn die Produktionsmaschinerie der Architektur einen Gang höher schaltet und so richtig in Schwung kommt, ist sie – in finanzieller, logistischer und technischer Hinsicht – eine höchst effiziente und mächtige Maschinerie. Das ist zugleich auch der entscheidende Moment für ein konsequent pragmatisches Vorgehen jenseits von Konzept und Theorie. Für mich ist daher der ganzheitliche Bauhaus-Ansatz die perfekte Inspirationsquelle.

Ein Gesamtkunstwerk zu schaffen, ist kein Kinderspiel. Es stimmt zwar, dass Architektur wie alle Kunstformen ein Handwerk ist, doch in ihrer Ausführung ist Handwerkskunst ein extrem technischer und hochkomplexer Vorgang. Und der Versuch, wieder an verwandte Kunstformen anzuknüpfen, ist für mich die probate Möglichkeit, einen ansonsten sehr technischen Prozessablauf zu stören und kreativ zu verbessern.

Ich habe das Bauhaus stets für seine Fähigkeit bewundert, die Grenzen zwischen Funktionalität und Ästhetik zu überschreiten. Als es die Architektur von ihrer Ornamentik befreite, verband es die beiden in gewisser Weise. Funktionalität wurde zu einer ästhetischen Erfahrung, und die Ästhetik war streng funktional.

Beim Entwurf des Wadden Sea Centre an der Westküste Dänemarks hatte ich die seltene Gelegenheit, funktionale Architektur mit Handwerkskunst zu verbinden. Die auf Zweckmäßigkeit angelegten, ineinander übergehenden Ausstellungsräume, das Gebäude an sich, das skulpturale Reetdach und die beeindruckende, karge Landschaft wurden eins – man könnte fast von einem Gesamtkunstwerk sprechen.

Dorte Mandrup

Man plans and God laughs

As the daughter of an architect, I came across the word "Bauhaus" early in life. My father, who was born in 1910, belonged to a generation in which architects, artists, poets, architectural critics and writers were all lumped together. It seemed to be widely accepted that all those professions had something very basic in common. My father's first job was working for the Bata shoe company, and I was born at the outset of the Second World War. My mother left the maternity hospital with me, her newly born infant, on the same day that Zlin – which was built by Bata and the only modern town in the world to be built between two world wars – was being occupied by the German Army, their soldiers marching through the streets. The town later became a kind of sanctuary for people who opposed fascism – their lives would be in danger if they lived in Prague. There were not many public places where friends could meet without fear at the time and our house became a meeting place for all my new "uncles" and "aunties" who had certainly come together because of their political views and their love of art and the country.

I was too little to understand the conversations on the Bauhaus and what happened to it. But I did pay attention whenever my father saw my little creative projects and said: "I will send her to the Bauhaus when life becomes normal again..."

My parents' home was very modern, in contrast to many of the buildings where my friends lived. We had a so-called Frankfurt Kitchen, designed by Margarete Schutte-Lihotzky, and many other modernist objects, such as Eileen Gray's Transat Chair and her black and white rug, and china and ceramics from UVA, to name a few. Those things sat comfortably in our small, standard home, the kind built by Bata for all of its employees, with the interior designed by my father in the style of 1930s.

"Man plans and God laughs," goes an old saying, and reality took a course contrary to my father's ideas and hopes. The war ended six years after my birth, but "normal life" after the end of the war lasted only two-and-a-half years, until February 1948 when the Communists took over. For us, what followed was a period of darkness, a totalitarian regime that left no space for freedom. Like fascism before it, the new regime could not cope with free thinking – so the free thinkers of the Bauhaus and that splendid organization again became a forbidden memory.

In 1956, I began studying architecture in Prague, and despite very strict party policies, most of my professors were of a generation that was either Bauhaus-influenced or Bauhaus-friendly or even Bauhaus-educated. Not surprisingly, as students always look for forbidden fruit, we secretly tried to discover traces of the Bauhaus and its history among banned books.

Der Mensch denkt und Gott lenkt

Als Tochter eines Architekten kam ich schon in jungen Jahren mit dem Wort „Bauhaus" in Berührung. Mein Vater, Jahrgang 1910, gehörte zu einer Generation, für die Architekten, Künstler, Dichter, Architekturkritiker und Schriftsteller zur selben Spezies gehörten – man war sich weitgehend darüber einig, dass die genannten Künste und Berufe etwas sehr Grundlegendes miteinander verband. Mein Vater hatte seine erste Anstellung bei Baťa, einer großen Schuhfabrik in Mähren, und ich wurde buchstäblich am Vorabend des Zweiten Weltkriegs geboren: Meine Mutter verließ das Krankenhaus genau an dem Tag, als die Deutschen in Zlín einmarschierten. Zlín, Hauptsitz von Baťa, war mit der Fabrik zu einem urbanen Industriezentrum angewachsen und in der Zeit zwischen den Kriegen architektonisch wie städtebaulich die wohl einzige moderne Stadt der Welt. Später wurde sie zu einem Rückzugsort für die Gegner des Faschismus. Es gab nicht allzu viele Orte, an denen man sich angstfrei treffen konnte, und unser Haus wurde zum Treffpunkt meiner neuen „Onkel" und „Tanten", die ihre politischen Ansichten miteinander verband und ihre Liebe zu Kunst und Land. Ich war noch zu klein, um Gespräche über das Bauhaus zu verstehen, aber ich erinnere mich noch gut daran, dass mein Vater, wenn er mir beim Spielen zusah, häufig sagte: „Wenn das Leben wieder normal wird, schicke ich sie ans Bauhaus." Das Haus meiner Eltern war sehr modern. Wir hatten eine original Frankfurter Küche nach dem Entwurf von Margarete Schütte-Lihotzky und jede Menge an aktuellem Design wie etwa Eileen Grays Transat-Stuhl. All diese Dinge fügten sich harmonisch in den Typ Siedlungshaus ein, wie es Baťa all seinen Angestellten zur Verfügung stellte, und dessen Inneneinrichtung mein Vater im Stil der 1930er-Jahre entworfen hatte. „Der Mensch denkt und Gott lenkt", lautet ein Sprichwort, und die Realität entwickelte sich nicht nach den Vorstellungen und Hoffnungen meines Vaters. Der Krieg endete zwar sechs Jahre später, doch das sogenannte normale Leben hielt nur zweieinhalb Jahre an. Im

Eva Jiřičná

Februar 1948 übernahmen die Kommunisten die Macht, und es folgte die düstere Ära eines totalitären Regimes, das der Freiheit keine Spielräume ließ und wie der Faschismus nicht mit dem freiem Denken und den freien Denkern des Bauhaus zurechtkam, sodass diese wunderbare Schule einmal mehr zur verbotenen Erinnerung wurde.

1956 begann ich, in Prag Architektur zu studieren, und trotz der strengen Parteirichtlinien war die Mehrzahl meiner Professoren Bauhaus-freundlich, -beeinflusst – oder hatte sogar am Bauhaus studiert. Da Studenten immer auf der Jagd nach verbotenen Früchten sind, gingen wir in den weggesperrten Büchern heimlich auf Spurensuche nach dem Bauhaus und seiner Geschichte.

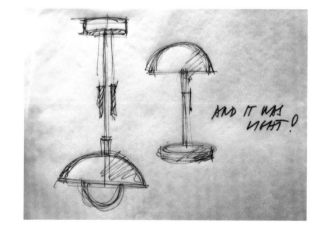

Total compartmentalization Gesamtkunstwerks frighten me. It was the Bauhaus's declared ambition to unite architecture with all other arts to become exactly that. I am not sure why they give me such a feeling of unease, as I find today's architectural world of total compartmentalization at least as troubling. It is almost as if the totalizing ambition of the cultural institution of the Bauhaus were being countered by a substantial fracturing in much of architectural practice these days.

In designing a national cultural institute, for instance, our office, FAR, is currently confronted by the fact that its bare-bone shell and furnishings are funded by different sources. This makes it largely impossible for us to engage in the debate on how the building will be outfitted. We are also being sanctioned from discussing the project with its actual future users. For this same cultural institute, an art-in-architecture competition will be held to select a work of art that – hopefully – engages in a dialogue with our building. My request to participate as member of the jury was denied, as I am an architect and not an artist.

Today, one could argue that Gesamtkunstwerks are used mainly to create all-encompassing brand experiences. It is probably this aspect that explains my initial unease. But the Gesamtkunstwerk's implied premise of unity and coherency seems to provide a helpful counterpoint – existing in opposition to the mundane unambiguousness in which individual experts hold exclusive competence and power over fragments of a project.

Totale Fragmentierung Gesamtkunstwerke machen mir Angst. Es war das erklärte Ziel des Bauhaus, die Architektur mit den anderen Künsten zu vereinen, um genau das zu werden. Ich weiß nicht genau, warum mir solche Ansätze ein derartiges Unbehagen bereiten, da ich die heutige Welt der totalen Kleinteiligkeit in der Architektur nicht minder beunruhigend finde. Es ist beinahe so, als wirke dem ganzheitlichen Ziel der Kulturinstitution Bauhaus heute ein Zergliederungsprozess in der architektonischen Praxis entgegen.

Unser Büro FAR entwirft derzeit etwa ein nationales Kulturinstitut und ist damit konfrontiert, dass der Rohbau und das Interieur aus unterschiedlichen Quellen finanziert werden. Das macht es für uns beinahe unmöglich, über die Ausstattung des Gebäudes zu diskutieren. Des Weiteren ist es uns untersagt, das Projekt mit den künftigen Nutzern zu besprechen. Für besagtes Kulturinstitut wird ein Kunst-am-Bau-Wettbewerb ausgeschrieben, und das ausgewählte Kunstwerk soll – so hoffe ich zumindest – mit unserem Gebäude in Dialog treten. Mein Wunsch, als Jurymitglied an diesem Prozess teilzunehmen, wurde abgelehnt mit der Begründung, ich sei Architekt und kein Künstler.

Man könnte sagen, dass der primäre Zweck eines Gesamtkunstwerks heute darin besteht, einheitliche Markenerlebnisse zu erzeugen. Dieser Aspekt erklärt wahrscheinlich mein anfängliches Unbehagen. Doch die implizite Prämisse der Einheit und Kohärenz eines Gesamtkunstwerks scheint ein sinnvolles Gegengewicht zur banalen Eindeutigkeit zu sein, bei der individuelle Experten die alleinige Kompetenz und Kontrolle über einzelne Fragmente des Projekts beanspruchen.

Marc Frohn

Frei Otto exhibition, Zentrum für Kunst und Medien Karlsruhe, 2016, design by FAR frohn&rojas. Otherwise mundane lighting cables are transformed into a totalizing infrastructure. They link technical, spatial, atmospheric as well as narrative dimensions by referencing Frei Otto's hanging models and his cosmos of artistic and scientific experimentation.
Frei Otto Ausstellung, Zentrum für Kunst und Medien Karlsruhe, 2016, Entwurf: FAR frohn&rojas. Die vorgeblich profanen Elemente der Beleuchtungskabel werden dabei in eine alles überwölbende Infrastruktur verwandelt. Sie verbinden die technischen, räumlichen, atmosphärischen und narrativen Dimensionen durch den Verweis auf Frei Ottos hängende Modelle und sein Universum künstlerischer und wissenschaftlicher Experimente.

Armchair designed and manufactured by Jan Feichtinger (above), Adaptation of the "Acapulco" armchair by Dietmar Feichtinger, Designer anonymous, Mexico
Fauteuil entworfen und hergestellt von Jan Feichtinger (oben), Adaptation Fauteuil „Acapulco" von Dietmar Feichtinger, Designer anonym, Mexiko (unten)

Pioneers of the future

It is inconceivable to think of the Bauhaus in isolation. But it is possible to think of contemporary architecture as a continuation of modernism, and of the Bauhaus as its elementary component. Does it follow that we can consider architecture as an "expression of craftsmanship and art as its perfection"? How romantic can architects be? Where are the craftsmen who enrich the work with their competence? Construction management takes the pen out of our hands and forces us into the corset of planning efficiency. The solution is called BIM. Does 3D printing replace the carpenter and the joiner? Architecture is sluggish, it's slow to develop. The industrialization of architecture remains limited. Architecture keeps us on the ground, gives us stability. The desire for sustainability can help to promote quality standards. Can we communicate these values to the architects of the next 100 years? Can we conceive of architecture as a balance to a virtual world, as a concrete expression of materiality, authenticity and appropriateness? The Bauhaus is 100 years old and points our way forward.

Wegbereiter der Zukunft

Das Bauhaus isoliert wahrzunehmen, ist undenkbar. Doch zeitgenössische Architektur als Fortsetzung der Moderne, das Bauhaus als deren elementarer Bestandteil und folglich: „Architektur als Ausdruck des Handwerks und Kunst als dessen Vollendung"? Wie romantisch können Architekten sein? Wo sind die Handwerker, die durch ihre Kompetenz das Werk bereichern? Das Baumanagement nimmt uns den Stift aus der Hand, es zwingt uns in das Korsett der Planungseffizienz. Die Lösung heißt BIM. Ersetzt der 3D-Druck den Zimmerer, den Tischler? Architektur ist behäbig. Sie entwickelt sich langsam. Die Industrialisierung der Architektur ist noch immer beschränkt. Architektur hält uns auf dem Boden, gibt Halt. Der Wunsch nach Nachhaltigkeit kann helfen, den Qualitätsanspruch zu fördern. Können wir den Architekten der nächsten 100 Jahre diese Werte vermitteln? Architektur als Ausgleich zu einer virtuellen Welt, als konkreter Ausdruck von Materialität, Echtheit, Angemessenheit? Das Bauhaus ist 100 Jahre alt und hat den Weg vorgegeben.

Dietmar Feichtinger

The artisan's way

By placing the process at the centre of our work, we share with the Bauhaus an interest in the artisan's way of doing things. This means valuing the physical condition of the material with which things are made, not appraising it through the transitive nature of inspiration, but instead recognising its quality as a thing, identical with itself at any moment of a project.

At the 16th Venice Biennale in 2018, we presented the development process of one of our recent projects, displaying all of the material we produced along the way, together with intermediate and unfinished documents. If a work is always the sum of the materials used during its conception, it should be possible to explain it through each one of these materials. This gives importance to the making of things as a way of finding a rhythm that does not depend on the effects of causality, of the commission or of the circumstances.

Auf Handwerkerart

Mit dem Bauhaus verbindet uns das Interesse an einer handwerklichen Arbeitsweise, weil bei uns der Prozess des Machens im Mittelpunkt steht. Das bedeutet eine echte Wertschätzung des Materials, aus dem etwas entsteht – nicht indem es im flüchtigen Licht der Inspiration erscheint, sondern durch eine Anerkennung seiner konkreten physischen Realität und Qualität als etwas, das zu jedem Zeitpunkt eines Projekts mit sich selbst identisch ist.

Auf der 16. Architekturbiennale in Venedig 2018 haben wir den Entwicklungsprozess eines unserer jüngsten Projekte vorgestellt und das gesamte dabei produzierte Material ebenso wie vorläufige und unfertige Unterlagen präsentiert. Wenn ein Werk stets die Summe der Materialien ist, die im Laufe seiner Konzipierung verwendet wurden, dann sollte es sich auch durch jedes einzelne dieser Materialien erklären lassen. Damit rückt der Herstellungsprozess von Dingen in den Vordergrund, und es eröffnet sich die Möglichkeit, einen Rhythmus zu finden, der nicht von irgendeiner Kausalität, vom Auftrag oder den Umständen abhängt.

Ricardo Flores, Eva Prats

Liquid Light, Biennale Architettura 2018

Work in progress

Tokyo, December 2011: we are throwing a party. The Folded House, my office's first project, has just been completed. The sculptor A., a dear acquaintance, hands me a simply wrapped box.

Later, all by myself in the new building, I open the present and stare into the space unfolding on the paper. Josef Albers's "Ascension" weaves lines, each of them the purest expression of the two-dimensional, into an intricate spatial construct.

A century rushes through my mind. In the early 1920s, Albers moved to Weimar and became part of the most visionary movement of its time. At Black Mountain College 20 years later, he worked on "Ascension" as part of his "Graphic Tectonic" series. The Bauhaus, defying its forced shutdown 10 years earlier, was living on through many of its minds, and perhaps striving in ways that a single location could not have achieved. "Thus we cannot remain in a single viewpoint; we need more for the sake of Free Vision," reads a quote from the catalogue of the Cincinnati Art Museum exhibition "Josef Albers", from 1949, stuck to the back of the print's frame. Today, as we still seem to be pursuing similar paths, much of the Bauhaus is alive. And like anything alive, it keeps evolving.

Work in progress

Tokio, Dezember 2011: Wir geben eine Party. Das Folded House, erstes Projekt meines Büros, ist gerade fertig geworden. Der Bildhauer A., ein lieber Bekannter, überreicht mir eine schlicht verpackte Schachtel.

Als ich später ganz allein in den neuen Räumen bin, öffne ich das Geschenk und blicke erstaunt in den Raum, der sich vor mir auf dem Papier entfaltet: Josef Albers' Zeichnung „Ascension" verwebt parallele Linien – und jede einzelne die Reinform von Zweidimensionalität – zu einem verschlungenen räumlichen Konstrukt.

Ein Jahrhundert rauscht mir durch den Kopf. Anfang der 1920er-Jahre zog Albers nach Weimar und wurde Teil der visionärsten Bewegung seiner Zeit. Zwanzig Jahre später arbeitete er am Black Mountain College an „Ascension" als Teil seiner Graphic Tectonic-Serie. Das Bauhaus trotzte seiner Zwangsschließung, die zehn Jahre zuvor erfolgt war, und lebte durch viele seiner Köpfe weiter. Und vielleicht genau dadurch entfaltete es eine weit größere Strahlkraft, als dies ein einzelner Standort je hätte erreichen können. „Daher können wir nicht in einer einzigen Sichtweise verharren; für eine freie Sicht benötigen wir mehr", lautet ein Zitat aus dem Katalog der Ausstellung „Josef Albers" im Cincinnati Art Museum von 1949, das auf der Rückseite des Rahmens der Grafik klebt. Noch heute verfolgen wir oft Ideen, die ursprünglich vom Bauhaus ausgingen. Das Bauhaus ist am Leben — und wie alles Lebendige hört es nicht auf sich weiterzuentwickeln.

Florian Busch

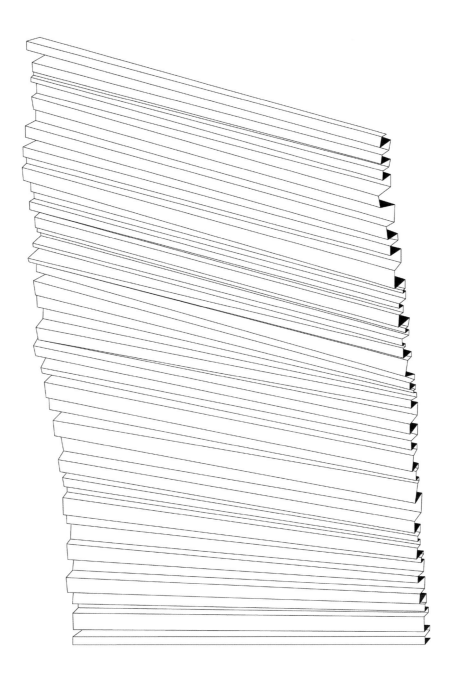

Study for Folded House
Studie für das Folded House

From vision to legacy

Perhaps there are beliefs passed on to me through generations of teachers, or maybe a conscious personal selection of inspirational ideas that happen to coincide with those of the Bauhaus. For example, I have a passionate interest in the links between architecture, design and art, which was at the core of Bauhaus teaching. There is also my driving curiosity about how things are made, which is exactly mirrored in the meaning of "Bauhaus" when it is translated as the "house of construction".

Gropius envisioned a time when buildings would be mass-produced in factories, and their component parts assembled like toy bricks – he designed cars, trains and, with Konrad Wachsmann, he experimented with modular systems for housing. As technology and materials have advanced, this thinking is even more relevant. We frequently utilize prefabricated components and we have worked at the scale of prefabricating entire buildings, with the development of a new, innovative system for the large-scale production of individual homes. The potential for three-dimensionally printing a building is arguably an extension of the Bauhaus philosophy. I am particularly interested in how these methods could be used to improve the quality of life in some of the world's poorest communities.

Von der Vision zum Vermächtnis

Es gibt vielleicht Überzeugungen, die über Generationen von Lehrern an mich weitergegeben wurden, oder vielleicht habe ich bewusst die Inspirationen ausgewählt, die sich zufällig mit denen des Bauhaus überschneiden. So interessiere ich mich zum Beispiel sehr für die Verbindungen zwischen Architektur, Design und Kunst, die im Mittelpunkt der Lehre am Bauhaus standen. Außerdem bin ich unendlich neugierig darauf, wie die Dinge gemacht werden – und genau das spiegelt sich in der Bedeutung des Wortes „Bauhaus" wider, wenn man es mit „Haus des Bauens" übersetzt.

Gropius sah eine Zeit voraus, in der Gebäude serienmäßig in Fabriken produziert und ihre Einzelteile wie Bauklötze zusammengefügt würden – er entwarf Autos und Züge und experimentierte mit Konrad Wachsmann an einem Fertighaussystem. Je mehr sich Technik und Materialien weiterentwickeln, umso wichtiger ist dieses Denken. Wir verwenden häufig vorgefertigte Elemente und haben schon ganze Gebäude vorgefertigt, wobei wir ein neues innovatives System zur Großproduktion einzelner Häuser entwickelt haben. Das Potenzial, ein Haus im 3D-Druck herzustellen, ist wohl eine Fortsetzung der Bauhaus-Philosophie. Besonders interessiert mich, wie man mithilfe dieser Methoden die Lebensqualität in einigen der ärmsten Regionen der Welt verbessern könnte.

Norman Foster

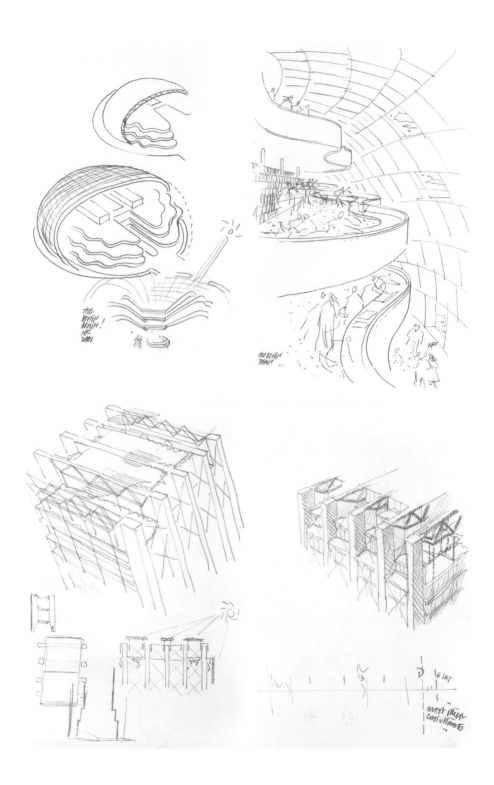

**Free University Berlin (above / oben),
Hongkong and Shanghai Bank Headquarters (below / unten)**

Constructive pros & cons
How do we engage in discourse? How do we talk to each other, when the personally appreciative, friendly or at least polite, discursive way of dealing with other views and opinions seems to be disappearing from the public arena? When theories and ideas can no longer be argued for, when dogmatic aggressiveness gains the upper hand in the exchange of opinions and the conversation level and word choice sink into the abyss, we should recall the circumstances surrounding the closure of the Bauhaus – when, for example, "fake news" was circulated, claiming that the modern functionalist style of the Neues Bauen movement was "Bolshevik" in nature. They are partial rays of hope when we see that it is sometimes possible to prove our personal greatness by standing up for those who think differently, even if their beliefs differ from ours. Even today, I am impressed by how Theodor Fischer, a proponent of "reform architecture" in Munich, participated in the debate on the impending closure of the Bauhaus in Dessau, when he wrote in 1927 (Theodor Fischer, "Um das Bauhaus," DIE KUNST, vol. 34/1, October 1927, p. 32.): "...and although I have a whole load of detailed reservations against the methods practiced there, and suspect that I myself have never enjoyed any special sympathies there, I recognize and admit that this undertaking has experienced important development and can still do so. I know that our time cannot march uniformly and, since I consider myself entitled and compelled to experiment, I know that others must also be granted the right to experiment. As for those who don't want to know anything about experiments (but who as a rule like to use the results to their benefit) or who want to dwell in tasteful comfort, I don't deny them the right to be as they are."
In other words, it's not about fighting against each other, but about standing up for each other. And not only at the Bauhaus.

Für ein konstruktives
Pro & Contra
Wie führt man Diskurse? Wie spricht man miteinander, wenn das persönlich wertschätzende, das freundliche oder zumindest höfliche, diskursive Umgehen mit anderen Ansichten und Meinungen in der Öffentlichkeit verschwindet? Wenn Thesen und Ideen nicht mehr argumentativ vertreten werden können, wenn dogmatische Aggressivität im Meinungsaustausch die Oberhand gewinnt und Gesprächsniveau und Wortwahl ins Bodenlose sinken, erinnert man sich an die Umstände der Schließung des Bauhaus – als beispielsweise „fake news" von der „bolschewistischen Natur des neuen Bauens" kolportiert wurden. Es sind dann partielle Lichtblicke, wenn man bemerkt, dass es manchmal gelingen kann, persönliche Größe zu beweisen und sich für Andersdenkende einzusetzen, selbst wenn man deren Thesen nicht teilt. So beeindruckt mich auch heute noch das Eintreten des Münchner Reformarchitekten Theodor Fischer in die Debatte um die drohende Schließung des Bauhaus in Dessau, als er 1927 schrieb (Theodor Fischer, „Um das Bauhaus", Die Kunst, 34. Jg., Nr. 1, Oktober 1927, S. 32): „.... und obwohl ich eine ganze Last von Bedenken im einzelnen gegen die dort geübten Methoden habe, obwohl ich mutmaße, dass ich selbst dort niemals besondere Sympathien genossen habe, erkenne und bekenne ich, dass diesem Unternehmen eine wichtige Entwicklung zugefallen ist und noch zustehen kann. Ich weiß, dass unsere Zeit nicht einheitlich marschieren kann und dass, da ich mich zu Versuchen berechtigt und genötigt glaubte, anderen das Recht zu Versuchen zugestanden werden muss. Ich gehe weiter: auch denen die von Versuchen nichts wissen wollen (die aber in der Regel die Ergebnisse sehr gern für sich benützen) oder in geschmäcklerischem Behagen verweilen wollen, auch denen spreche ich das Recht, zu sein, wie sie sind, nicht ab."
Also: nicht aufeinander, sondern füreinander eintreten. Nicht nur beim Bauhaus.

Matthias Castorph

Theodor Fischer, Stairwell in the home for unmarried persons, Munich 1927
Theodor Fischer, Treppenhaus im Ledigenheim München, 1927

Colour theories

When I think of the Bauhaus, their many colour theories come to mind. These ranged from those scientifically derived to poetically intuited and understood by only a few.

Colour theories are used everywhere today for inspiration and production, particularly in the design industry and the art world. The Bauhaus succeeded in introducing colour theory to designers as well as the pigment industry, who were the only ones to give colours their names.

With our Catastrophe Colours, we take a critical approach to how colours are chosen and applied in architecture. The name of each of our Catastrophe Colours is associated with a human disaster, and so the selection of a colour becomes a conscious act. Catastrophes stay in our memories as a name, which when you think about it, is connected to a dominant colour visualized by the media when it happens.

While scientific approaches to colour today may be state of the art, the poetics of colour needs a serious update. Colours have long been in the hands of an industry that has assigned them cheerful, empty names. They make colour an embellishment, like flowers in the living room. Flowers but no plants. Medication but no prevention. The names given to colours always seem to be related to nature, flowers and fruits – it's a world of fake.

Catastrophe Colours reconnects colours to today's world, so that we can understand how our choice of colour is loaded with meaning.

Wieder richtig Farbe bekennen

Wenn ich an das Bauhaus denke, kommen mir seine vielen Farbtheorien in den Sinn – von wissenschaftlich fundiert bis poetisch erfühlt –, die nur von wenigen verstanden wurden.

Heute sind Farbtheorien zu Inspirations- oder Produktionszwecken überall im Einsatz, besonders in Kunst und Design. Dem Bauhaus ist es gelungen, Kreative und Farbhersteller an das Thema heranzuführen – seine Vertreter waren die Einzigen, die ihren Farben Namen gaben.

Mit unseren „Katastrophenfarben" setzen wir uns kritisch mit der Auswahl und Anwendung von Farbe in der Architektur auseinander. Jede einzelne ist über ihren Namen mit einer menschlichen Katastrophe verbunden. Die Wahl einer Farbe wird so zu einer bewussten Entscheidung. Katastrophen bleiben uns als Name im Gedächtnis, der tatsächlich mit einer ganz bestimmten Farbstimmung korrespondiert – nämlich jener, die die Berichterstattung durch die Medien dominiert.

Während die wissenschaftliche Farbforschung heute vielleicht auf dem neuesten Stand ist, bedarf der ästhetische Aspekt von Farbe einer gründlichen Überholung. Die Farben befinden sich schon viel zu lange in den Händen einer Industrie, die ihnen heitere, sinnentleerte Namen verliehen hat. Sie machen Farbe zum zierenden Beiwerk, wie Blumen im Wohnzimmer. Blumen, aber eben keine Pflanzen. Medizin, doch ohne Prävention. Die Namen, die man den Farben gibt, suggerieren stets einen Bezug zur Natur, zu Blumen und Früchten, doch das ist nur vorgetäuscht.

Katastrophenfarben dagegen bringen Farben wieder mit der Welt von heute in Verbindung – damit wir verstehen, wie sehr unsere Farbwahl mit Bedeutung aufgeladen ist.

Pierre Jorge Gonzalez

"Catastrophe Colours / Katastrophenfarben", Gonzalez Haase AAS

Thinking about the Bauhaus Bauhaus is not translated. It is itself.

It's amazing that it only lasted 14 years, but it still lasts.

The Bauhaus is a well, from which we draw crystal clear refreshment again and again, being reminded of imagination, co-operation, inventiveness, craft.

A place of making and thinking; the workshop as the basis of education; testing, understanding, pushing materials; finding beauty; fusing architecture, weaving, sculpture, carpentry...

Imagine this group of individuals:
Wassily Kandinsky, Helena Borner, Anni Albers, Gunta Stolzl, Josef Albers, Marcel Breuer, Walter Gropius, Mart Stam, Ludwig Hilberseimer, Johannes Itten, Paul Klee, Mies van der Rohe, László Moholy-Nagy, Marcel Breuer...
...researching "visual facts" and surrounded by:
Oscar Schlemmer's Stick Dance; Fritz Schleifer's Bauhaus poster; Gunta Stolzl's multi-coloured weave; Josef Hartwig's chess set; Marianne Brandt's teapot.

When we discovered a book with images of Bauhaus party costumes, it was a revelation, representing the important ingredient in the inventive, creative process: play, which, combined with the design and making of artefacts and buildings for daily life, at all its scales and in all its forms, was a key lesson to us.

Making and playing, thinking and imagining... a Play-Haus Bauhaus!

Nachdenken über das Bauhaus „Bauhaus" ist unübersetzbar. Es bleibt stets es selbst.

Es ist schon verblüffend, dass es nur 14 Jahre bestand, doch es besteht noch immer.

Das Bauhaus ist eine nie versiegende Quelle, aus der wir unentwegt kristallklare Inspiration schöpfen – ein ständiger lebendiger Appell an unsere Imagination, unseren Erfindergeist und die Wertschätzung von Kooperation und Handwerk.

Ein Ort des Machens und Denkens; die Werkstatt als Basis der Ausbildung; Materialien ausprobieren, verstehen, puschen; Schönheit entdecken; die Architektur mit der Textilkunst, der Bildhauerei, dem Schreinerhandwerk vereinen ...

Man stelle sich allein folgende Gruppe von Persönlichkeiten vor:
Wassily Kandinsky, Helene Börner, Anni Albers, Gunta Stölzl, Josef Albers, Marcel Breuer, Walter Gropius, Mart Stam, Ludwig Hilberseimer, Johannes Itten, Paul Klee, Mies van der Rohe, László Moholy-Nagy, Marcel Breuer ...
... die „visuelle Fakten" untersuchten und umgeben waren von:
Oskar Schlemmers Stäbetanz, Fritz Schleifers Bauhaus-Plakat, Gunta Stölzls bunten Webmustern, Josef Hartwigs Schachspiel, Marianne Brandts Teekanne.

Als wir ein Buch mit Bildern von Kostümen der Bauhaus-Feste entdeckten, war das für uns wie eine Offenbarung, denn sie symbolisieren die wichtigste Ingredienz des kreativen Prozesses: das Spiel, das wir neben dem zweckorientierten Entwerfen von Design und Architektur in seiner Schlüsselfunktion als unentbehrlich wertzuschätzen lernten.

Machen und spielen, denken und imaginieren ... das Bauhaus als Spielhaus!

Shelley McNamara, Yvonne Farrell

*Con Wells Coates, Walter Gropius
e Pat Crook a Londra, 1951* 1951

Confrontational solidarity

When I was still a student, I had the rare privilege to be invited to the CIAM Congress in Hoddesdon, England in 1951. Franco Albini and I went there by train and shared a room in a student dormitory. I still remember that the theme "The Heart of the City" somehow led to questions about the relationships between project, history and context. But what impressed me much more profoundly was the one week I spent in the circle of Le Corbusier, Van Eesteren, Gropius and other greats minds. It was an inspiring atmosphere that led to true friendships – even with the (then) youngest of us. It was as if the avant-garde of the 1920s were revived in all its confrontational solidarity – a solidarity among people who were firmly convinced they were on the right side of history (and they were right!). At some point, Gropius sat down next to me casually, as if he were really only interested in me at that moment – even if that was probably part of his routine as a teacher. I still remember admiring his elegance, which reminded me very much of Thomas Mann.

Streitlustige Solidarität

Als ich noch studierte, wurde ich 1951 zum CIAM Kongress im englischen Hoddesdon eingeladen – das war ein rares Privileg. Franco Albini und ich fuhren im Zug dorthin und teilten uns ein Zimmer im Studentenwohnheim. Ich erinnere mich noch, dass das Thema „The Heart of the City" irgendwie zu Fragen der Relation zwischen Projekt, Geschichte und Kontext führte. Doch was mich viel nachhaltiger beeindruckte, war die eine Woche im Kreise von Le Corbusier, Van Eesteren, Gropius und anderen Größen, in einer inspirierenden Atmosphäre, die zu echten Freundschaften führte – auch mit uns (damals) Jüngsten. Es war, als ob die Avantgarde der 20er-Jahre wiederaufleben würde in ihrer ganzen streitlustigen Solidarität – einer Solidarität unter Menschen, die felsenfest davon überzeugt waren, auf der richtigen Seite der Geschichte zu stehen (und sie hatten Recht!). Irgendwann setzte sich Gropius ganz zwanglos neben mich, als ob er sich in diesem Moment wirklich nur für mich interessierte – auch wenn das vermutlich zu seiner Routine als Lehrer gehörte. Ich erinnere mich noch, dass ich seine Eleganz bewunderte, die mich sehr an Thomas Mann erinnerte.

Vittorio Gregotti

A culture of curiosity

To many people, Henning Larsen is known for his prodigious work in architecture that distinctively plays with the powers of daylight. However, to those who knew and worked with him, his legacy is just as much his curious approach to the world. His greatest inspiration was the people around him.

The idea of working as a community, as advanced by the Bauhaus, rather than as a hierarchy drove the culture at Henning Larsen from the company's beginning. The best idea won regardless of authorship. One of the most important tasks for me as a leader has been – and still is – to ensure that this spirit remains and is present in our organization.

Today, Henning Larsen is a community of thinkers and doers from different academic and practical backgrounds who work collectively to explore the boundaries of design. What characterizes our work, more than anything else, is that every single project is the result of a dialogue between different art forms, skill sets and cultures. As such, Henning Larsen shares the core ideology of interdisciplinary collaboration that guided the Bauhaus.

Henning Larsen's curious nature brought him to Riyadh in Saudi Arabia – a part of the world no one else in Scandinavia had previously thought about exploring. Henning Larsen designed the winning proposal for the Ministry of Foreign Affairs (MoFA) in 1980. The project was completed in 1984.

MoFA is in many ways the epitome of Henning Larsen's unique method of approaching architecture from different perspectives; fusing different architectural styles, cultural and historic references, and, of course, listening to people to try to understand their needs and background.

Although designed in the 1980s, MoFA remains an inspiration today and serves as a constant reminder to always be curious about other cultures, ask questions and appreciate diversity.

Eine Kultur der Neugier

Viele verbinden den Namen Henning Larsen mit seiner außergewöhnlichen Architektur, die auf so unverwechselbare Weise mit der Kraft des Tageslichts spielt. Für alle jedoch, die ihn näher kannten und mit ihm gearbeitet haben, liegt sein Vermächtnis nicht minder in seiner großen Neugier, mit der er an die Welt und die Dinge heranging. Seine größte Inspirationsquelle waren die Menschen um ihn herum.

Das kollektive Miteinander im Gegensatz zur hierarchischen Struktur des Bauhaus war von Anfang an bestimmend für die Arbeitskultur im Hause Larsen. Die beste Idee setzte sich durch, egal von wem sie kam. Eine der wichtigsten Aufgaben für mich als Führungsperson war und ist es, dafür zu sorgen, dass dieser Geist in unserem Unternehmen erhalten und präsent bleibt.

Heute ist Henning Larsen eine Gemeinschaft von Denkern und Machern mit verschiedenen Backgrounds und unterschiedlichen praktischen Erfahrungen, die gemeinsam die Grenzen der Gestaltung erforschen. Und jedes einzelne Projekt ist das Ergebnis eines Dialogs zwischen verschiedenen Kunstformen, Qualifikationen und Kulturen. In diesem Punkt stimmt Henning Larsen voll überein mit dem Konzept von interdisziplinärer Zusammenarbeit, das dem Bauhaus ja zugrunde lag.

Henning Larsens Aufgeschlossenheit führte ihn nicht zuletzt auch ins saudische Riad – einen Teil der Welt, der bis dahin für jeden in ganz Skandinavien absolutes Neuland war. Und es war Henning Larsen, der sich 1980 dort mit seinem Entwurf für das Außenministerium (MoFA) durchsetzte. 1984 wurde es fertiggestellt.

Das MoFA ist in vielerlei Hinsicht der Inbegriff von Henning Larsens einzigartiger Methode, sich an Projekte aus verschiedenen Perspektiven heranzutasten, unterschiedliche Stile und Bezüge kultureller wie historischer Art miteinander zu vereinen – und natürlich bei alldem den betroffenen Menschen zuzuhören, um ihre Bedürfnisse und ihr Umfeld besser zu verstehen.

Auch wenn es in den 1980er-Jahren entworfen wurde, ist das MoFA heute noch immer eine architektonische Inspirationsquelle – und eine ständige Mahnung, stets neugierig und offen gegenüber anderen Kulturen zu sein, Fragen zu stellen und Vielfalt wertzuschätzen.

Mette Kynne Frandsen

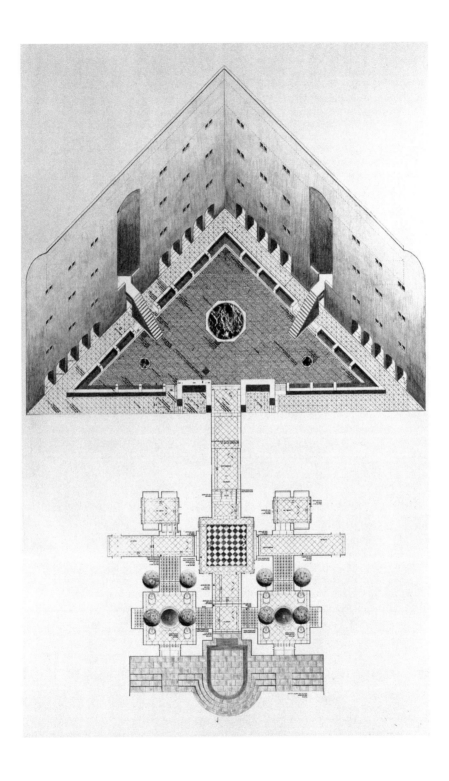

Concreteness instead of abstraction

In Vienna after 1945, the rediscovery and reappraisal of international and Austrian Modernism was undertaken not by art historians, but by architects. For this reason, it had a productive influence on design thinking. Architect Friedrich Kurrent described the sense of "confusion and uncertainty" felt by himself and other young architects – already well-versed in such movements as the Bauhaus, De Stijl, Constructivism, Le Corbusier, etc., upon encountering the works of Josef Frank, which criticized the meanderings of modernism in establishing itself as a new style.

Adolf Loos himself once wrote that the approach taken by the next generation of anti-ornament architects "conceals my struggle and falsifies it at the same time." Loos did not speculate about how form should appear in the future in a different culture that had yet to be created. He did not rethink every detail from scratch. In order to communicate new ideas, one cannot use a new language at the same time. Josef Frank continued Loos's anti-dogmatic criticism of modernism, while managing to prevent Loos's own concept of culture from becoming doctrinaire.

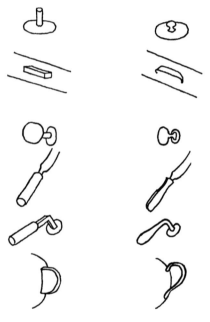

a) "Bauhaus" handles. They all have basic geometric shapes, making them quite "simple", yet not very practical when it comes to handling.

b) Handles for the same purpose, as they usually appear, especially when industrially manufactured. They fulfil a function, but who would ever call them "functionalist"

Frank's argumentation from 1934 (pictured above) has proven to be futile, for decades now: What the industry delivers on its own has long since become more ridiculous and uncomfortable than what lofty theories could ever have imagined. The justification of form through abstraction, asceticism and geometry must be countered by concreteness, comfort and informality. And architecture, of course, needs both these approaches. But if architects must reinvent the wheel with every new generation, we should at least ensure that we are not always starting out from a square.

Hermann Czech

Konkretheit statt Abstraktion

In Wien fand nach 1945 die Wiederentdeckung und Aufarbeitung der internationalen und österreichischen Moderne nicht durch Kunsthistoriker, sondern durch Architekten statt. Deshalb hatte sie einen produktiven Einfluss auf das Entwurfsdenken. – Friedrich Kurrent beschreibt die „Verwirrung und Verunsicherung", die nach der Rezeption von Bauhaus, De Stijl, Konstruktivismus, Le Corbusier etc. das Erlebnis Josef Franks hervorrief, der den Irrweg der Moderne, ein neuer Stil zu werden, bloßgelegt hatte.

Schon Adolf Loos meinte über seine ornamentlose Nachfolge: Sie „verschweigt meinen kampf und verfälscht ihn zugleich". Er stellt nicht die Frage, wie Form in Zukunft in einer anderen, erst zu schaffenden Kultur aussehen müsste. Er erdenkt nicht jede Einzelheit von Grund auf neu. Wer neue Gedanken mitteilen will, kann sich nicht gleichzeitig einer neuen Sprache bedienen. — Josef Frank setzt Loos' anti-dogmatische Kritik fort, bewahrt aber sogar dessen eigenen Kulturbegriff davor, doktrinär zu werden.

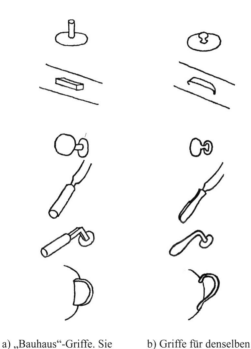

a) „Bauhaus"-Griffe. Sie haben alle geometrische Grundformen. Sind also sehr „einfach", aber wenig geeignet zum Angreifen mit der Hand

b) Griffe für denselben Zweck, wie sie gewöhnlich ausschauen und wie sie die Industrie herstellt. Sie erfüllen eine Funktion, wer würde sie aber jemals „funktionalistisch" nennen

Dieses Argument Franks von 1934 geht freilich seit Jahrzehnten ins Leere: Was die Industrie von sich aus liefert, ist längst lächerlicher und unbequemer als das, was sich abgehobene Theorien ausdenken konnten. Der Begründung von Form durch Abstraktion, Askese, Geometrie ist die Begründung durch Konkretheit, Komfort, Informalität entgegenzustellen. — Natürlich braucht Architektur beide Herangehensweisen. Aber wenn wir Architekten schon in jeder Generation das Rad neu erfinden müssen, sollten wir wenigstens darauf achten, dass es nicht zunächst immer eckig ist.

Hermann Czech

Bauhaus as dogma

As an architectural office, we see the Bauhaus primarily as a formal experiment of the 1920s, which admittedly had an incredible influence on the time that followed. This was the result of its enormously successful combination of ideological and formal content, which was conveyed by particularly charismatic individuals. As practicing architects, however, we are closer to the practical orientation of the Werkbund (German Association of Craftsmen), for instance, than to the Bauhaus. We do not feel compelled to adopt the formal language of the international style which emerged from the Bauhaus. Instead, we appreciate the great variety of regional building types, which we also enjoy referencing in our work. The actual legacy of the Bauhaus, it seems, lies with the universities. To this day, no serious attempts have been made to convey its basic doctrine in any way other than how it was supposedly developed in Weimar and Dessau. Designs are thought exclusively from simplified volumes, following a stylizing approach. Irrespective of whether this does justice to the Bauhaus as a whole: that the dominance of this dogma in architectural education has gone unchallenged is the true secret behind its continued widespread presence in public discourse.

Das Bauhaus als Dogma

Als Architekturbüro nehmen wir das Bauhaus in erster Linie als formales Experiment der 20er-Jahre wahr, das in der Folgezeit eine zugegebenermaßen unglaubliche Wirkmächtigkeit entfalten konnte. Sie ist ein Ergebnis der enorm erfolgreichen Verknüpfung ideologischer und formaler Inhalte, die zudem von besonders charismatischen Personen transportiert wurden. Als praktizierenden Architekten jedoch ist uns die handwerkliche Orientierung etwa des Werkbundes näher als das Bauhaus. Auch die Formensprache des internationalen Stils, der sich ausgehend vom Bauhaus etabliert hat, müssen wir uns nicht zu eigen machen. Zu sehr schätzen wir die Vielfalt regionaler Gebäudetypen, auf die wir in unserer Arbeit ebenfalls gerne Bezug nehmen. Das eigentliche Erbe des Bauhaus scheint man an den Hochschulen zu finden. Bis heute gibt es keinen ernstzunehmenden Versuch, die Grundlehre anders zu vermitteln, als sie vermeintlich in Weimar und Dessau entwickelt wurde. Entwürfe werden dabei, einem stilisierenden Ansatz folgend, ausschließlich von vereinfachten Volumen her gedacht. Ganz unabhängig von der Frage, ob dies dem Bauhaus in seiner Gesamtheit überhaupt gerecht wird: Die ungebrochene Dominanz dieses Dogmas in der Architektenausbildung ist das eigentliche Geheimnis hinter seiner anhaltend breiten Präsenz im öffentlichen Diskurs.

Andreas Hild, Dionys Ottl, Matthias Haber

Everything Bauhaus

Ah, the Bauhaus... I see it every morning, while seasoning my breakfast egg with Wagenfeld's salt shaker. I was introduced to Mies's wonderful homes for Esters and Lange in Krefeld early on. As a youth, I spent my summers at Monte Verità Hotel in Ascona, surrounded by furniture and pictures by Stam, Breuer, Wagenfeld, Klee, Feininger and everything else that Baron von der Heydt possessed. Fahrenkamp, who was commissioned to build that hotel instead of Mies, was never at the Bauhaus himself, but he designed marvellous buildings as if he had been there – until he started working for the Nazis. My work has occasionally brought me into uncomfortably close "contact" with that of Wilhelm Kreis, Emil Fahrenkamp and in Stuttgart, Paul Bonatz, a non-Bauhausler or also anti-Bauhausler, who perhaps for this reason also succumbed to the temptations of the Nazi regime. So I've had a very personal, productive struggle with these gentlemen. I admire Hans Scharoun, whom Gropius did not want in 1923, but whom Mies (!) then invited in 1927 to work on the Weissenhof estate. I had the honour of reinstalling Max Bill's sculpture in Karlsruhe, and respect Otl Aicher, his co-founder in Ulm. I put my clothes on the Barcelona stool designed by Lily Reich and Mies, and collect his photos and montages (see picture) – the culmination of an almost outrageous search for eternal beauty. So, yes, much of which I know and admire is connected to the Bauhaus. But my love also goes to the Härings and the Scharouns, to the exiles, to Neutra, Schindler, Frey and Lautner as well as Eames, Ellwood, Fuller, Frei Otto and all others who wanted to go even further, freer and, as Tom Wolfe might say, sought to be less humourless, and in doing so, have found and are finding their own way.

Alles Bauhaus oder was?

Ja, das Bauhaus ... Ich begegne ihm bereits morgens beim Salzen meines Frühstückseis mit Wagenfelds Salzstreuer, bin mit Mies' wunderbaren Häusern für Esters und Lange in Krefeld sehr früh vertraut gemacht worden, habe im Hotel Monte Verità in Ascona die Sommer meiner Jugend verbracht, inmitten der Möbel und Bilder von Stam, Breuer, Wagenfeld, Klee, Feininger und allem anderen, was Baron von der Heydt besessen hatte. Fahrenkamp, der anstelle von Mies den Auftrag zum Bau des Hotels erhielt, war selbst nie am Bauhaus, baute aber so wunderbare Häuser, als sei er es gewesen – bis er sich den Nazis andiente. Bin beruflich in teils zu engem „Kontakt" mit Wilhelm Kreis, Emil Fahrenkamp geraten – und nicht zuletzt in Stuttgart mit Paul Bonatz, Nicht- oder auch Anti-Bauhäusler, vielleicht deshalb auch den Verlockungen des NS-Regimes erlegen. Habe also meinen ganz persönlichen, produktiven Kampf mit diesen Herrschaften gehabt, bewundere Hans Scharoun, den Gropius '23 nicht dabei haben wollte, den Mies (!) aber '27 zur Weißenhofsiedlung einlud, hatte die Ehre, Max Bills Skulptur in Karlsruhe neu aufstellen zu dürfen, habe seinen Ulmer Mitgründer Otl Aicher verehrt, lege meine Kleider auf Lilly Reichs und Mies' Barcelona-Hocker ab, sammle die Fotos und Montagen von Mies (s. Abb.), Kulmination einer fast schon unverschämten Suche nach ewiger Schönheit. Also, ja, ich kenne und verehre vieles und viele, die mit dem Bauhaus verbunden waren. Aber meine Liebe gilt den Härings, Scharouns, den Exilanten, Neutra, Schindler, Frey, Lautner, auch Eames, Ellwood, Fuller, Frei Otto und allen anderen, die es noch weiter, freier und, wie Tom Wolfe sagen würde, weniger humorlos wollten und dafür ihren jeweils eigenen Weg fanden und finden.

Christoph Ingenhoven

Glass Skyscraper Project "Wabe" (Honeycomb), Ludwig Mies van der Rohe, Berlin, 1922
Glashochhausprojekt „Wabe", Ludwig Mies van der Rohe, Berlin, 1922

Modernism as a philosophy in practice

My ambivalence towards the Bauhaus is best reflected by my time at the Institute of Technology in Chicago. There I sat in Mies van der Rohe's Crown Hall, a building whose almost transcendental quality only reveals itself through the time spent in it – and not by looking at its form. This is where I both despaired and enthused about Visual Training, a Bauhaus exercise by Walter Peterhans, until I almost physically felt that it was never about the result, but always about the process. Dealing with the traditionally-minded teaching staff, which was divided into two camps, enabled me to experience the power and radicality of modernism as a practised philosophy. But I also experienced the speechlessness and aloofness of this thinking. In Chicago, the loss of narrative and the related trivialization of the canon of forms in the commercial glut of postwar architecture could only be experienced too well. But as part of the mockingly dismissed "Funky Form Boys" faction, we were – in search of meaning(s) in a constantly changing system – interested in design approaches that could allow everything without dogmatic restrictions. What remains is a deep sympathy for those who are passionate about their ideas, for teachers who look over your shoulder and whisper in your ear: "Do you really care about the line? I mean do you really, really care…?"

Die Moderne als gelebte Haltung

Meine Ambivalenz gegenüber dem Bauhaus spiegelt sich am besten in meiner Zeit am Institute of Technology in Chicago. Dort saß ich nun in Mies van der Rohes Crown Hall, einem Gebäude, dessen fast schon transzendentale Qualität sich erst durch die darin zugebrachte Zeit offenbart – und eben nicht durch die Betrachtung seiner Form. Hier verzweifelte ich und begeisterte mich zugleich am Visual Training, einer Bauhaus-Übung von Walter Peterhans, bis ich geradezu körperlich spürte, dass es nie um das Resultat, sondern stets um den Prozess ging. Die Auseinandersetzung mit dem traditionsbewahrenden Teil des in zwei Lager gespaltenen Lehrkörpers machte mir die Kraft und Radikalität der Idee der Moderne als gelebte Haltung erfahrbar. Aber auch die Sprachlosigkeit und Hermetik dieses Denkens. In Chicago war der Verlust der Narration und die damit verbundene Banalisierung des Formenkanons im kommerziellen „Würfelhusten" der Nachkriegsarchitektur nur zu gut erlebbar. Als Teil der spöttisch belächelten „Funky Form Boys"-Fraktion waren wir dagegen – auf der Suche nach Bedeutung(en) in einem sich ständig verändernden System – an Entwurfshaltungen interessiert, die ohne dogmatische Einschränkungen alles zulassen konnten. Was bleibt, ist die tiefe Sympathie für Menschen, die leidenschaftlich für ihre Idee einstehen, für Lehrer, die sich von hinten über deine Schulter beugen und dir ins Ohr flüstern: „Do you really care about the line? I mean do you really, really care …?"

Peter Ippolito

The Bauhaus effect

For the past decade, I have been working in Jaffa, on a project located within the walls of the Crusader citadel, with views north across the roofs of the ancient port town to the "White City" of Tel Aviv, so called because it is made up of the largest concentration of Modern Movement architecture in the world. In the evenings, one of my great pleasures has been to walk along the White City's quiet streets of apartments, enjoying glimpses into spatially refined, bookish interiors when dusk falls and the lights go on, designed by architects who had trained in Europe. It is impossible to overestimate the place of the Bauhaus in the development of modernism. For me personally, it is likewise impossible to overestimate the impact of the school's third and last director, Mies van der Rohe, on my architectural thinking. Mies's Seagram Building is the most beautiful skyscraper in the world. To move around it is to see a continual shift between the transparency of its glass facade and the apparent solidity of the carefully drilled, bronze-finished steel beams. All the visual clutter and banality of detail that threatens to invade even the most ambitious architecture has been eliminated.

Der Bauhaus-Effekt

Die letzten zehn Jahre habe ich an einem Projekt in Jaffa gearbeitet, das sich innerhalb der Mauern der Kreuzfahrerzitadelle befindet. Von dort aus blickt man im Norden über die Dächer der alten Hafenstadt in Richtung Tel Aviv – auch bekannt als „Weiße Stadt", weil sie die weltweit größte Sammlung von Architektur der Moderne darstellt. Abends ist es ein wahrer Genuss, die ruhigen Wohnstraßen entlang zu spazieren, bei Einsetzen der Dämmerung und den ersten Lichtern flüchtige Blicke in die raffiniert geschnittenen Innenräume voller Bücher zu werfen – alles Entwürfe von Architekten, die in Europa ausgebildet wurden. Man kann die Bedeutung des Bauhaus für die Entwicklung der Moderne gar nicht genug betonen. Ähnliches gilt, was mich angeht, für den Einfluss des dritten und letzten Leiters des Bauhaus, Mies van der Rohe, auf mein architektonisches Denken. Sein Seagram Building ist der schönste Wolkenkratzer der Welt. Wandert man um ihn herum, bemerkt man einen steten Wechsel zwischen der Transparenz seiner Glasfassade und der scheinbaren Solidität der sorgfältig gebohrten, mit Bronze überzogenen Stahlträger. Alle optische Überfrachtung, alle banalen Details, die selbst die ambitionierteste Architektur zu überwältigen drohen, wurden beseitigt.

John Pawson

Architectural déjà-vu

Design approach, history of architecture and technology studies are an intrinsic part of an architectural education. They shape the instinct of an architect and find themselves expressed in a drawing, a sketch or an informal chat. I would call it architectural déjà-vu. Bits of the school in Dessau are still floating in the air of contemporary architectural institutes and universities.

Projects are reminiscent of the past and visions for the future. Bauhaus is embodied in fine structural details, in the openness of a building towards the city and in the lightness of a glass facade. An infinite array of buildings, including some of our designs, unconsciously feature a hint of Mies.

Architektonisches Déjà-vu

Design, Architekturgeschichte und ein Technikstudium gehören zur Architekturausbildung ganz wesentlich dazu. Sie schärfen den Instinkt des Architekten und zeigen sich ganz nebenbei in einer Zeichnung, einer Skizze oder einem informellen Gespräch. Ich würde das als architektonisches Déjà-vu bezeichnen. Auch heute noch spürt man den Geist der Dessauer Schule in den Architektur-fakultäten und Universitäten.

Architektonische Projekte gemahnen stets an die Vergangen-heit und sind doch zugleich immer auch Zukunftsvisionen. Das Bauhaus manifestiert sich in subtilen baulichen Details, in der Offenheit eines Gebäudes gegenüber der Stadt oder der Leichtig-keit einer Glasfassade. Unendlich viele Bauten, darunter auch einige unserer eigenen, enthalten unbewusst einen Hinweis auf Mies.

Kees Kaan

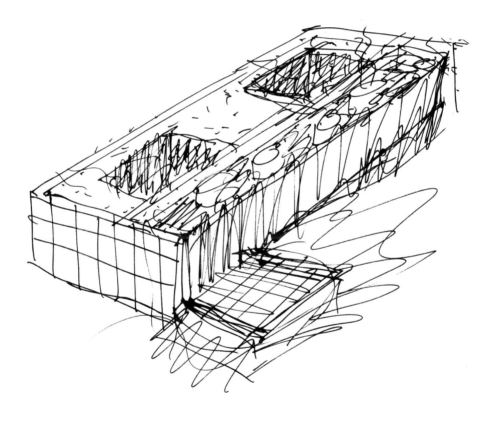

Appeal to the future

Much of what surrounds us in everyday life has a bit of Bauhaus to it. We can sense its aim to break with the existing to create a more just world, for it to literally take shape. Unfortunately, the term "Bauhaus" has also been to market cars, furniture and, yes, architecture. Banal, functional buildings are often praised as "timeless" or "functional" in the sense of the Bauhaus idea, even if they are its glaring opposite. The Bauhaus propagated the interdisciplinarity of composition, the quality of craftsmanship and the democratization of design. A design plan without the slightest too much or too little requires a high degree of dedication, time and the brain power of all involved in its development. But the aesthetic quality of a building does not lie in reduction alone – something that today is all too often elevated to dogma. For all its practicality, at its core the Bauhaus strove for beauty; for the sculptural power and playful elegance of form. I hope that its sensuality, multidimensionality and love of experimentation will spark again. Let's not see Bauhaus as a label for a style, but as a mission to continue its interdisciplinary approach, to remain relevant and think about the future of society.

Appell an die Zukunft

Vieles, was uns im Alltag umgibt, ist ein Stück Bauhaus. Wir spüren darin dessen Anspruch, mit Bestehendem zu brechen, um eine gerechtere Welt zu schaffen, buchstäblich Form werden zu lassen. Leider muss der Begriff Bauhaus aber auch herhalten zur Vermarktung von Autos, Möbeln und, ja, Architektur. Banale Funktionsbauten werden dann gern als „zeitlos" oder „sachlich" im Sinne des Bauhaus-Gedankens gepriesen, auch wenn sie sich schon auf den ersten Blick als sein Gegenteil entpuppen. Das Bauhaus propagierte die Interdisziplinarität der Gestaltung, die Qualität des Handwerks und eine Demokratisierung des Designs. Ein Entwurf ohne das geringste Zuviel oder Zuwenig setzt in der Entwicklung ein hohes Maß an Hingabe, Zeit und das Hirnschmalz aller Beteiligten voraus. Doch die ästhetische Qualität eines Objekts liegt nicht in der Reduktion allein – was heute allzu oft zum Dogma erhoben wird. Bei aller Sachlichkeit wohnt(e) dem Bauhaus das Streben nach Schönheit inne, nach skulpturaler Kraft und spielerischer Eleganz der Form. Ich wünsche mir, dass seine Sinnlichkeit, Mehrdimensionalität und die Lust am Experiment wieder neu entflammt. Auf dass wir Bauhaus nicht verstehen als Label eines Stiles, sondern als Auftrag, seine interdisziplinäre Haltung fortzuführen – um zukunftsfähig zu bleiben und die Gesellschaft weiterzudenken!

Kilian Kada

Embedded in our architectural DNA

We feel very fortunate to be surrounded by Bauhaus projects in the streets of Tel Aviv, the "White City", which are a constant reminder of the importance of modesty and functionality in architecture. Most importantly, however, they are a great example of design for a human scale.

We have always been fascinated by the way in which spaces are formed by implementing the renowned breakthrough Bauhaus concept of the free plan, allowing spaces to flow one into the other. We have reinterpreted this incredible concept in section form. The aspiration for a free section is evident in our first project from the 1980s, which is our current place of residence. Using similar interests, we later designed a single-family home in northern Tel Aviv, in which a recessed glass facade sits between a white plaster mass and an exposed concrete wall.

Israel is a young country, in which many followers of the Bauhaus movement arrived in the 1930s and shaped the architectural language of the newly founded socialist state in 1948. What was then a revolution in Europe, for us was a given built environment – the context of our work and part of our architectural DNA.

Teil unserer architektonischen DNA

Wir schätzen uns glücklich, in den Straßen von Tel Aviv, der Weißen Stadt, von Bauhaus-Projekten umgeben zu sein. Sie gemahnen uns permanent an die Bedeutung von Bescheidenheit und Funktionalität in der Architektur. Vor allem aber sind sie ein großartiges Beispiel für gelungene Entwürfe im menschlichen Maßstab.

Es hat uns schon immer fasziniert, wie es dem Bauhaus mit seinem bahnbrechenden Konzept des offenen Grundrisses gelang, Räume so zu gestalten, dass sie fließend ineinander übergehen. Wir haben dieses unglaubliche Konzept auf den Schnitt übertragen und auf diese Weise neu interpretiert. Der von uns angestrebte freie Schnitt zeigt sich schon in unserem ersten Projekt aus den 1980er-Jahren, in dem wir aktuell wohnen. Ähnliche Beweggründe führten uns später zum Entwurf eines Einfamilienhauses im Norden Tel Avivs, bei dem eine zurückgesetzte Glasfassade zwischen einer weißen Gipsmasse und einer Sichtbetonwand liegt.

Israel ist ein junges Land. In den 1930er-Jahren kamen viele Bauhaus-Anhänger hierher und prägten die Architektursprache des 1948 neu gegründeten sozialistischen Staates. Was seinerzeit in Europa eine Revolution war, war für uns das gegebene Geschenk einer gebauten Umwelt – der Kontext unserer Arbeit und ein Teil unserer architektonischen DNA.

Etan Kimmel, Michal Kimmel Eshkolot

Curse and blessing

The Bauhaus drove out musty Wilhelmine architecture and design: its motto was light, air and equality for all. Design became justifiable – and ideally readable. Manufacturing processes were used as the basis for design, bringing it closer to engineering. Architecture became the representation of a functional diagram. Over the next generations, university curricula were determined by these principles, which were sometimes ideologically exaggerated. My professors were also still strongly influenced by the Bauhaus dogma and the assessment criteria it gave rise to, as "pros and cons" and "right or wrong". Already at the beginning of my studies, the works of Heinrich Tessenow and Richard Riemerschmid were cast aside as antiquated. For us students, this black-and-white thinking and reflecting on it served as a good "guide" in terms of form finding and defining our own style.

The proverbial Bauhaus "box" has since become a metaphor for our uniform cities. The construction industry has taken a liking to them and abused them for its purposes. When real estate brokers find themselves at a loss for words, they simply add "Bauhaus style" to the description. Everything looks the same – a horde of white cubes that differ only in small details. What has gone lost is creative diversity: individuality, craft as well as sensuality.

We must free ourselves from the mainstream and bring back traditional building methods, regional characteristics and even ornamentation – both in teaching and in practice. Because the best stories are still told by the buildings whose layers of life cannot be fathomed by a functional diagram or a manufacturing process.

Fluch und Segen

Das Bauhaus vertrieb den wilhelminischen Muff aus Architektur und Design: Licht, Luft und Gleichberechtigung für alle, hieß die Devise. Die Gestaltung wurde begründbar – im Idealfall ablesbar –, Fertigungsprozesse fungierten als Gestaltgeber, und es fand eine Annäherung an das Ingenieurwesen statt. Architektur verkam zum Abbild eines Funktionsdiagramms. Die Lehre an den Hochschulen wurde über die nächsten Generationen hinweg durch diese Prinzipien bestimmt und zum Teil ideologisch überhöht. Auch meine Professoren waren noch stark geprägt vom Dogma Bauhaus und den daraus resultierenden Beurteilungskriterien „pro und contra", „richtig oder falsch". Schon zu Beginn meines Studiums wurden die Werke von Heinrich Tessenow oder Richard Riemerschmid als antiquiert beiseite gelegt. Für uns Studenten war dieses Schwarz-Weiß-Denken und die Reflexion darüber ein guter „Leitfaden" auf dem Weg zur Formfindung und einer eigenen Handschrift.

Die sprichwörtliche Bauhaus-„Schachtel" ist mittlerweile zur Metapher für unsere uniformierten Städte geworden. Die Bauindustrie hat sich mit Vorliebe auf sie gestürzt und für ihre Zwecke missbraucht. Und wenn die Makler nicht mehr weiter wissen, schreiben sie einfach „Bauhaus-Stil" ins Exposé. Alles sieht gleich aus – viele weiße Kuben, die sich nur in kleinen Details unterscheiden. Dabei verloren gegangen ist die gestalterische Vielfalt – das Individuelle, das Kunsthandwerkliche, aber auch die Sinnlichkeit.

Wir müssen uns freischwimmen vom Mainstream und traditionelle Bauweisen, regionale Besonderheiten, aber auch das Ornament wieder stärker in den Fokus rücken – sowohl in der Lehre als auch in der Praxis. Denn die besten Geschichten erzählen immer noch die Häuser, deren Lebensschichten nicht durch ein Funktionsdiagramm oder einen Fertigungsprozess zu erfassen sind.

Gerhard Landau

A comprehensive school of modernism

What the Bauhaus can still teach us today is actually a relevant question for me. Its reputation long preceded it – the Bauhaus has become a myth. At its core, it was a school that combined a variety of disciplines: architecture, industrial design, photography, graphics, theatre, painting and many more. For the first time, artistic, artisanal and technical forms of expression that were previously considered incompatible were united under one roof. The individual departments overlapped and enriched each other in many ways. For this reason, in my opinion, the Bauhaus is based on a humanist approach – not in the classical sense, but in a thoroughly modernist sense. This understanding of modernism would be inconceivable without the Bauhaus. In this respect, its approach serves as the foundation and structure of an entire epoch, and as a school it has influenced diverse creative branches and people. I try to put this idea into practice every day of my life.

Eine Gesamtschule der Moderne

Was uns das Bauhaus heute noch zu sagen hat, ist für mich tatsächlich eine relevante Frage. Sein Ruf eilt ihm ja längst voraus – es ist zum Mythos geworden. Dabei war es vom Grundgedanken her vor allem eine Gesamtschule für unterschiedliche Disziplinen: Architektur, Industriedesign, Fotografie, Grafik, Theater, Malerei und viele mehr. Bis dahin unvereinbar erscheinende künstlerische, handwerkliche und technische Ausdrucksformen waren zum ersten Mal unter einem Dach vereint. Die einzelnen Fachbereiche überlagerten und bereicherten sich auf vielfältige Weise. Von daher liegt dem Bauhaus für meine Begriffe ein humanistischer Ansatz zugrunde – nicht im klassischen, sondern in einem durch und durch modernen Sinne. Dieses Verständnis von Moderne wäre ohne das Bauhaus nicht denkbar. Insofern ist sein Ansatz Fundament und Struktur einer ganzen Epoche und prägend als Schule für unterschiedliche kreative Bereiche und Menschen. Diese Idee versuche ich, in meinem Leben jeden Tag aufs Neue in die Tat umzusetzen.

Piero Lissoni

A new debate culture

If only we had the courage, the enthusiasm, the optimism and the debate culture that made up the Bauhaus! Then we wouldn't have to dream about it. Architects, painters, sculptors and craftsmen were brought together in the old Bauhaus. Today, we have two Bauhauses. The one is virtual: a home for project managers, financiers, construction lawyers, naysayers and nitpickers. The other: an Eldorado for do-it-yourself pensioners. Architecture doesn't deserve either of them.

Für eine neue Streitkultur

Ach, hätten wir nur den Mut, die Begeisterung, den Optimismus und die Streitkultur, die das Bauhaus ausmachten! Dann bräuchten wir nicht davon zu träumen. Architekten, Maler, Bildhauer, Kunstgewerbler tummelten sich im alten Bauhaus. Heute haben wir zwei Bauhäuser. Das eine ein virtuelles: Heimat für Projektsteuerer, Finanziers, Baurechtler, Bedenkenträger, Kaninchenfurzfänger. Das andere: ein Eldorado für heimwerkelnde Rentner. Die Architektur hat beide nicht verdient.

Arno Lederer

On a sidenote
      "Founder Walter Gropius believed
that women thought in two dimensions,
while men could grapple with three."
      Jonathan Glancey, The Guardian,
7 November 2009

Eine Randbemerkung
      „Der Gründer Walter Gropius war der
Ansicht, Frauen dächten in zwei Dimensionen,
während Männer sich mit dreien auseinander-
setzen könnten."
      Jonathan Glancey, The Guardian,
7. November 2009

Marie-José van Hee

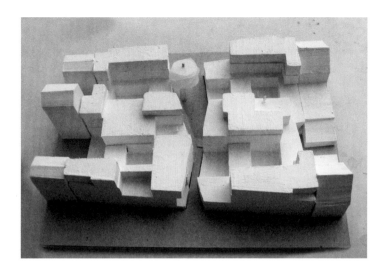

Housing complex between Tuinstraat & Nieuwstraat, Kortrijk 2006 (above),
Paul Klee, Rhythmic, 1930 (below)
Gebäudekomplex zwischen Tuinstraat & Nieuwstraat, Kortrijk 2006 (oben),
Paul Klee, Rhythmisches, 1930 (unten)

A planning paradigm

As an experimental approach that tends to synthesize painting, sculpture, theatre, poetry and architecture, the Bauhaus catalyses the energy of art and formalizes the connection between arts and crafts and industrial design.

As a painter, I'm inspired daily by the work of Paul Klee, whose theories on colour and form are expressed through paintings that show a realistic perception of nature without reproducing it analytically. Klee consciously turns and shapes his soulful marks, passing from figurativism to abstractionism without losing expressiveness in his pieces.

As an architect, I often associate the Bauhaus with Tel Aviv. The city was designed according to Patrick Geddes's urban plan by architects educated at the renowned Weimar school, and populated by buildings built on pilotis, aesthetically based on asymmetry and the introduction of curved lines. Here, concrete served as an innovative material signalling a view towards the future in a city traditionally built with Jerusalem stone; because of this material, Tel Aviv is now known as the "White City".

The Bauhaus can be summed up with the Bauhaus slogan "from the spoon to the city" – and from the city to the spoon, I would add. This planning paradigm is a representation of the overall idea of design: through figurative and plastic arts, the architect designs every single object, being conscious of its specific environmental belonging.

Ein Planungsparadigma

Als experimenteller Ansatz, der eine Synthese aus Malerei, Skulptur, Theater, Poesie und Architektur anstrebt, katalysiert das Bauhaus die Energie der Kunst und formalisiert die Beziehung zwischen Kunsthandwerk und Industriedesign.

Als Maler bin ich immer wieder aufs Neue von den Werken Paul Klees inspiriert, dessen Theorien zu Farbe und Form sich in Bildern widerspiegeln, die eine realistische Wahrnehmung der Natur zeigen, ohne sie analytisch zu reproduzieren. Klee wendet und formt bewusst ihren Gefühlswert und wechselt vom Figürlichen zum Abstrakten, ohne dabei an Ausdruck zu verlieren.

Als Architekt assoziiere ich das Bauhaus häufig mit Tel Aviv. Die Stadt entstand nach dem Masterplan von Patrick Geddes und wurde gebaut von Architekten, die ihre Ausbildung an der berühmten Schule in Weimar erfahren hatten. So entstanden Gebäude, die asymmetrisch und auf Pilotis aufgeständert waren und erstmals geschwungene Linien aufwiesen. In einer Stadt, die traditionell aus Jerusalem-Stein gebaut war, stellte Beton ein innovatives und zukunftsweisendes Material dar. Er verlieh Tel Aviv zudem den Beinamen „Weiße Stadt".

Das Bauhaus lässt sich am besten zusammenfassen mit seinem eigenen Slogan „vom Löffel zur Stadt" – und von der Stadt zum Löffel, würde ich ergänzend hinzufügen. Dieses Planungsparadigma repräsentiert den Grundgedanken jeglicher Gestaltung: Durch figurative und bildende Kunst entwirft der Architekt jedes einzelne Objekt – im steten Bewusstsein seines umweltspezifischen Kontexts.

Massimiliano Fuksas

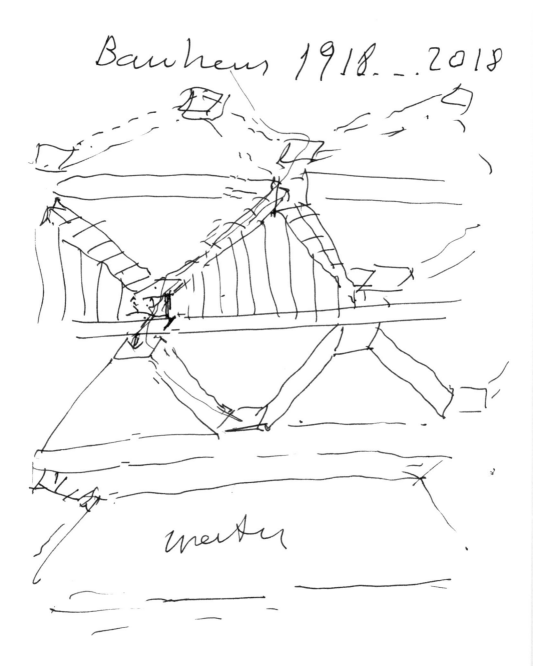

100 Years of Bauhaus:	100 Jahre Bauhaus:
An architectural drama in 2 acts	ein Architekturtheater in 2 Akten

I. The initial spark

I. Die Initialzündung

Bauhaus: A holistic approach
Paul Klee: A childhood love
Gropius: A master
Otl Aicher: A continuation at the Hochschule für Gestaltung Ulm
Tubular furniture: The start of reproducibility

Bauhaus: ein holistischer Ansatz
Paul Klee: eine Jugendliebe
Gropius: ein Meister
Otl Aicher: ein Weitermacher in der Hochschule für Gestaltung Ulm
Stahlrohrmöbel: der Start in die Multiplizierbarkeit

* * * * *

* * * * *

II. Inspired by the Bauhaus

II. Vom Bauhaus beflügelt

40 years ago, an explosion occurred:
Memphis
Impossible without the Bauhaus!

Vor 40 Jahren platzte die Bombe:
Memphis
Ohne Bauhaus wäre sie nie geplatzt!

* * * * *

* * * * *

We were fed up:
Our clients from the industry
wanted the "grey Bauhaus mouse"

Wir hatten die Nase voll:
Unsere Auftraggeber aus der Industrie
wollten die „graue Bauhaus-Maus"

A Bauhaus misunderstanding –
Form follows function –
Function follows boredom –
predictable moulds ...

Ein Bauhaus-Missverständnis –
Form folgt Funktion –
Funktion folgt Langeweile –
vorhersehbare Formhülsen ...

We commissioned ourselves in a kind of
cellar theatre –
Not always logical ...
De-axial, colourful objects –
Filled with emotion –
Beyond functional standards ...
Form followed a new function –
Function followed emotion

Wir beauftragten uns selbst in einer Art
Kellertheater –
nicht immer schlüssig ...
de-axiale, bunte Objekte –
mit Emotionen gefüllt –
jenseits funktionaler Maßstäbe ...
Form folgte einer neuen Funktion –
die Funktion folgte der Emotion

* * * * *

* * * * *

– An emotion that would never have come about
without the Bauhaus

– einer Emotion, die ohne Bauhaus nie zustande
gekommen wäre

I thank the Silver Princes on behalf of all
Memphisians

Ich bedanke mich bei den Silberprinzen im
Namen aller Memphisianer

Matteo Thun

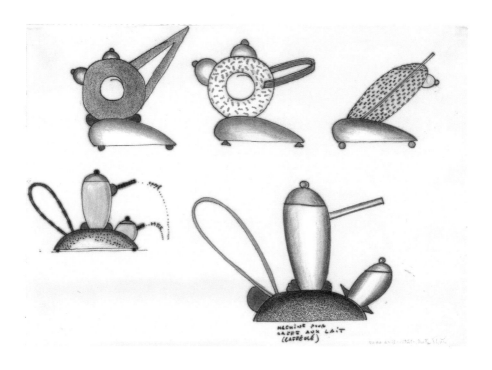

What do we associate with the Bauhaus?
It is the unity of function, shape and material-specific construction. It is the rational use of resources. But it is also sensuality, haptics and colour. This spirit accompanies us every day – in our stairwell from 1890 on the way to our office, in our work and in how we approach our building projects.

Was verbinden wir mit dem Bauhaus?
Es ist die Einheit von Funktion, Gestalt und materialgerechter Konstruktion. Es ist der rationale Umgang mit Ressourcen. Es ist aber auch Sinnlichkeit, Haptik und Farbe. Täglich begleitet uns dieser Geist – in unserem Treppenhaus von 1890 auf dem Weg zum Schreibtisch, in unserer Arbeit und in der Haltung gegenüber unseren Bauvorhaben.

Andreas Meck, Axel Frühauf

California Bauhaus

When I was in school, I never really liked the Bauhaus. I was supposed to; we were all supposed to. It was a moment of division in architecture, with a fight between post-modernist formal historicism and late modernism. It mattered to all of us. I sided instead with the contemporary, which was an uneasy bedfellow of the modern. I was gravitating toward a complexity that modernism, and the Bauhaus in particular, seemed uncomfortable with.

After graduation, I began my work in Los Angeles. A land filled with the accomplishments of many designers, but none more present and influential than the emigres who arrived from Bauhaus Europe in the Second World War. Their experiments were everywhere, and the resulting efforts of their ideas and work was a foundation for the post-war architecture that became the style of Southern California. In the work of Neutra (and sometimes Schindler), and then Ain, Soriano, Ellwood, Koenig and of course, the Eameses, the purity of the original Bauhaus ideals began to loosen in the service of an architecture that was emerging from a culture and social soup made from informality, capitalism, expediency, openness, the sun and the cheap.

I loved that mashup and the vitality that came with it, and I still do. Over the years, I began to lose my ambivalence toward the Bauhaus as I had greater distance from it, allowing me to see just how present its influence continued to be in the work here. Its history became our history too. The Bauhaus evolved from an immutable doctrine to something more sustainable. An idea that continues to be a provocation, even today.

Das kalifornische Bauhaus

An der Uni mochte ich das Bauhaus nie besonders. Dabei hätte ich es mögen sollen, wir alle sollten es mögen. Die Architektur zerfiel in zwei Lager: den formalen Historismus der Postmoderne auf der einen Seite, die Spätmoderne auf der anderen. Wir nahmen das alles sehr wichtig. Ich stellte mich dagegen auf die Seite des Zeitgenössischen, das mit der Moderne ein seltsames Gespann bildete. Ich tendierte zu einer Komplexität, mit der die klassische Moderne, insbesondere das Bauhaus, sich unwohl zu fühlen schienen.

Nach dem Abschluss begann ich, in Los Angeles zu arbeiten. Die USA hatten eine Fülle an guter Architektur zu bieten, aber keine war so präsent und einflussreich wie die der Emigranten, die im Zweiten Weltkrieg aus „Bauhaus-Europa" eintrafen. Ihre Experimente waren allgegenwärtig, und ihre Ideen und Werke waren die Basis für die amerikanische Nachkriegsarchitektur, die sich als (süd)kalifornischer Stil etablierte. In den Entwürfen von Neutra (bisweilen auch bei Schindler), später dann Ain, Soriano, Ellwood, Koenig und nicht zu vergessen denen der beiden Eames' lockerten sich die strengen Bauhaus-Ideale allmählich zugunsten einer Architektur, die einem Kultur-und-Sozial-Mix entsprang mit den Zutaten Ungezwungenheit, Zweckmäßigkeit, Offenheit plus einer Prise Kapitalismus, kalifornischer Sonne und günstigem Preis.

Mir gefiel diese Mischung und ihre Vitalität, und ich mag sie noch immer. Im Laufe der Jahre und mit größerem Abstand überwand ich schließlich mein zwiespältiges Verhältnis zum Bauhaus. Mir wurde klar, wie stark sein Einfluss noch immer ist. Seine Geschichte wurde auch unsere Geschichte. Das Bauhaus entwickelte sich von einer unumstößlichen Doktrin zu etwas Nachhaltigerem. Einer Idee, die weiterhin provoziert, selbst heute noch.

Michael Maltzan

Tract homes in Levittown (above / oben)
Highway Interchange (below / unten)

Experimentation and craftsmanship

When I think of the Bauhaus, one of the things that immediately comes to mind are its many artisanal workshops, which formed the core of its legendary curriculum. It also relates to something that I have pursued in my own work, my produzione privata: cultivating a practice of experimentation and craftsmanship. The evolution of the world continues to be based on the profound connections between traditional craft culture and contemporary industrial culture.

Experiment und Handwerkskunst

Wenn ich ans Bauhaus denke, kommen mir unmittelbar die zahlreichen Werkstätten in den Sinn, die das Herzstück seines legendären Unterrichts bildeten. Zugleich sehe ich eine Verbindung zu dem, was ich in meiner eigenen Arbeit anstrebe, meiner „produzione privata" sozusagen: die Pflege von Experiment und Handwerkskunst. Denn die künftige Entwicklung der Welt beruht auch weiterhin auf der tiefen Verbindung zwischen traditioneller Handwerkskultur und zeitgenössischer Industriekultur.

Michele De Lucchi

Learning from the Bauhaus

When I began my studies to become an architect, the first book I was given was a beautiful monograph on the Bauhaus. I used it so much that over the years it actually lost its cubic shape and now it's on my shelf as a very soft-shaped volume. The sharp corners have all become rounded and a few pages may even be missing.

I was impressed by everything I read in it: Gropius, Klee, Kandinsky, Moholy-Nagy, Itten, Breuer, Lilly Reich... It was the first time I realized that such a radical artistic attitude could have its roots in a sort of mystical research.

With that book in mind, I plunged into the architecture adventure.

The heroic, the playful and the experimental. A school, playing as a collective like a symphony with a soul...

Did I ultimately learn something from all of that?

Lernen vom Bauhaus

Als ich mit dem Architekturstudium begann, war das erste Buch, das ich in die Hand bekam, eine wunderschöne Monografie über das Bauhaus. Ich benutzte sie so oft, dass sie im Laufe der Jahre ihre klare kubische Form verlor und heute als ein eher lappriges, unförmiges Ding in meinem Regal steht. Ihre einst scharfen Kanten sind ziemlich rund geworden, und vermutlich fehlen sogar ein paar Seiten.

Alles in diesem Buch beeindruckte mich: Gropius, Klee, Kandinsky, Moholy-Nagy, Itten, Breuer, Lilly Reich ... Zum ersten Mal wurde mir bewusst, dass eine derart radikale künstlerische Haltung das Ergebnis einer Art von mystischer Erfahrung sein konnte.

Mit diesem Buch im Kopf habe ich mich auf jeden Fall in das Abenteuer Architektur gestürzt.

Das Heroische, das Spielerische, das Experimentelle – all das fand ich hier. In einer Schule, die als Kollektiv zusammenwirkte, wie eine Symphonie mit einer Seele ...

Habe ich letztendlich aus all dem etwas gelernt?

Benedetta Tagliabue

Morning Breeze Villa, 2018

Creating values

In my opinion, the scope of thinking on which the Bauhaus was grounded is the true common denominator for the authentically timeless architecture and industrial design of the past 100 years. "God is in the details," Mies van der Rohe famously said. This dictum resonates with me deeply as I consider my own work, in which the equation of details guides the composition of my projects. When I say "equation of details", I mean the method by which I address every project, whether it's a building or a small object. A process which, by means of logical synthesis, balances form, materials and technology, allowing me to achieve a convincing equilibrium in every work I undertake.

The movement that began with the Bauhaus is still extraordinarily topical. Today, more than ever, the crossover between art and method, thanks to technological innovation, is proving itself as an engine for sustainable development in many parts of the world. Creating "neutral" spaces and objects, based on honest design and integrity of thought, is still today, in my opinion, the measure to which we should refer in order to create value. This has been made possible by a process that began at the Bauhaus 100 years ago.

Ideelle Werte schaffen

Der allumfassende Denkansatz des Bauhaus ist meiner Meinung nach der wahre gemeinsame Nenner für die authentische Zeitlosigkeit der Architektur und des Industriedesigns der letzten 100 Jahre. „Gott steckt im Detail", lautet das berühmte Zitat von Mies van der Rohe. Dieses Diktum stößt bei mir auf größten Widerhall, wenn ich mein eigenes Werk betrachte, bei dem die Balance der Details das Leitprinzip der Komposition ist. Wenn ich Balance der Details sage, meine ich die Herangehensweise an ein Projekt, sei es ein Gebäude oder ein kleines Objekt. Ein Verfahren, das Form, Material und Technik durch logische Synthese in ein ausgewogenes Verhältnis zueinander bringt und es mir erlaubt, in jeder meiner Arbeiten ein überzeugendes Gleichgewicht herzustellen.

Die Bewegung, die mit dem Bauhaus begann, ist noch außerordentlich aktuell. Dank einer fortschreitenden technischen Entwicklung erweist sich der Crossover zwischen Kunst und Methode heute mehr denn je als Triebkraft für eine weltweit nachhaltige Entwicklung. Das Schaffen „neutraler" Räume und Objekte, die auf ehrlichem Design und integrem Denken basieren, ist meiner Ansicht nach noch immer das Maß, an dem wir uns bei der ideellen Wertschöpfung orientieren sollten. Möglich geworden ist dies durch einen Prozess, der vor 100 Jahren am Bauhaus begann.

Monica Armani

Provocation and collective practice

The Bauhaus was a critical part of my formation as an architect and a teacher: an educational model embodying an immense cultural shift; a complete rethinking of art, design, graphics, photography and architecture; a unique synthesis generating out of the interdisciplinary connections, research and investigations of faculty as diverse as Albers, Breuer, Moholy-Nagy, Kandinsky, Klee and Lissitzky. The Bauhaus school gave us a provocative and absolutely incendiary model for collective practice that was foundational to our own trajectories.

Provokation und kollektive Praxis

Das Bauhaus war ein wichtiger Teil meiner Ausbildung als Architekt und als Lehrer – ein Unterrichtsmodell, das einen grundlegenden Kulturwandel bedeutete; ein vollständiges Umdenken in Kunst, Gestaltung, Fotografie und Architektur; eine einzigartige Synthese, die aus dem interdisziplinären Austausch in Experiment und Analyse entstand – unter der Ägide von so unterschiedlichen Lehrern wie Albers, Breuer, Moholy-Nagy, Kandinsky, Klee und Lissitzky. Das Bauhaus lieferte uns das provokante und absolut rebellische Modell einer kollektiven Praxis, das für unseren eigenen Werdegang von grundlegender Bedeutung war.

Thom Mayne

B.O.T. 1/1

Blue Orange Composite1

Sami Parliament building, Kiruna, Sweden

Dialogue and free thought

As a student, I studied the elegant Barcelona Pavilion in depth. There was so much to analyse: function, proportions, material and how they were all put together. Mies van der Rohe was the last responsible teacher at the Bauhaus before it became politically impossible and the school was closed by the authorities. For me, his architecture is far more than the Bauhaus ideology that stood for the integration of architecture, art and graphical form.

The Bauhaus broke new ground, showing a new direction through its way of thinking freely. And the times were ready for that. For example, in his work for the Stockholm Exhibition in 1930, whose architecture greatly affected me, Gunnar Asplund must also have been influenced by the Bauhaus. The Bauhaus was the result of ideas and discussion among people thinking radically beyond convention, before nationalism became strong and the school was perceived as a threat, not as an opportunity.

Unfortunately, there are parallels today with the spread of strong nationalist views, while openness, trust and curiosity in community construction is being threatened. What we need today is not more high walls and protectionism but an environment that works, inviting us to engage with one another in dialogue and creativity – all that Bauhaus stood for.

Dialog und freies Denken

Als Student beschäftigte ich mich sehr eingehend mit dem eleganten Barcelona-Pavillon. Es gab so viel zu analysieren: Funktion, Proportionen, Material und wie sie miteinander kombiniert waren. Mies van der Rohe war der letzte Leiter des Bauhaus, bevor es für die Nazis politisch untragbar wurde und man die Schule schloss. Für mich ist seine Architektur weit mehr als die Bauhaus-Ideologie, die Architektur, Kunst und Grafik zu vereinen suchte.

Das Bauhaus beschritt neue Wege und zeigte durch sein freies Denken eine völlig neue Richtung auf. Die Zeit war reif dafür. Auch Gunnar Asplund muss vom Bauhaus inspiriert gewesen sein, als er die wegweisende „Stockholm Ausstellung 1930" inszenierte, deren Architektur großen Einfluss auf mich hatte. Das Bauhaus war das Ergebnis von Ideen und Gesprächen zwischen Menschen, die radikal und jenseits aller Konventionen dachten. Nach dem Erstarken des Nationalismus wurde die Schule nicht mehr als Chance, sondern als Bedrohung wahrgenommen.

Leider gibt es Parallelen zur heutigen Ausbreitung nationalistischer Ideen, die jegliche Offenheit sowie das Vertrauen und die Neugier gegenüber Konzepten gemeinschaftlichen Bauens vermissen lassen. Was wir heute brauchen, sind weder hohe Mauern noch Protektionismus, sondern eine Umgebung, die im guten Sinne funktioniert und uns dazu animiert, miteinander in einen kreativen Dialog zu treten – all das, wofür das Bauhaus stand.

Hans Murman

What do I have to do with the Bauhaus?
Less and less...
My time as a student was extremely influenced by my reflec-
tions on modernist architecture and its continuation – thinking
back today, it was the formal aspects that were most important.
Our first independent projects therefore followed this tradition.
But I'm not really interested in that anymore. It took me 20 years to
get away from what I was taught in school. Today, I prefer to think
about buildings that have a strong relationship to their context
and its tradition in their form, materials and construction. I am
particularly interested in how we can build "correctly" in terms of
social responsibility, the use of resources and the construction
process, and what kinds of form or architecture can develop from
this.
Maybe this has something to do with the Bauhaus after all.

Was habe ich eigentlich mit dem Bauhaus zu tun?
Immer weniger ...
Meine Studienzeit war extrem geprägt von der Reflexion über
die Architektur der Moderne und ihre Weiterschreibung – aus
heutiger Sicht standen dabei die formalen Aspekte im Vordergrund. Unsere ersten eigenen Projekte folgten daher auch dieser
Tradition. Doch das interessiert mich eigentlich überhaupt nicht
mehr. Ich habe 20 Jahre gebraucht, um mich von dem zu lösen,
was mir im Studium beigebracht wurde. Heute mache ich mir viel
lieber Gedanken zu Häusern, die in Form, Material und Konstruktion einen starken Bezug zu ihrem Kontext und seiner Tradition
haben. Dabei interessiert mich vor allem, wie wir im Hinblick auf
soziale Verantwortung, den Einsatz von Ressourcen und Fragen
des Bauprozesses „richtig" bauen und welche Form oder Architektur sich daraus entwickeln kann.
Vielleicht hat das ja doch was mit dem Bauhaus zu tun.

Florian Nagler

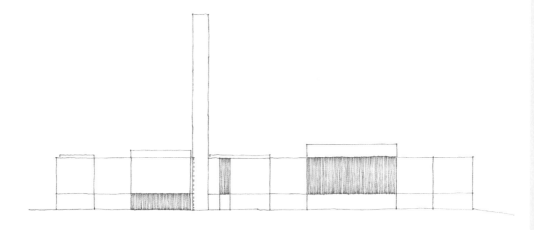

Riem church centre, 1999 (above), House in Franconia, 2018 (below)
Kirchenzentrum Riem 1999 (oben), Haus im Fränkischen 2018 (unten)

A multidisciplinary crucible

The early manifestos of the Bauhaus have infiltrated our everyday lives as designers and architects. At Neri&Hu, we take on a multiplicity of disciplines and their productions (architecture, interior, product, graphics and branding) while bridging the gap between craft and industry in the way we think about almost every project. Our work could take us from a building construction site to a furniture woodshop to a photography printing review, all in one day. We often wonder if our practice would be set up like this, crossing disciplines and intersecting varying scales of design, without precedent from such strong theoretical and conceptual foundations of the Bauhaus school. We take it for granted that things could be this way today, forgetting that the Bauhaus was an incredibly forward-thinking crucible for creating breakthroughs in design and art!

Ein multidisziplinärer Schmelztiegel

Unser tägliches Leben als Designer und Architekten ist durchdrungen vom Geist des Bauhaus. Unser Büro beschäftigt sich mit den unterschiedlichsten Fachgebieten (Architektur, Innenarchitektur, Produktdesign, Grafik und Branding) und schlägt unserem Ansatz entsprechend bei fast jedem Projekt eine Brücke zwischen Handwerk und Industrie. Unsere Tätigkeit kann uns von einer Baustelle zu einer Möbelschreinerei bis zur Überprüfung eines Fotoprints im Grafikstudio führen – und das alles an einem einzigen Tag. Wir fragen uns oft, ob unser Büro mit seiner multidisziplinären Ausrichtung und den unterschiedlichen, sich überschneidenden Entwurfsformaten wohl so eingerichtet worden wäre, hätte es nicht das Beispiel des Bauhaus mit seinen stark theoretischen und konzeptionellen Grundlagen gegeben. Heute erachten wir das alles für selbstverständlich und vergessen dabei gerne, was für ein unglaublich weitblickender Schmelztiegel das Bauhaus doch für bahnbrechende Neuerungen in Kunst und Design war!

Lyndon Neri, Rossana Hu

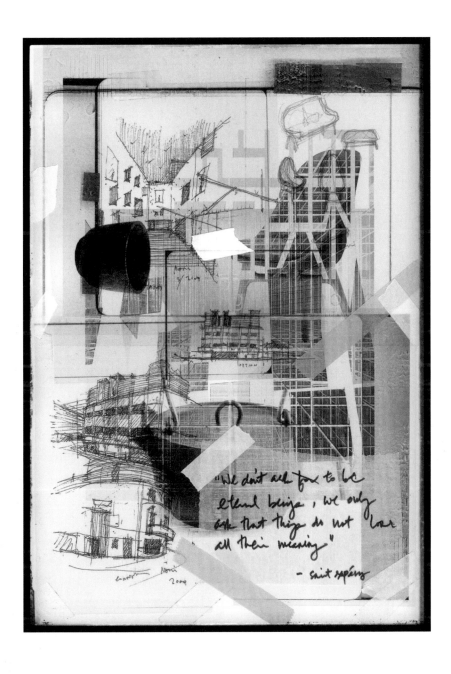

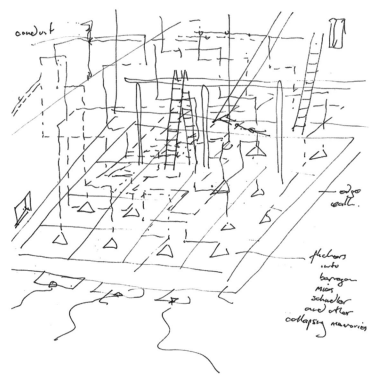

Paul Klee

The Pathos of Fertility.
Mural from The Temple of
Longing.
The Tightrope Walker.
Uncomposed in Space.
City in the Intermediate Realm.
The Way Out Discovered.
Wandering Artist. A Poster.

When I was first asked to design a building for people with dementia, I spent a lot of time trying to think about what it is that they experience. What do we have that they are losing? I researched all of the expert documents and professional guidance, but this did not answer the underlying question. The interaction of memory, projection and navigation are essential to our ability to situate ourselves. Architects speak blithely about space all the time, but what do we mean by it, and how did we come to acquire a sense of ourselves as belonging in space?

For all my reading, it was the drawings of Paul Klee that taught me most about this aspect of the human predicament. In continuous precise lines, he traces our journey from the womb to adulthood to the fragility of age as though he were describing a tightrope walk. He understood that we learn as infants to navigate the world, and this ability is fundamental to what we are. People with dementia lose this infinitely fine cat's cradle of memories, plans and associations, and with it they eventually lose themselves.

I worked with Yeoryia Manolopoulou and many of our ex-students to make a piece for the Venice Biennale in 2016, which tried to draw the world as experienced by people with dementia. Paul Klee was our guiding spirit. Amid the tragedy and terror of the condition we tried to rescue some fleeting fragments of beauty and connection.

Paul Klee

Das Pathos der Fruchtbarkeit.
Wandbild aus dem Tempel
der Sehnsucht.
Der Seiltänzer.
Nichtkomponiertes im Raum.
Stadt im Zwischenreich.
Der gefundene Ausweg.
Wander-Artist. Ein Plakat.

Als man mich bat, ein Haus für Demenzkranke zu entwerfen, musste ich erst einmal lange darüber nachdenken, was sie wohl erleben. Was haben wir, das sie allmählich verlieren? Ich vertiefte mich in Fachliteratur und professionelle Ratgeber, doch die grundlegende Frage blieb unbeantwortet. Das Zusammenspiel von Gedächtnis, Vorausschau und Orientierungsvermögen ist der wesentliche Faktor einer gelungenen Selbstverortung. Wir Architekten sprechen immerzu ganz unbekümmert vom Raum – doch was meinen wir eigentlich damit und wie haben wir ein Gefühl für unsere Zugehörigkeit zum Raum entwickelt?

Trotz all der Lektüre waren es die Zeichnungen Paul Klees, von denen ich am meisten über diesen Aspekt der menschlichen Realität lernte. In präzisen durchgehenden Linien zeichnet Klee unseren Weg nach vom Mutterleib über das Erwachsenwerden bis zur Gebrechlichkeit im Alter, als beschriebe er einen Seiltänzer. Er begriff, dass wir als Kinder lernen, uns durch die Welt zu bewegen, und diese Fähigkeit ist ein fundamentaler Bestandteil unseres Seins. Menschen mit Demenz verlieren den Faden in diesem unendlich feinen Spiel aus Erinnerungen, Plänen und Assoziationen – und damit sich selbst.

Für die Architekturbiennale 2016 in Venedig habe ich zusammen mit Yeoryia Manolopoulou und vielen unserer ehemaligen Studierenden an einem Projekt gearbeitet, das die Welt so zu zeichnen versucht, wie Menschen mit Demenz sie erleben. Unser Vorbild war dabei Paul Klee. Inmitten der Tragik und des Schreckens, die dieses Leiden mit sich bringt, haben wir versucht, wenigstens einige flüchtige Fragmente der Schönheit zu retten und „die losen Enden" wenigstens nicht ganz zu verlieren.

Níall McLaughlin

A memory

We are aware that the Bauhaus is much more than a building. Architecture, art, typography and industrial design are all parts of a Gesamtkunstwerk, a total work of art, which represents the spirit of an era, an idea, an aspiration that is for us a permanent reference and motivation. But as architects, we cannot avoid associating the Bauhaus with its building. The transformation of concepts into realities is strongly influenced by the physical space in which they can be developed. The building by Gropius in Dessau is hence itself a manifesto. In our memories, architecture and travel intersect: both share a link with memory and imagination, so that when we visited the Bauhaus for the first time, we experienced the past even as we discovered spaces that would become part of future memories. It was a late visit and therefore greatly desired, not long after the fall of the Berlin Wall. The photo that we found – though barely recognizable – reminds us of the emotion of the day when we visited a building that was in itself the construction of an idea. Today, that distant journey remains engraved in our memory. It evokes the uncertain, but decisive, time of transition between the years of our foundational academic training, and the years of our practical training – a time that would deeply impact our vision of architecture.

Eine Erinnerung

Wir wissen natürlich, dass das Bauhaus viel mehr ist als ein Gebäude. Architektur, Kunst, Typografie und Industriedesign sind allesamt Teil eines Gesamtkunstwerks, das den Geist einer Ära verkörpert, eine Idee und ein Ziel, das für uns ein ständiger Bezugspunkt und eine ständige Triebfeder ist. Doch als Architekten können wir gar nicht anders, als das Bauhaus mit seinem Gebäude in Verbindung zu bringen. Die Verwandlung von Konzepten in Realitäten wird stark durch den physischen Raum geprägt, in dem sie stattfindet. Gropius' Gebäude in Dessau ist daher als solches ein Manifest. In unseren Erinnerungen überschneiden sich Architektur und Reisen: In beiden verbindet sich das Erinnerte mit der Imagination, und so erlebten wir bei unserem ersten Besuch des Bauhaus die Vergangenheit und entdeckten zugleich auch Räume, die Teil zukünftiger Erinnerungen werden sollten. Es war ein später und daher sehnsüchtig erwarteter Besuch kurz nach dem Fall der Berliner Mauer. Ein ziemlich vergilbtes Foto aus dieser Zeit erinnert uns an die Emotionen jenes Tages, an dem wir ein Gebäude besichtigten, das den Bau einer Idee verkörperte. Diese Reise ist uns im Gedächtnis geblieben. Sie erinnert uns an die ungewisse, aber prägende Zeit des Übergangs von der Grundlagensammlung unserer Lehrjahre zu den praktischen Erfahrungen unserer Wanderjahre, die unser Architekturverständnis nachhaltig prägen sollten.

Enrique Sobejano, Fuensanta Nieto

When architecture lost its meaning

100 years since its establishment, the ideals of the Bauhaus seem both novel and outdated. In approaching design as a multidisciplinary pursuit, combining theory with practice, Walter Gropius's Bauhaus Manifesto of 1919 qualifies as avant-garde for most architects even today. Since Gropius, however, the words "multidisciplinary" and "practice" have acquired new meanings – less about architects, painters, sculptors and other artists jointly working towards the Gesamtkunstwerk than about financial experts, technical specialists, quantity surveyors and real estate consultants, knocking themselves out over viable design propositions. The architect has the honorary role of presiding over all of them. A century ago, architecture practice implied craftsmanship; nowadays it is mostly an act of mediation between the interests of investors, the policies of municipalities and the expertise of consultants.

The curriculum diagram of the Bauhaus had "building" at its centre, even though it didn't have an architecture department until 1927. In hindsight, that might have been the moment architecture started losing its relevance (by 1930, under Mies van der Rohe, the teaching of design had been reduced to a matter of mere aesthetics). If we are to imagine teaching not architecture but "building" once more, what kind of training would be relevant?

Als die Architektur ihre Bedeutung verlor ...

100 Jahre nach seiner Gründung erscheinen die Ideale des Bauhaus neu und antiquiert zugleich. Durch seinen multidisziplinären gestalterischen Ansatz und die Verbindung von Theorie und Praxis nimmt sich Walter Gropius' Bauhaus-Manifest von 1919 selbst für viele Architekten von heute geradezu avantgardistisch aus. Die Begriffe „multidisziplinär" und „Praxis" haben inzwischen allerdings eine neue Bedeutung erlangt – sie bezeichnen weniger Architekten, Maler, Bildhauer und andere Künstler, die gemeinsam auf ein Gesamtkunstwerk hinarbeiten, als vielmehr Finanzexperten, Techniker, Kostenplaner und Immobilienberater, die sich in Bezug auf machbare Entwurfsvorschläge gegenseitig lahmlegen. Dem Architekten kommt dabei die ehrwürdige Rolle zu, den Vorsitz über sie alle zu führen. Vor einem Jahrhundert bedeutete die architektonische Praxis noch Handwerkskunst – heute ist sie zumeist eine Mittlertätigkeit zwischen den Interessen von Investoren, der Politik von Städten und Gemeinden und der Expertise von Beratern.

Im Idealschema der Bauhaus-Lehre stand der „Bau" im Mittelpunkt allen Handelns, auch wenn es bis 1927 keine eigene Architekturabteilung gab. Rückblickend war dies vielleicht der Augenblick, in dem die Architektur ihre Bedeutung zu verlieren begann – unter Mies van der Rohe wurde die Gestaltungslehre 1930 auf eine Frage der bloßen Ästhetik reduziert. Wie müsste eine Ausbildung aussehen, die mehr auf den Prinzipien des Bauens basiert als auf denen der Architektur?

Reinier de Graaf

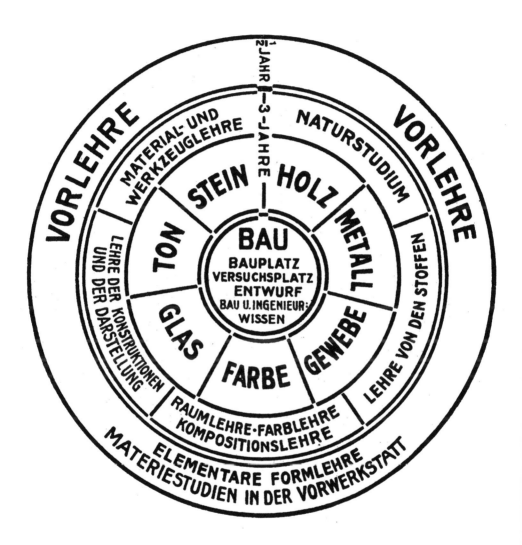

Walter Gropius, Bauhaus curriculum diagram, 1923
Walter Gropius, Schema zum Aufbau der Lehre am Bauhaus, 1923

Josef Hartwig, Chess Set / Schachspiel, 1924

Connecting the dots

In 1919, Walter Gropius claimed in his Bauhaus manifesto: "Art rises above all methods; in itself, it cannot be taught, but the crafts certainly can be." As a framework for these lessons, the school proposed to encourage "friendly relations between masters and students outside of work".

The traditional Arts & Crafts structure of masters and apprentices was respected in the new Bauhaus institution. Its aim was to provide every student with proper tools as a kind of "base camp" to reach the top in one's field, but also to pass on solid and valuable knowledge on teaching a profession to the students. This basis could be understood as the minimum requirement to go deeper into modern approaches and concepts that intended to be incorporated, developed and nurtured in the school. At the same time, the staff likely recognized that creativity's richest results often appear while not paying too much attention, and made strong use of that to expose singularity. Design – embracing and intertwining with life itself – thus becomes all the better.

Sometimes, what a creative mind needs in order to connect all the dots is simply a pretext to look around for a while, to steal a glance through the window, to grab a cup of coffee and listen to casual but profound words spoken by a distracted partner during a walk or a game of chess, just for fun, no worries. Then it's back to the drawing board, because somehow a dose of joy during the process is not a mere supplement, detour or excuse, but a necessity to push creativity. Only then can endless attempts be turned into games to be taken seriously.

Die hohe Schule der Absichtslosigkeit

In seinem Bauhaus-Manifest von 1919 verkündete Walter Gropius: „Kunst steht über allen Methoden, sie ist an sich nicht lehrbar, wohl aber das Handwerk." Im Rahmen dieser Lehre sollte die Schule den „freundschaftlichen Verkehr zwischen Meistern und Studierenden außerhalb der Arbeit" pflegen.

Die traditionelle Hierarchie von Meister und Lehrling, wie im klassischen Handwerk üblich, wurde dennoch auch am Bauhaus respektiert. Die Absicht dahinter war, den Studenten in einer Art „Grundkurs" die richtigen Werkzeuge in die Hand zu geben, um sie zu führenden Vertretern ihres Faches zu machen. Zugleich wollte man ihnen so auch ein solides Wissen und wichtige Erkenntnisse über ihren Beruf vermitteln. Es war die Mindestanforderung, um tiefer in die neuen Ansätze und Konzepte einzusteigen, die in der Ausbildung entwickelt, integriert und kultiviert werden sollten. Zugleich war dem Lehrpersonal jedoch bewusst, dass die kreativsten Ergebnisse häufig aus reiner Absichtslosigkeit entstanden, und sie legten größten Wert darauf, diese Erkenntnis als eine „Methode" zu propagieren, die absolut einzigartige Ergebnisse hervorbringt. Je mehr der Gestaltungsprozess das Leben einzubinden versteht, desto besser die Qualität des Designs.

Um sich neu zu sortieren und ordnen zu können, braucht ein kreativer Kopf manchmal nichts weiter als einen guten Vorwand, für eine Weile einfach nur dazusitzen und völlig „absichtslos" aus dem Fenster zu schauen, sich einen Kaffee zu holen, auf einem Spaziergang oder bei einer Partie Schach den beiläufig dahingesagten Worten eines Partners oder Gegenübers zu lauschen. Nur so zum Vergnügen. Ohne Verpflichtung. Dann geht's umso beschwingter zurück ans Reißbrett. Denn eine kleine Portion Spaß während der Arbeit ist mehr als eine bloße Ablenkung, ein überflüssiger Umweg oder die pure Ausrede – es ist eine Notwendigkeit, um den Kopf frei zu kriegen und die Inspiration zu beflügeln. Nur so können die endlosen, mühsamen Anläufe in lockere, kreative Spiele münden, die zugleich auch ernst zu nehmen sind.

Rok Oman, Špela Videčnik

Lost in transition

Why is it so difficult for me to write about my relationship with the Bauhaus?
Is it because I have no relationship with the Bauhaus?
And yet... I do.
A very vague one, though.

I

The cover of an architectural book I received at the age of 13 depicts the Bauhaus building in Dessau. For a boy who had been socialized in an Upper Bavarian suburb with a farmhouse wardrobe and corner bench, this was the first time I encountered the full force of modernism.

II

During a trip to Israel I saw the so-called White City for the first time while flying into Tel Aviv. At that moment, I understood that the Bauhaus was not only about objects. An entire urban space had been built there according to a preconceived order. With similarly formatted buildings all painted in the same colour. And yet in a nevertheless impressive variety of spatial situations, both inside the buildings and outside on the street.
Not like Dammerstock. Not like Törten. Not a settlement. But part of the city.

III

I visited Weimar for the first time in 2003. A small, comfortable, sedate town in the shadow of Goethe and classical music. How could van de Velde and Gropius stand it here, I thought at the time. Was it that explicitly familiar and provincial atmosphere that sparked the autonomous idea of collectively creating a modern world?

IV

On a recent trip through Saxony-Anhalt I also visited the Bauhaus in Dessau.
A campus, not a cosmos.
Only committed to itself.
But empty.

Freshly renovated. A museum. It was only there that I finally grasped what an incredible teaching concept was practised at the Bauhaus. The textiles, prints, drawings and furniture shown are compelling products of the spirit of:

All together!
All together!

For me, the Bauhaus phenomenon itself itself has lost all momentum, relevance and potential for questioning, making and experimenting – in the museum-like, educated bourgeois cultural space into which it has been increasingly pushed over the last 100 years. What a pity.
With its cosmos of insight, ideas and methods in education and production, however, it can (and should) continue to exist.

So let's get going!

Lost in Transition

Warum fällt es mir so schwer, über mein Verhältnis zum Bauhaus zu schreiben?
Weil ich kein Verhältnis zum Bauhaus habe?
Doch. Hab ich.
Wenn auch ein sehr unbestimmtes.

I

Auf dem Umschlag eines Architekturbuchs, das ich mit 13 Jahren bekam, war das Bauhaus-Gebäude in Dessau zu sehen. Einem Jungen, der in einer oberbayerischen Vorstadt mit Bauernschrank und Eckbank sozialisiert worden war, offenbarte sich hier zum ersten Mal die ganze Wucht der Moderne.

II

Während einer Israelreise erblickte ich beim Anflug auf Tel Aviv erstmals die sogenannte „Weiße Stadt". Damals habe ich verstanden, dass es beim Bauhaus nicht nur um Objekte ging. Dort war ein ganzer Stadtraum gebaut worden. Nach einer erdachten Ordnung. Mit ähnlich formatierten, gleichfarbig gestrichenen Gebäuden. In dennoch beeindruckender feiner Vielfalt der räumlichen Situationen – im Inneren der Häuser wie auch draußen auf der Straße.
Kein Dammerstock. Kein Törten. Keine Siedlung. Ein Stück Stadt.

III

2003 besuchte ich zum ersten Mal Weimar. Dieses gemütliche, betuliche Städtchen im Schatten Goethes und der Klassik. Wie haben es van de Velde und Gropius hier nur ausgehalten, dachte ich mir damals. Schuf gerade das Vertraute, das Provinzielle die notwendige Atmosphäre für die autonome Idee der kollektiven Erschaffung einer modernen Welt?

IV

Auf einer Reise durch Sachsen-Anhalt war ich jüngst auch im Bauhaus, in Dessau.
Ein Campus, nein ein Kosmos. Nur sich selbst verpflichtet. Aber: leer.
Frisch renoviert. Ein Museum. Dabei habe ich dort erst wirklich verstanden, welch unglaubliches Lehrkonzept am Bauhaus praktiziert wurde. Die gezeigten Textilien und Drucke, Zeichnungen und Möbel sind überzeugende Produkte des

Alle zusammen!
Alles zusammen!

Das Phänomen Bauhaus selbst hat für mich in dem musealen, bildungsbürgerlich geprägten Kulturraum, in den es in den letzten 100 Jahren zunehmend geschoben wurde, jede Wucht, jede Relevanz und jegliches Potenzial des Hinterfragens, des Machens, des Ausprobierens verloren. Schade.
Mit seinem Kosmos von Erkenntnissen, Ideen und Methoden in Ausbildung und Fertigung kann (und soll) es jedoch weiter bestehen.

Los geht's!

Peter Scheller

Margarete Dambeck, Buttons, collage, 1927 (Exhibition Bauhaus Dessau Foundation)
Margarete Dambeck, Druckknöpfe, Collage, 1927 (Ausstellung Stiftung Bauhaus Dessau)

Bauhaus meets farmhouse

We architects are shaped by the Bauhaus way of thinking in modules and its timeless, simple aesthetics. For a long time, this was also my reference system and an aesthetic language that I could expand at will, like the variations of light and dark in a pencil drawing. But coming from the Bavarian Forest, I often questioned the international vocabulary of the Bauhaus, its humourless and listless rigidity, its unpoetic, timeless, severity and its dogma. When we rebuilt Cilli, our farmhouse in the Bavarian Forest, the timelessness and ahistoricity of the Bauhaus became a dilemma. It seemed impossible to renovate a historical building shaped by certain social structures with the limited means of Bauhaus modernism, without destroying it. So, first of all, we dealt intensively with the historical building techniques of old regional homes. It was in their serial, reduced approach to materials that we finally discovered a link to Bauhaus ideals. This enabled us to play with its vocabulary and expand the existing building using a modern design language – while simultaneously preserving the building's history.

Bauhaus trifft Bauernhaus

Wir Architekten sind geprägt vom Bauhaus-Denken in Modulen und seiner zeitlosen, schlichten Ästhetik. Lange war das auch mein Bezugssystem und eine ästhetische Sprache, die ich nach Belieben erweitern konnte wie die Variationen von hell und dunkel in einer Bleistiftzeichnung. Doch als überzeugter Bayerwäldler (ver)zweifelte ich immer wieder am internationalen Vokabular des Bauhaus, seiner genauso humorlosen wie lustlosen Rigidität, seiner unpoetischen, zeitlosen Strenge und seinem Dogma. Als wir unser Bauernhaus Cilli im Bayrischen Wald umbauten, geriet die Zeit- und Geschichtslosigkeit der Bauhaus-Sprache dann zum Dilemma. Es schien unmöglich, ein historisches, durch bestimmte gesellschaftliche Strukturen geprägtes Gebäude mit den begrenzten Mitteln der Bauhaus-Moderne umzubauen, ohne es dabei zu zerstören. Also beschäftigten wir uns erst einmal intensiv mit den historischen Bautechniken alter Waidlerhäuser. In deren seriellem, reduziertem Umgang mit dem Material entdeckten wir schließlich eine Verwandtschaft mit den Bauhaus-Idealen. So war es uns also möglich, auch weiterhin mit ihrem Vokabular zu spielen und das Bestandsgebäude durch eine moderne Formensprache zu erweitern – bei gleichzeitiger Wahrung seiner Geschichte.

Peter Haimerl

Sober mistranslation

We like to think that everything we learn from a foreign source is in fact the feeble echo of a bad translation. We embrace the mistranslation in its unintentional authority. The very notion of Neue Sachlichkeit, one of the tangential dictums of the Bauhaus myth, has been interpreted as new objectivity, new realism, new matter-of-factness, new restraint, new dispassion or new sobriety, depending on the context. The German word "sachlich" not only refers to the factual, framed by objects outside the subject, but also to a rather moralistic attitude of being impartial or unbiased. An attitude that expresses itself as the flat blankness or crystalline glassness of modern abstract surfaces. With such an ideological model – as idealistic as the romantic expressionism that was criticized at the time – the neutral or generic, without special character, was institutionalized. If one understands that the quality of plain disinterest is the choice for unspecific possibilities, a radical indifference beyond good and evil, one has to assume that the "New Objectivity", in its distorted mistranslation as mere resignation, also implied a submissive acceptance, a degree of giving up, of sensitive failure or a form of liberation that has always intrigued us.

Ein Lob der Fehlauslegung

Wir glauben, dass alles, was aus einer ausländischen Quelle stammt, in Wahrheit nur das schwache Echo einer schlechten Übersetzung ist. Wir bekennen uns zur Fehlauslegung in ihrer ungewollten Autorität. Schon der Begriff „Neue Sachlichkeit", eine der sekundären Maximen des Bauhaus-Mythos, ist je nach Kontext als „Neue Objektivität", „Neuer Realismus", „Neue Zurückhaltung", „Neue Leidenschaftslosigkeit" oder „Neue Nüchternheit" interpretiert worden. Das deutsche Wort „sachlich" bezieht sich nicht nur auf das rein Faktische, wie es sich außerhalb des Subjekts konstituiert, sondern konnotiert zugleich auch eine eher moralisch gefärbte innere Haltung von Objektivität und Wertfreiheit. Eine Haltung, die sich in der leeren Glätte und kristallinen Gläsernheit moderner abstrakter Oberflächen manifestiert. Mit einem solchen ideologischen Modell – das im Kern so idealistisch ist wie der seinerzeit heftig kritisierte romantische Expressionismus – konnte sich der Begriff einer vorgeblich neutralen Architektur etablieren, die ohne jeglichen spezifischen Charakter ist. Wenn man jedoch begreift, dass die Qualität von Desinteresse, einer radikalen Gleichgültigkeit jenseits von Gut und Böse, in der Eröffnung unbegrenzter Möglichkeiten liegt, dann darf man wohl annehmen, dass die neue Sachlichkeit in ihrer Fehlauslegung als bloße Resignation zugleich auch ein fügsames Akzeptieren bedeutet, ein gewisses Maß an Aufgabe und sensiblem Scheitern – oder eine Form der Befreiung, die uns seit jeher fasziniert.

Mauricio Pezo, Sofia von Ellrichshausen

Pezo von Ellrichshausen, Ines plan (UBB Innovation Centre, 2015-),
both oil on canvas 30 × 30 cm, 2016.

This pair of paintings is the neutral representation of two opposite floor plans of a five-storey building. While the white centre depicts a void that decreases its diameter, the corner circles depict a private room that increases its size upon ascension. The resulting relationship between core and perimeter is inversely proportional. Objectively seen, the reflection on the glass facade will complete the other three-quarters of the curved inner wall.

Pezo von Ellrichshausen, Ines plan (UBB Innovation Centre 2015-),
Öl auf Leinwand (je) 30 × 30 cm, 2016.

Dieses Bilderpaar ist die neutrale Darstellung zweier gegensätzlicher Grundrisse eines fünfstöckigen Gebäudes. Während der weiße Mittelpunkt einen Hohlraum andeutet, der den Durchmesser verringert, beschreiben die Eckkreise einen privaten Raum, der größer wird, je höher man steigt. Die daraus entstehende Beziehung zwischen Mittelpunkt und Umfang ist umgekehrt proportional. Objektiv vervollständigt die Spiegelung an der Glasfassade die anderen drei Viertel der gekrümmten Innenwand.

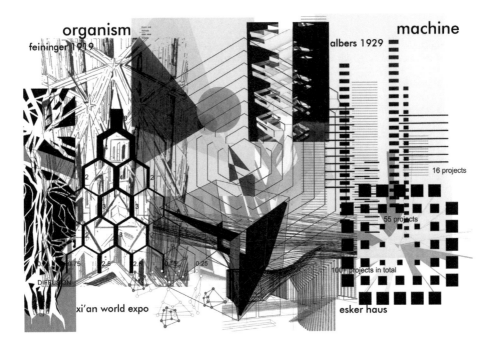

Creative backbone
for the future

The Bauhaus, as the foremost incubator and synonym of modernism, transformed the world structurally and aesthetically in all-encompassing and ubiquitous ways, shaping the very structures and processes of social interaction, business, production and knowledge. Despite the emergence of the post-Fordist "network society", this modernist structure still underpins our world today.

Yet because we have grown weary of the pure and honest representations of those relentless patterns of repetition, elements and determinations, they have become concealed beneath veneers of interface and signification. This deception is inadequate and needs to be absolved but any real new order and language will have to absorb and sublimate this modernist system.

To look beyond the seemingly coherent brand of the Bauhaus and its icons and see the manifold, tense and often contradictory strands of thinking and working, and understanding the Bauhaus as a transient laboratory shifting from organism to machine, offers a trajectory that when inverted could turn modularity and repetition (back) into coherence and unity.

By creatively mediating between fundamental dialectical positions, the processes and structures employed at the Bauhaus 100 years ago offer a perspective and a creative backbone to the social and technological transformation of our world ahead.

Kreatives Rückgrat
für die Zukunft

Als Geburtshelfer und Impulsgeber der Moderne verwandelte das Bauhaus die Welt baulich und ästhetisch auf grundlegende und allgegenwärtige Weise. Es hat unsere Ökonomie- und Produktionsstrukturen, Erkenntnisprozesse und Kommunikationsformen total verändert. Und obwohl wir mittlerweile in einer postfordistischen „Netzwerkgesellschaft" leben, ist dieser Ansatz der Moderne noch immer eine tragende Säule unserer heutigen Welt.

Doch weil wir seine puristischen Konzepte in der rigiden Wiederholung ihrer Muster und Regeln leid geworden sind, haben wir sie mit Furnierschichten von Bedeutung überzogen. Eine solche „Verblendung" ist natürlich völlig unangemessen und muss dringend beendet werden. Denn jede wirkliche Neuordnung wird nicht umhin kommen, den grundlegenden Ansatz des Bauhaus aufzunehmen und zu verfeinern.

Erst wenn man über die vermeintlich kohärente Marke Bauhaus hinausschaut und es in seiner Vielfalt und Widersprüchlichkeit begreift – als ein temporäres Labor, das sich von einem Organismus zu einer Maschine entwickelte –, entsteht eine Verlaufskurve, die bei ihrer Umkehrung Modularität und Wiederholung in Geschlossenheit und Einheit (zurück) verwandeln könnte.

Die am Bauhaus vor 100 Jahren verwendeten Verfahren und Strukturen schlagen eine Brücke zwischen fundamental entgegengesetzten Positionen und bieten so eine Perspektive und ein kreatives Rückgrat für den sozialen und technologischen Wandel der Welt von morgen.

Holger Kehne

Interplay of the arts

What was a matter of course for centuries, and central to the Bauhaus, is often completely missing in architectural education today: the interplay of the arts. For us, painting and sculpture are not only important sources of inspiration; we are directly involving artists in our projects more and more. With our office building for the pharmaceutical company CROMA in Leobendorf near Vienna, Ingo Nussbaumer designed the restaurant area and Esther Stocker the staircase. Our aim was to enliven a highly rational architecture with emotional moments. Ingo Nussbaumer also helped to make our ODO housing project in Vienna a Gesamtkunstwerk in the cityscape, endowing the balcony parapets with aluminium-shaped pipes in different heights and colours. Meanwhile, Heimo Zobernig developed the concept behind the play of colours for the Citygate Tower in Vienna. The design of the walls, rising over 100 metres high, reflects the percentage distribution of different colours associated with the term "sociability", according to a study conducted by the colour psychologist Eva Heller. At Museum Liaunig, Esther Stocker and Brigitte Kovanz each transformed a corridor into a work of art. For our ACW office building near Vienna, a motif printed on a truck tarpaulin, designed by Stefanie Lichtwitz and Kriso Leinfellner, causes a sense of spatial irritation. And at the Vienna headquarters of the Federal Property Association (BIG), Heimo Zobernig's ceiling-high letters composed of small black dots serve as camouflage for the unsightly existing walls.

Zusammenspiel der Künste

Was über Jahrhunderte ohnehin selbstverständlich war, für das Bauhaus jedoch zentral, ist in der heutigen Architekturausbildung leider oft gänzlich abhandengekommen: das Zusammenspiel der Künste! Für uns liefern Malerei und Bildhauerei nicht nur wichtige Inspirationen, wir binden zunehmend auch Künstler direkt in unsere Projekte mit ein. So gestaltete Ingo Nussbaumer den Restaurantbereich und Esther Stocker das Treppenhaus im Bürogebäude der Pharmafirma CROMA in Leobendorf bei Wien. Hier ging es darum, eine extrem nüchterne Architektur mit emotionalen Momenten zu beleben. Unser Wiener Wohnbauprojekt ODO wiederum wurde durch Ingo Nussbaumer zu einem Gesamtkunstwerk im Stadtbild, indem er die Balkonbrüstungen mit Aluminiumformrohren in verschiedenen Höhen und Farbtönen versah. Von Heimo Zobernig stammt das Konzept zum programmatischen Farbspiel des Wiener Citygate Towers: Die Farbgebung der Wände folgt über 100 Meter Höhe exakt den Prozentsätzen, mit denen die einzelnen Töne – laut einer Untersuchung der Farbpsychologin Eva Heller – dem Begriff „Geselligkeit" zugeordnet sind. Esther Stocker und Brigitte Kovanz haben jeweils einen Gang des Museums Liaunig als Kunstobjekt umgesetzt. Ein auf LKW-Plane gedrucktes Motiv von Stefanie Lichtwitz und Kriso Leinfellner sorgt bei unserem Bürogebäude ACW in der Nähe von Wien für eine räumliche Irritation. Und bei der Wiener Verwaltungszentrale der Bundesimmobiliengesellschaft (BIG) dienen Heimo Zobernigs raumhoch folierte Buchstaben aus kleinen schwarzen Punkten als Camouflage für die unschönen Bestandswände.

Jakob Dunkl

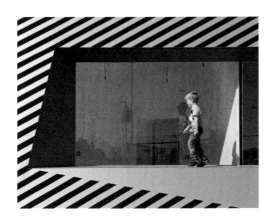

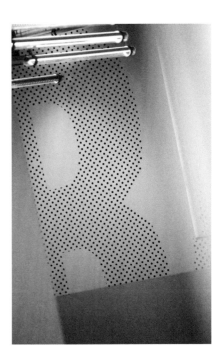

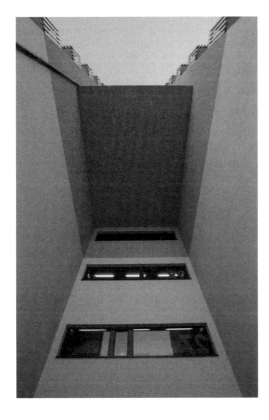

Incomparable vitality

The Bauhaus speaks for itself. In its combination of art and craftsmanship and a dynamic resulting from the interaction of heterogeneous positions and personalities, it released a maximum of creative energies. It marks a unique historical moment of incomparable vitality, which has lost none of its radiance to this day and will always remain a point of reference. Even abstracted from its contents, it embodies everything that is indispensable for a renewal and further development of architecture: a willingness to make formal breaks, an openness towards new manufacturing processes and materials, and the courage to embrace utopia as a dream of a better world with new possibilities and ways of life. It was the start of a new era that stood up to a dark past. The Bauhaus stands for the spirit of modernity par excellence. Although we do not directly draw on it formally, the Bauhaus is an inspiration for our research project, La Vila. With it, we want to create a world that may one day have a positive influence on future generations – just like the Bauhaus.

Unvergleichliche Vitalität

Das Bauhaus spricht für sich selbst. In seiner Zusammenführung von Kunst und Handwerk und einer Dynamik, die aus dem Zusammenspiel heterogener Positionen und Persönlichkeiten entstand, setzte es ein Höchstmaß an kreativen Energien frei. Es markiert einen einzigartigen historischen Moment von unvergleichlicher Vitalität, der bis heute nichts von seiner Strahlkraft verloren hat und immer ein Referenzpunkt bleiben wird. Auch abstrahiert von seinen Inhalten verkörpert es all das, was für jedwede Erneuerung und Weiterentwicklung der Architektur unabdingbar ist: die Bereitschaft zum formalen Bruch, die Offenheit gegenüber neuen Herstellungsprozessen und Werkstoffen und der Mut zur Utopie als Traum von einer besseren Welt mit neuen Möglichkeiten und Lebensweisen. Es war der Beginn eines Aufbruchs, der sich gegen eine dunkle Vergangenheit behauptet. Das Bauhaus steht für die Moderne schlechthin. Wenn auch nicht direkt von seinen Ideen inspiriert, ist es dennoch zugleich eine Referenz für unser Forschungsprojekt La Vila. Wir möchten damit eine Welt schaffen, die vielleicht eines Tages einen positiven Einfluss auf die nachfolgenden Generationen hat – genau wie das Bauhaus.

Rafael Aranda, Carme Pigem, Ramon Vilalta

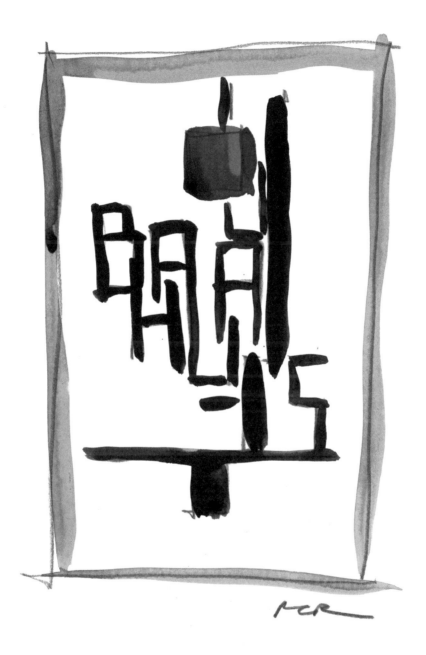

Bauhaus, RCR, watercolour ink and pencil on Canson Imagine paper (200 g / m²),
29.7×42 cm
Bauhaus, RCR, Aquarell-Tusche und Bleistift auf Canson Imagine Papier (200 g / m²),
29.7×42 cm

Pragmatism with humour

Dancing, costumes and creative delight are what first come to mind when I think of the Bauhaus. But also the clear, austere buildings by Mies van der Rohe, and the bright colours of the Masters' Houses in Dessau. When I immersed myself in Berlin's architectural scene in the early 1990s, my studies in Glasgow had not really prepared me for the realities of being a German architect. So it was in Berlin that I first learned architecture as a craft. I grew up with the functionalist buildings of modernism, and paired with my Swedish pragmatism, this led to my own Realarchitektur. Driven by the search for a solution that embodies the task, my goal is to create spaces that provide added value to all those who live in them. For example, when the young performance artist Goro Tronsmo came to me to convert her very normal apartment in Berlin-Neukölln, this provided me with an opportunity to challenge myself and the artist. We took the general functions that an apartment has and changed their situational position in the space. The result is a place of communication – with humour, creativity and a sense of craftsmanship, in short: with Bauhaus character.

Pragmatismus mit Humor

Das Tanzen, die Kostüme, die kreative Fröhlichkeit sind meine ersten spontanen Assoziationen zum Bauhaus. Hinzu kommen die klaren, strengen Bauten Mies van der Rohes und die bunten Farben der Meisterhäuser in Dessau. Als ich Anfang der 90er-Jahre in das Berliner Architekturgeschehen eintauchte, hatte mein Studium in Glasgow mich nicht wirklich auf die Realitäten des deutschen Architekten-Daseins vorbereitet. Architektur als Handwerk habe ich daher erst in Berlin gelernt. Ich bin aufgewachsen mit den funktionalistischen Bauten der Moderne, und gepaart mit meinem schwedischen Pragmatismus ist Realarchitektur entstanden. Angetrieben von der Suche nach einer Lösung, die das verkörpert, was der Aufgabenstellung entspricht, ist es mein Ziel, Räume zu schaffen, die für alle, die darin leben, einen Mehrwert haben. Als etwa die junge Performance-Künstlerin Goro Tronsmo zu mir kam und ihre ganz normale Neuköllner Wohnung umbauen wollte, war das die Gelegenheit, mich selbst wie auch die Künstlerin herauszufordern. So nahmen wir die Funktionen, die eine Wohnung im Allgemeinen hat, und veränderten einfach ihre situative Lage im Raum. Entstanden ist ein Ort der Kommunikation – mit Humor, Kreativität und einem Gefühl fürs Handwerk, kurz: mit Bauhaus-Charakter.

Petra Petersson

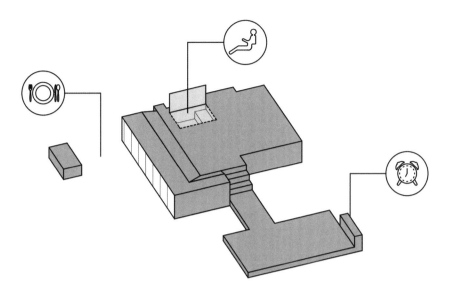

BoG, Panierstrasse

Grandchildren and grandparents

While designing the Federal Environment Agency (UBA) in Dessau, we often wondered how much Bauhaus was in it and to what extent the new building could be compared with Gropius's buildings. In a way, it was its antithesis: while the proponents of the Bauhaus blithely ignored ecological approaches, with the UBA one of our priorities was minimizing the need for fossil fuel energy. Nevertheless, we were increasingly surprised to see how much we were in harmony with the Bauhaus's efforts to aestheticize everyday life. The productive meeting of creative minds with different ways of thinking, as so uniquely practiced by the Bauhaus, is a model for us, and the aesthetic power of its architecture is still a valid measure. Like the modernist architects, we are convinced that we can solve the problems of the present through prudent use of our planning and technical intelligence. Unlike our grandparents, however, we grandchildren are no longer concerned with establishing an exclusively dominant relationship with the (natural and artificial) environment, but rather a symbiotic one.

Enkel und Großeltern

Als wir das Umweltbundesamt (UBA) in Dessau entwarfen, haben wir uns oft gefragt, wie viel Bauhaus wohl in ihm steckt und inwieweit das neue Gebäude sich mit den Bauten von Gropius vergleichen ließ. In gewisser Weise war es ja die Antithese: Während die Bauhäusler ökologische Ansätze unbekümmert ignorierten, ging es uns beim UBA nicht zuletzt auch darum, den Bedarf an fossilen Ressourcen auf ein Minimum zu reduzieren. Wir waren jedoch erstaunt, mehr und mehr festzustellen, wie sehr wir mit dem Bemühen des Bauhaus um eine Ästhetisierung des Alltags in Einklang standen. Das produktive Zusammentreffen kreativer Köpfe unterschiedlichster Denkart, wie es das Bauhaus so einzigartig praktizierte, hat für uns Vorbildcharakter, und die ästhetische Kraft seiner Architektur ist nach wie vor ein gültiger Maßstab. Wie die Architekten der Moderne sind auch wir davon überzeugt, mit dem richtigen Einsatz von planerischer und technischer Intelligenz die Probleme der Gegenwart lösen zu können. Im Gegensatz zu unseren Großeltern geht es uns Enkeln allerdings nicht mehr um ein ausschließlich dominierendes, sondern vielmehr um ein symbiotisches Verhältnis zur (natürlichen und künstlichen) Umwelt.

Matthias Sauerbruch, Louisa Hutton

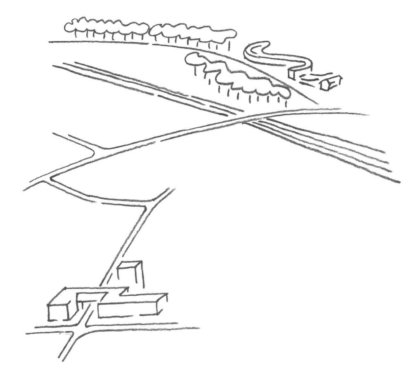

Unity of art and space

The studio we use when we need some peace and quiet is located in Zwenkau in Saxony – far removed from the hustle and bustle of our city office in Leipzig. Zwenkau is also home to Haus Rabe, which embodies the Bauhaus spirit like no other. Adolf Rading and Oskar Schlemmer built it in 1930 as a Gesamtkunstwerk, a total work of art that fuses architecture and the fine arts. This building inspired us to collaborate with Korean artist Jong Oh, who designed a fragile installation of metal rods, strings, pencil lines, black paint and a small carbon ball for the gable wall of our studio space. The geometric forms of his "Wall Drawing (monochrome) #1" react to their spatial environment by imitating formats and gestures of architectural elements. This work of art and the space around it visually merge because they pursue the same strategy: elements and how they are joined are reduced to the essential. Clarity and precision determine perception. The elegance and beauty of simple things are rendered visible. This approach only works when it understands how to combine comprehensive artistic understanding with constructive thinking.

Die Einheit von Kunst und Raum

Unser Atelier für stille Stunden liegt im sächsischen Zwenkau – weitab vom Trubel des Leipziger Innenstadtbüros. Hier steht auch Haus Rabe, das wie kein zweites den Bauhaus-Geist verkörpert. Adolf Rading und Oskar Schlemmer schufen es 1930 als Gesamtkunstwerk, das Architektur und Bildende Kunst miteinander verschmilzt. Uns inspirierte es zu einer Zusammenarbeit mit dem koreanischen Künstler Jong Oh, der für die Giebelwand unseres Atelierraums eine fragile Installation aus Metallstäben, Schnüren, Bleistiftlinien, schwarzer Farbe und einer kleinen Carbonkugel entwarf. Die geometrischen Formen seines „Wall Drawing (monochrome) #1" reagieren dabei auf ihr räumliches Umfeld, indem sie Formate und Gestik von architektonischen Elementen nachahmen. Kunstwerk und Raum gehen optisch ineinander über, weil sie dieselbe Strategie verfolgen: Elemente und Fügung werden auf das Wesentliche reduziert. Klarheit und Präzision bestimmen die Wahrnehmung. Die Eleganz und Schönheit der einfachen Dinge wird sichtbar. Ein Ansatz, der nur funktioniert, wenn er gesamtkünstlerische Bildung und konstruktives Denken miteinander zu verbinden weiß.

Ansgar Schulz Benedikt Schulz

Jong Oh, Wall Drawing (monochrome) #1, 2015
Metal rods, cord, pencil lines, black paint, ball
Jong Oh, Wall Drawing (monochrome) #1, 2015
Metallstäbe, Schnur, Bleistiftlinien, schwarze Farbe, Kugel

Bauhaus Dessau (left / links)
Wildcoast House facade prototype (right / rechts)
Wildcoast House (below / unten)

Striving for the Gesamtkunstwerk

When the German government decided to close the Bauhaus in 1933, they unwittingly provided the world with a remarkable gift. The influence of the Bauhaus still pulsates across the globe, 100 years after its inception, as it first did when luminaries such as Mies van der Rohe, Walter Gropius and Marcel Breuer continued their extraordinary work and research away from Europe and the troubles of that time. The Bauhaus managed to capture the zeitgeist of Germany in the 1920s and the complex fusing of the Arts and Crafts movement with the expediencies of mass production resulted in a New Objectivity – an extraordinary explosion of rational design that was to become the bedrock of 20th century art and architecture in the western world.

Now, in this disturbing age of globalized homogenization, my office still aspires to the Bauhaus ideal of Gesamtkunstwerk in every project that we undertake.

Auf der Suche nach dem Gesamtkunstwerk

Als die Nazi-Regierung 1933 die Schließung des Bauhaus beschloss, machte sie der Welt ungewollt ein bemerkenswertes Geschenk. Denn sein Einfluss pulsiert auch 100 Jahre nach seiner Gründung noch immer rund um den Globus – genau wie damals, als Berühmtheiten wie Mies van der Rohe, Walter Gropius und Marcel Breuer ihre einzigartige Arbeit und Forschung in der Fremde fortsetzten, fern der Heimat und dem Ungeist jener Jahre. Dem Bauhaus gelang es perfekt, den Spirit der 1920er-Jahre in Deutschland einzufangen. Die komplexe Verschmelzung der Arts-and-Crafts-Bewegung mit den Zielsetzungen der Massenproduktion führte zur Neuen Sachlichkeit – einer wahren Explosion von rationalem Design, die in der westlichen Welt zum Fundament der Kunst und Architektur des 20. Jahrhunderts werden sollte.

In diesem höchst verstörenden Zeitalter globalisierter Homogenisierung verfolgt mein Büro noch immer bei jedem unserer Projekte das Bauhaus-Ideal des Gesamtkunstwerks.

Sean Godsell

Understanding comes from doing

"Architects, sculptors, painters – we all must return to craftsmanship!" says Walter Gropius in his Bauhaus Manifesto. Our office was founded on one great commission, the transformation of the Bungenäs peninsula – an old military exercise ground and limestone quarry on the Swedish island of Gotland in the Baltic Sea, which had been closed off to the public since the 1960s.

When we first came to Bungenäs in 2010, we had just finished our architectural education and were looking for something that had not been taught in our schools: a knowledge of craftsmanship. For us, understanding comes from doing. Therefore, testing things became a method not only to master different crafts but also to absorb a language to be used to communicate with contractors.

The types of crafts needed at Bungenäs have been specific to the site. The visible traces of its former uses are always present, the landscape was transformed by the quarry and destroyed by military use, rutted by heavy tanks, and what has been left behind abounds with bunkers and trenches.

Craft here means the understanding of concrete structures, excavation of covered bunkers, cutting through metre-thick walls, making moulds for concrete and wood detailing.

Seven years later, Bungenäs remains our school after school, a 165-hectare-large workshop.

Verstehen kommt von Machen

„Architekten, Bildhauer, Maler, wir alle müssen zum Handwerk zurück!", fordert Walter Gropius in seinem Bauhaus-Manifest. Unser Büro ging aus einem Großauftrag hervor: der Umgestaltung der Halbinsel Bungenäs auf Gotland, einem alten Truppenübungsplatz und Steinbruch, der seit den 1960er-Jahren nicht mehr öffentlich zugänglich war.

Als wir 2010 das erste Mal nach Bungenäs kamen, hatten wir gerade unser Architektur-studium beendet und suchten nach etwas, das man uns an der Universität nicht beigebracht hatte: handwerkliches Können. Für uns kommt Verstehen von Machen. Das Ausprobieren wurde zur Methode – nicht nur um verschiedene Techniken zu beherrschen, sondern auch um eine Sprache zu entwickeln, in der wir mit den Baufirmen kommunizieren konnten.

Die in Bungenäs benötigten Gewerke mussten der Örtlichkeit angepasst werden. Überall waren die Spuren ehemaliger Nutzungen unübersehbar präsent – die Landschaft zerstört durch den Kalkabbau und zerfurcht von schwerem Gerät. Was davon übrig blieb, war mit Bunkern und Schützengräben übersät.

Handwerk bedeutete hier den Umgang mit Betonstrukturen, den Aushub von überwucherten Bunkern, das Durchschneiden meterdicker Wände, die Herstellung von Formen für Beton- und Holzdetails.

Sieben Jahre danach bleibt Bungenäs unsere Schule nach der Schule, eine 165 Hektar große Werkstatt.

Skälsö Arkitekter

Mindre bunker 18

Cross-professional collaborations

Whenever the Bauhaus is mentioned, there is a slight sense of unease that spreads among those present. The reason might be that Bauhaus is commonly referred to as "the" Bauhaus. By using "the" as a determiner, we have no option but to accept the absoluteness embedded in its name. Therein lies both my fascination with a movement so far away from today's diverse and pluralistic reality and my fear of its fundamentalist approach to society.

Even if it was leaning on the 19th-century definition of Gesamtkunstwerk, the Bauhaus was still a child of its time. The dreadful destruction of the First World War forced society to allow the emergence of completely new, collaborative models.

To learn from the Bauhaus, we needed to decipher elements of its philosophy, split its statements into smaller parts and pull these elements into our own practice. Our self-defined method of "transpositioning" is directly related to cross-professional collaborations. Through this method, all individuals involved in the creative process may change profession with one another. Architect becomes engineer, philosopher becomes artist, client becomes designer, engineer becomes landscape architect, artist becomes architect, and so on. We release forces beyond the professions and relieve the professionals from their regular responsibilities. This thinking would not have been possible without the Bauhaus.

Ein interdisziplinärer Ansatz

Immer, wenn vom Bauhaus die Rede ist, macht sich unter den Anwesenden ein gewisses Unbehagen breit. Das könnte daran liegen, dass es im Allgemeinen als „das" Bauhaus bezeichnet wird. Durch die Verwendung des Bestimmungswortes „das" bleibt uns nichts anderes übrig, als die mit dem Namen einhergehende Absolutheit zu akzeptieren. Daher rührt meine Faszination für eine Bewegung, die sehr weit von unserer heutigen vielfältigen und pluralistischen Realität entfernt ist, aber auch meine Angst vor seinem fundamentalistischen gesellschaftlichen Ansatz.

Obwohl sich das Bauhaus an eine Definition des gesamtkunstwerklichen Ansatzes aus dem 19. Jahrhundert anlehnte, war es ein Kind seiner Zeit. Die schrecklichen Zerstörungen des Ersten Weltkriegs zwangen die Gesellschaft, völlig neue gemeinschaftliche Modelle zuzulassen.

Um vom Bauhaus zu lernen, mussten wir die Elemente seiner Philosophie erst einmal entschlüsseln, seine Statements in kleinere Teile zerlegen und diese wiederum in unsere eigene Praxis integrieren. Die von uns ausgearbeitete Methode des „Transpositionierens" bezieht sich direkt auf Formen berufsübergreifender Zusammenarbeit. Nach dieser Methode können alle am kreativen Prozess Beteiligten ihr Betätigungsfeld wechseln. Der Architekt wird zum Ingenieur, der Philosoph zum Künstler, der Bauherr zum Designer, der Ingenieur zum Landschaftsarchitekten, der Künstler zum Architekten und so weiter. Wir setzen Kräfte jenseits der Berufsfelder frei und befreien die Experten von ihren üblichen Aufgaben. Dieses Denken wäre ohne das Bauhaus nicht möglich gewesen.

Kjetil Trædal Thorsen

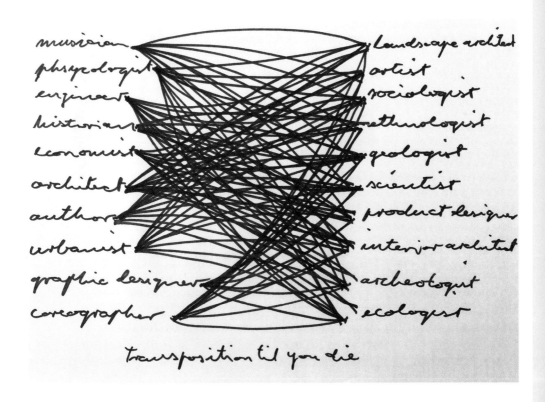

How to experience the world

Unsuspectingly, our world and work is steeped in Bauhaus ideology. It was there in our first project, "Pole Dance", a participatory Gesamtkunstwerk for the Museum of Modern Art in New York, which combined abstract systems and forms with colour, movement, dance and sound referencing Oskar Schlemmer's "Pfauentanz". And it continues to be present in "L'air pour l'air", a recent collaborative work for the Chicago Architecture Biennial consisting of an ensemble of air-filtering mesh enclosures worn by performing musicians. Our work is inherently optimistic, integrative and multifaceted. So we naturally absorbed this underpinning, its abstraction, the use of structure to frame space, movement as experience... it all seems obvious now. More than forms and shapes, it's our way of experiencing the world – our way of living, that one could call "our Bauhaus".

Eine Art, die Welt zu erleben

Mit unserer Arbeit und unserer Weltsicht stecken wir tiefer in der Ideologie des Bauhaus, als uns bislang klar war. Das zeigte sich schon bei unserem ersten Projekt „Pole Dance", einem partizipatorischen Gesamtkunstwerk für das Museum of Modern Art in New York, das in Anlehnung an Oskar Schlemmers „Pfauentanz" abstrakte Systeme und Formen mit Farbe, Bewegung, Tanz und Klang verknüpfte. Und es wird genauso spürbar in „L'air pour l'air", einer jüngeren Gemeinschaftsarbeit für die Architekturbiennale in Chicago, bei der sich in Netzkokons gehüllte und performende Musiker als lebende Luftfilter betätigten. Unsere Arbeiten sind grundsätzlich optimistisch, integrativ und vielgestaltig. Daher haben wir uns selbstverständlich diesen ideologischen Unter- und Überbau zu eigen gemacht – in seiner Abstraktion, seiner Verwendung von Struktur zur Gestaltung von Raum und der Bewegung als Erfahrung ... Heute scheint das alles offensichtlich. Jenseits von Formen und Gestalten handelt es sich um unsere Art, die Welt zu erleben – unsere Lebensweise, die man als „unser Bauhaus" bezeichnen könnte.

Florian Idenburg

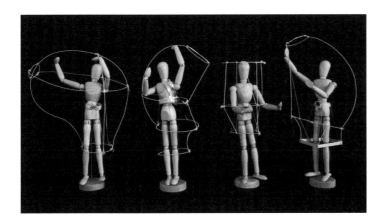

Bauhaus as integration

The Bauhaus, for me, stands for integration. Integration of shape, logic, function, form, materials, surroundings, histories and the human body. Integration of different categories of architecture, art, performance, texts, music, dance, movies and so on. So the Bauhaus is always with me, because integration is the most essential thing for me when I think about architecture.

The spirit of Bauhaus is the foundation of my thinking.

Synthese und Integration

Das Bauhaus steht für mich für Synthese und Integration: die Integration von Gestalt, Logik, Funktion, Form, Material, Kontext, Geschichte(n) und den menschlichen Körper; die Synthese verschiedener Kategorien von Architektur, Kunst, Performance, Texten, Musik, Tanz, Filmen und so weiter. Das Bauhaus begleitet mich also ständig, weil Synthese und Integration für mich das Wichtigste ist, wenn ich an Architektur denke.

Der Geist des Bauhaus ist das Fundament meines Denkens.

Sou Fujimoto

Serpentine Pavilion, London 2013

Digital perfection

The first time I encountered the Bauhaus was in the form of a Barcelona Chair at my parents' house. I remember finding it quite uncomfortable as a child. Today I work almost daily with the Bauhaus, because we are expanding the Bauhaus Archive in Berlin. In connection with this project, I was asked how our intervention actually relates to the architecture of the Bauhaus. The answer could only be to seek a programmatic connection rather than a formal one: experimentation – didactics – discourse. These programmatic contents are made visible in the new entrance tower. The tower's design also reflects the digital influence on the planning and construction process. Just as industrialization did at the beginning of the last century, digitization is transforming our work today. Our tower is an example of a supporting structure that is made possible by the digital process.

Digitale Vollendung

Das erste Mal ist mir das Bauhaus in Form eines „Barcelona-Chairs" im Haus meiner Eltern begegnet. Ich kann mich noch erinnern, dass ich ihn als Kind recht ungemütlich fand. Heute habe ich fast täglich mit dem Bauhaus zu tun, da wir das Archiv in Berlin erweitern. Im Zusammenhang mit diesem Projekt wurde ich vor die Frage gestellt, in welcher Relation unser Eingriff eigentlich zur Architektur des Bauhaus steht. Die Antwort konnte nur sein, keine formale, sondern eine programmatische Verbindung zu suchen: Experiment – Didaktik – Diskurs. Diese programmatischen Inhalte werden im neuen Eingangsturm sichtbar. Darüber hinaus dokumentiert seine Konstruktion den digitalen Einfluss auf die Planung und den Bauprozess. Wie die Industrialisierung im beginnenden letzten Jahrhundert verändert heute die Digitalisierung unsere Arbeit. Unser Turm ist ein Beispiel für ein Tragwerk, das durch den digitalen Prozess so erst möglich wird.

Volker Staab

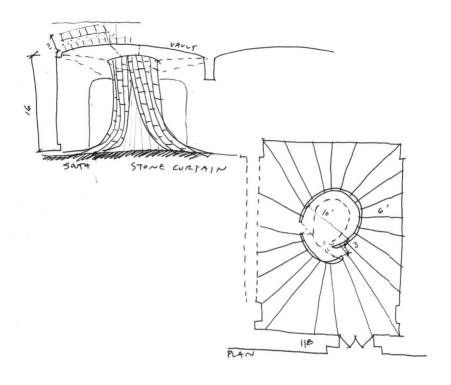

Marble curtain, sketch and snapshot

The art of building
For me, the Bauhaus connotes the art of building. In my work, I often think about building, and when I think about building, I think about materials – approaching them with the same kind of curiosity and experimentation that the Bauhaus encouraged. I ask myself, what are the material's inherent qualities? What qualities could it gain if we harness newly available techniques and technologies? What is this material capable of doing, and has it been underestimated?

Sometimes this exploration leads to an expression of material thinness. The Marble Curtain installation, for example, cut 600 pieces of marble as thin as possible and interlocked them into a translucent structure hung in tension. At other times this way of working leads to an expression of the joint between materials, like the wood "cat's paw" that suspends the walkway of Writers Theatre from seemingly delicate timber battens. It can also lead to an expression of construction, as in the stacked cordwood that forms the masonry walls of the Arcus Center for Social Justice Leadership, or the expression of compression, like those same walls' gently arcing geometry.

To be a student of material as the Bauhaus taught is to be unafraid to ask new questions of the things and thinking we inherit, staying open to both failure and surprise. It is a method of discovery that remains equally potent today as ever.

Die Kunst des Bauens
Für mich steht das Bauhaus für die Kunst des Bauens. In meiner Arbeit denke ich oft über das Bauen nach, und wenn ich über das Bauen nachdenke, denke ich über Materialien nach – ich nähere mich ihnen mit derselben Neugier und Experimentierfreude, zu der das Bauhaus ermunterte. Die Fragen, die ich an ein Material stelle, sind folgende: Welches sind seine spezifischen Eigenschaften? Welche Qualitäten könnte es durch den Einsatz neuer Techniken und Technologien dazugewinnen? Wozu ist dieses Material in der Lage und inwieweit wurde es bislang unterschätzt? Diese Befragung kann zum Beispiel dazu führen, dass ich das betreffende Material in einer geringeren Stärke verwende. So wurden die 600 Marmorteile des Marble Curtain bei der Installation so dünn wie möglich geschnitten, zu einer transluzenten Struktur zusammengesteckt und straff gespannt.

Ein anderes Mal wirkt sich diese Arbeitsweise etwa auf die Verbindung von Materialien aus – so wie beim hölzernen Laufgang im Obergeschoss des Writers Theatre in Glencoe, Illinois, der vermeintlich an dünnen Latten aufgehängt ist. Meine Methode kann aber auch zu einer Offenlegung der Konstruktion führen, wie beim aufeinander geschichteten Klafterholz, aus dem die Wände des Arcus Center for Social Justice Leadership in Kalamazoo, Michigan, bestehen. Oder es ist ein Ausdruck von Verdichtung wie bei dem leichten Bogen, den eben jene Wände bilden.

Die Erforschung von Materialien, wie sie das Bauhaus lehrte, heißt keine Angst davor zu haben, an bekannte Dinge und tradierte Vorstellungen neue Fragen zu stellen und für Misserfolge ebenso offen zu sein wie für Überraschungen. Es ist eine wahre Entdeckungsreise. Und eine Methode, die heute so spannend und wirkungsvoll ist wie damals.

Jeanne Gang

An ethical challenge

I am a student of the Bauhaus. My early training as an architect was all with refugees from Germany coming directly from the Bauhaus. I studied at the Cooper Union School of Art in New York. My favourite professor, Hannes Beckmann, taught colour theory from his notebooks, which had been corrected by Wassily Kandinsky – so I had exactly the same course that was given at the Bauhaus. I learned a lot in those days. Even now, I continue to understand design according to the Bauhaus spirit: as an ethical challenge and a fundamental approach to forming a good society.

Eine ethische Herausforderung

Ich bin ein Bauhaus-Student. Meine frühe Ausbildung als Architekt erhielt ich von Flüchtlingen aus Deutschland, die direkt vom Bauhaus kamen. Das war an der Cooper Union School of Art in New York. Mein Lieblingsprofessor Hannes Beckmann lehrte Farbtheorie, seine Notizbücher für den Unterricht waren mit Anmerkungen von Wassily Kandinsky versehen. So genoss ich genau den Unterricht, der in dieser Form auch schon am Bauhaus stattgefunden hatte. Ich habe damals viel gelernt. Und noch heute verstehe ich Gestaltung im Sinne des Bauhaus – als eine ethische Herausforderung und einen grundlegenden Ansatz für den Aufbau einer besseren Gesellschaft.

Daniel Libeskind

Daniel Libeskind (far left / links außen), Cooper Union, 1969

Videolink: Redux House, This was not my dream

This is not my dream

In May 2014, I travel two hours from São Paulo to visit the Redux House to make sure everything is just right before the shoot. It has been some time since I last visited this house. The finished garden is pretty good, considering the small budget the landscape artist had. I notice the slab on the left side that is slightly deformed. I follow it back to the woods that surround the house but not too close because I am afraid of the monkeys that hang out there. I enter the house and explore the wooden volumes. One of the door handles is a bit crooked. One of the floor tiles has a small scratch. The lighting is good, but one of the bulbs is blown. I just can't have any pleasure when I visit a built work: I always see the problems and analyse what could have been done better. I never think a project is good. I go back to the living room, maybe there's a rug missing. I sit in the Costela lounge chair near the glass that is a little dirty. Maybe I'm becoming a grumpy old man. The house's caretaker serves me some orange juice that I shouldn't drink, but I down the whole thing anyway.

The movie that we're shooting tomorrow tells the story of a couple that lived in the house and then separated for architectural reasons. He wanted a neoclassical house and she wanted a modernist design. She knew the entire story of Bauhaus very well. It was her dream and she was determined to build it.

Ultimately, it's only a movie. I reflect on similar situations that I have experienced in my long professional life. I get up to adjust a vase on the shelf. I go to the veranda. They are building a house on a plot right below and it's messing up the beautiful view. I go for one last stroll past the front; the concrete is already dirty. Soon I'll head back to São Paulo. I stop and give myself some slack, mumbling: I like this house!

This is not my dream

Im Mai 2014 mache ich mich von São Paulo aus auf die zweistündige Reise zu meiner Casa Redux, um sicherzugehen, dass vor dem Videodreh für „This was not my dream" auch alles so weit stimmt. Es ist schon eine Weile her, dass ich zuletzt dort war. Bedenkt man das schmale Budget des Landschaftsarchitekten, ist der Garten eigentlich ganz schön geworden. Mir fällt nur die leicht verformte Platte links auf. Ich folge ihr in Richtung auf den kleinen Wald, der das Gebäude umgibt, wage mich aber nicht weiter hinein aus Angst vor den Affen, die hier gerne herumlungern. Ich betrete das Haus und begutachte die Volumen aus Holz. Einer der Türgriffe ist etwas krumm. Eine Bodenfliese weist einen kleinen Kratzer auf. Die Beleuchtung ist o.k., nur eine der Glühbirnen ist durchgebrannt – ich kann es einfach nicht genießen, eins meiner Gebäude zu besuchen: Ich sehe überall Probleme und stelle mir vor, was man alles hätte besser machen können. Für mich ist genug nie gut genug. Ich gehe zurück ins Wohnzimmer – fehlt da nicht vielleicht ein Teppich? Ich sitze im Costela Lounge Chair vor der Glaswand und stelle fest, dass sie leicht verschmiert ist. Werde ich schon zum ollen Griesgram? Mit wird ein Orangensaft gereicht, den ich nicht trinken sollte, aber dennoch hinunterkippe.

Der Film, den wir morgen drehen, soll die Geschichte eines Paares erzählen, das hier in diesem Hause lebt und sich dann wegen unvereinbarer Stilfragen total verkracht: Er hatte sich etwas Neoklassisches vorgestellt, sie einen klassischen Bau der Moderne. Sie war mit der Geschichte des Bauhaus sehr vertraut – es war ihr Traum. Und sie war fest entschlossen, ihn wahr zu machen.

Letztlich ist es ja nur ein Film. Aber er erinnert mich an ähnliche Situationen, die mir in meinem langen Berufsleben begegnet sind. Ich stehe auf, um eine Vase im Regal zurechtzurücken. Ich trete auf die Veranda hinaus: Sie bauen ein Haus auf dem Grundstück gleich unterhalb, und es blockiert brutal die schöne Aussicht. Ich gehe auf einem letzten Rundgang die Vorderseite entlang. Der Beton ist schon ganz schön fleckig. Höchste Zeit, wieder heimzufahren. Ich halte inne, mache mich kurz locker und murmle: Ich mag dieses Haus!

Marcio Kogan

My Bauhaus

I discovered the Bauhaus when I was teenager through my art teacher at school and later studied its principles when I was an architecture student. For me, the most fascinating aspect about the Bauhaus is its multidisciplinary approach, in which architecture is interlinked with other disciplines, as well as the collective and participative atmosphere between and among the students and teachers.

The spirit of the times when it was established, the beginning of the 20th century, was very particular – turning towards creativity, the avant-garde and openness.

Creating a new school needs vision, and the vision of those who established the Bauhaus resonated with the spirit of their innovative time.

I decided to launch my own school because it was clear to me that the architecture schools of our time were not reflecting the spirit of our own innovative time. I was especially inspired by the Black Mountain College that existed from the 1930s to the 1950s, where some of the previous Bauhaus faculty also taught. I have visited schools all around the world and seen how things have been done over the last decades. I discovered that in many architecture schools today, there is a sentiment that architectural education needs to evolve – to be more in coherence not only with our current and future ways of living, but also with new generations of students who have grown up in a digital and deeply connected world.

Taking up this vision, a new school was born at the beginning of the 21st century.

Mein Bauhaus

Dank meines Kunstlehrers entdeckte ich das Bauhaus schon als Teenager und beschäftigte mich später als Architekturstudentin mit seinen Prinzipien. Der faszinierendste Aspekt daran war und ist für mich sein multidisziplinärer Ansatz, die Verknüpfung der Architektur mit anderen Disziplinen wie auch die kollektive und partizipative Atmosphäre unter Studierenden und Lehrern. Der Zeitgeist zu Beginn des 20. Jahrhunderts war ein ganz besonderer – eine Hinwendung zu Kreativität, Avantgarde und Offenheit.

Die Gründung einer neuen Schule braucht Visionen, und die Vision jener, die das Bauhaus gründeten, entsprach dem Geist einer ausgesprochen innovativen Zeit.

Ich beschloss also, meine eigene Schule zu eröffnen, weil mir klar war, dass die heutigen Architekturschulen nicht dem kreativen Spirit unserer Zeit entsprachen. Ein großes Vorbild dabei war für mich das Black Mountain College, das von den 1930er-Jahren bis in die 1950er-Jahre bestand und an dem auch frühere Bauhaus-Lehrer unterrichteten. Ich habe Schulen auf der ganzen Welt besucht und mir angesehen, was sich in den letzten Jahrzehnten so getan hat. Die heute vorherrschende Meinung ist, dass sich die Ausbildung dringend weiterentwickeln müsse – im Einklang mit unseren gegenwärtigen und zukünftigen Lebensweisen sowie den neuen Generationen von Studierenden, die in einer digitalen und eng vernetzten Welt aufgewachsen sind.

Diese Vision habe ich aufgegriffen, und so entstand zu Beginn des 21. Jahrhunderts eine neue Schule.

Odile Decq

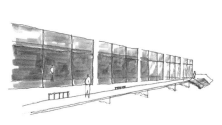

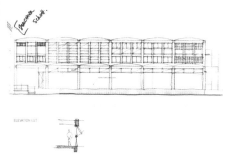

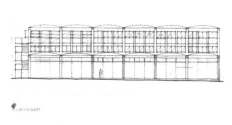

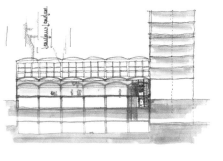

Confluence Institute, Lyon

From Dessau to Tokyo

We both received our undergraduate degrees in architecture at Musashi Institute of Technology (now Tokyo City University), which focused strongly on the Bauhaus style. One of its early tutors, the architect Chikatada Kurata, spent time at the Bauhaus in the early 1930s. Back in Japan, he went on to influence many modernist architects at the school, and some of them became our professors. The school has produced eight Architectural Institute of Japan prize winners, which is the most exclusive prize for Japanese architects. The most influential modernist in our school history was Kenji Hirose, who was known for his minimalist architecture with extremely thin and lightweight steel. His style left its imprint on us as students and even today some of us tend to pursue minimalist structures.

We also happen to be children of modernist architects. Both of our families used to live in an environment influenced by the Japanese Bauhaus style, which is not strictly minimalist but tends to grasp the Bauhaus style in a uniquely Japanese way. Takaharu's father, Yoshio Tezuka, was a site architect for the Imperial Palace in Tokyo designed by Junzō Yoshimura, who is considered to be one of the most important Bauhaus-style architects in Japan.

Perhaps the greatest influence we received from the Bauhaus is a sense of craftsmanship in architectural details – which clearly distinguishes the Bauhaus movement from functionalism. For all of our projects, we work closely with many artisans, with whom we have nurtured long-term partnerships.

Von Dessau nach Tokio

Wir haben beide unser erstes Architekturstudium am Musashi Institute of Technology (der heutigen Tokyo City University) absolviert. Diese Fakultät orientierte sich sehr am Bauhaus. Einer der ersten Lehrer des Instituts, der Architekt Chikatada Kurata, hatte zu Beginn der 1930er-Jahre einige Zeit dort verbracht. Zurück in Japan beeinflusste er zahlreiche zeitgenössische Architekten der Schule, von denen einige wiederum unsere Professoren wurden. Aus dem Musashi Institute sind allein acht Preisträger des Architectural Institute of Japan hervorgegangen, das den renommiertesten Architekturpreis Japans vergibt. Der wichtigste Vertreter der klassischen Moderne in der Geschichte unseres Instituts war Kenji Hirose, der für seine minimalistische Bauweise mit extrem dünnem und leichtem Stahl bekannt war. Sein Stil prägte uns als Studenten, und bis heute ist sein Einfluss in der Architektursprache vieler seiner Schüler sichtbar.

Wir sind beide zufällig Kinder von Architekten der klassischen Moderne. Unsere Familien lebten in einem Umfeld, das von der japanischen Variante des Bauhaus-Stils inspiriert war. Dieser ist streng genommen nicht minimalistisch, sondern spiegelt den klassischen Bauhaus-Stil auf einzigartig japanische Weise wider. Takaharus Vater Yoshio Tezuka war Bauleiter bei dem von Junzō Yoshimura entworfenen Kaiserpalast in Tokio – und Yoshimura gilt als einer der wichtigsten Vertreter des Bauhaus in Japan.

Die vielleicht nachhaltigste Spur in unserer Arbeit hat das Bauhaus mit seiner Betonung des Handwerks in architektonischen Details hinterlassen. Das unterscheidet die Bauhaus-Bewegung klar vom Funktionalismus. Bei all unseren Projekten arbeiten wir eng mit Handwerkern zusammen, denen wir in langjährigen Partnerschaften verbunden sind.

Takaharu Tezuka, Yui Tezuka

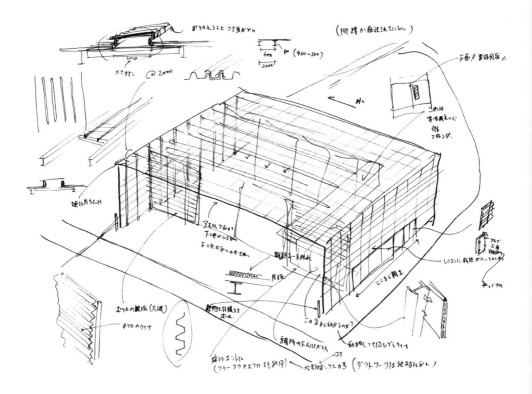

Toyota LF Hiroshima

Firm roots, fluid futures

As a movement, the Bauhaus continues to inspire us through its original utilitarian and optimistic ways of looking at the world with the ambition to merge art, craft and architecture into an entity that is relevant and accessible to everybody. We admire the craftsmanship visible in the well-studied and engineered solutions which, regardless of construction technique, simultaneously demonstrate a deep knowledge of tradition and strive for something new. The close look at the future possibilities of industrial production, while keeping an interest in the quality of materials and integrity of the specific artistic voice. We can relate to the rather straightforward approach to each task, which through open analyses can still generate experimental and surprising results that push the limits of preconceived concepts of living, working and socializing. The shift between abstract, transparent and real, solid. Between clear and open functionality, and lyrical, poetic meaning.

In the end, architecture is a form of history projected into the future; contemporary yet soon to become part of our common culture, acting as a backdrop for everyday life. The chances of success for any project can certainly be inspired by the Bauhaus legacy, which oscillates between a search for something new and its firm base in the entire history of architecture.

Fest verankert und völlig losgelöst

Als Bewegung inspiriert uns das Bauhaus noch immer durch seine originelle utilaristische und optimistische Weltsicht und die von ihm angestrebte Einheit von Kunst, Gestaltung und Architektur, die für jeden relevant und zugänglich ist. Wir bewundern das handwerkliche Können hinter den perfekt durchdachten Lösungen, die unabhängig von ihrer Konstruktionstechnik eine profunde Kenntnis der Tradition aufweisen und zugleich nach Neuem streben; die intensive Auseinandersetzung mit den künftigen Möglichkeiten der Industrieproduktion und das gleichzeitige Interesse an der Qualität des Materials und der Integrität des persönlichen künstlerischen Ausdrucks. Wir können uns identifizieren mit dieser sehr geradlinigen Herangehensweise an eine Aufgabe, die durch offene Analyse dennoch zu einem experimentellen und überraschenden Ergebnis führt – einem Ergebnis, das die Grenzen vorgefasster Konzepte von Wohnen, Arbeiten und Socializing überschreitet. Dem Wechsel zwischen abstrakt–transparent und konkret–solide. Zwischen klarer, offener Funktionalität und lyrischer, poetischer Bedeutung.

Architektur ist letzten Endes eine Art Geschichte, die in die Zukunft projiziert wird – Aktualität, die bald Teil unserer gemeinsamen Kultur und zur Kulisse unseres Alltags werden wird. Die Erfolgschancen eines jeden Projekts können vom Bauhaus-Erbe inspiriert sein – einem Erbe, das pendelt zwischen der Suche nach dem Neuen und seiner festen Verankerung in der Architekturgeschichte.

Bolle Tham, Martin Videgård

Humlegården apartment, Stockholm, 2006–2008

Bauhaus in context

One of the first architecture books that I became aware of as a student at the Technical University of Braunschweig was an exhibition catalogue on postmodernist architecture by Heinrich Klotz, the founding director of the German Architecture Museum (DAM) in Frankfurt am Main. So at the start of my studies in 1983, I had come into contact with this "reactionary" movement before grasping the significance of the Bauhaus, and I was immediately suspicious of it. I understood that a new direction, cultural epoch or "style" is usually a critical reaction to what preceded it.

Considering the sequence of the Romanesque, Gothic, Renaissance, Baroque, Classicism, Modernism and Postmodernism, this can be well understood. Then, when I worked in the office of Richard Meier in New York (1987/88), I became acquainted with Neomodernism – even before my involvement with Bauhaus modernism.

More than 30 years after those early experiences, I now see the Bauhaus as epochal, powerful, holistic and immensely important. It became the foundation for the development of my own architectural approach. Today, my practice is concerned with creating architecture that is sensual, atmospheric and rich, in terms of materiality, light and colour. Above all, it is a contextual architecture that increasingly deals with issues of social responsibility and less with formal or formalistic features. The Bauhaus is the starting point, reference and pioneer of this development in every respect. Its radical consistency and fundamental approach at the time are impressive. But history is constantly being written – making all recent reactions to the Bauhaus and its related movements perfectly reasonable.

Bauhaus im Kontext

Eines der ersten Architekturbücher, das ich als Student an der TU Braunschweig bewusst wahrnahm, war der Ausstellungskatalog „Revision der Moderne – Postmoderne Architektur" von Heinrich Klotz, dem Gründungsdirektor des Deutsches Architektur Museum (DAM) in Frankfurt am Main. Zu Beginn meines Studiums 1983 kam ich also zunächst gewissermaßen mit der „reaktionären" Strömung in Kontakt, bevor ich die Bedeutung des Bauhaus begriff, und ich war mit dieser „Postmoderne" sogleich kritisch ... So begriff ich, dass eine neue Richtung, kulturelle Epoche oder ein neuer „Stil" meist die kritische Reaktion

auf das Vorausgehende bedeutet: In der Abfolge Romanik, Gotik, Renaissance, Barock, Klassizismus, Moderne und Postmoderne lässt sich das gut nachvollziehen. Während meiner Bürotätigkeit für Richard Meier in New York (1987/88) machte ich dann auch Bekanntschaft mit der „Neomoderne" – noch vor meiner Auseinandersetzung mit der Moderne/dem Bauhaus.

Mehr als 30 Jahre nach diesen frühen Prägungen begreife ich das Bauhaus als epochal, kraftvoll, ganzheitlich und ungemein wichtig. Es wurde zur Basis für meine Entwicklung einer eigenen architektonischen Haltung. Worum es meinem Büro heute

geht, ist die Schaffung einer sinnlichen, atmosphärisch reichen und in Bezug auf Materialität, Licht und Farbe vor allem auch kontextuellen Architektur, die sich zunehmend mit Themen der sozialen Verantwortung und weniger mit formalen oder gar formalistischen Merkmalen befasst. Das Bauhaus ist in jeder Hinsicht Ausgangspunkt, Gradmesser und Vordenker dieser Entwicklung. Seine für die damalige Zeit radikale Konsequenz und Grundhaltung sind beeindruckend. Geschichte wird aber stets weitergeschrieben – somit sind alle jüngeren Reaktionen auf das Bauhaus und seine verwandten Strömungen nur folgerichtig.

Titus Bernhard

Haus SL (above / oben), Haus 11 × 11 (centre / Mitte), Villa Savoye project / Asmund Havsteen-Mikkelsen (below / unten)

Effective beauty
     Beauty guides the sensual person
to form and thinking;
through beauty the spiritual human being
is returned
to matter and the senses.
     Friedrich von Schiller

Wirkende Schönheit
     Durch die Schönheit wird der sinnliche
Mensch zur Form und zum Denken geleitet;
durch die Schönheit wird der geistige Mensch
zur Materie zurückgeführt
und der Sinnenwelt wiedergegeben.
     Friedrich von Schiller

Martin Rein-Cano

The many faces of Bauhaus
The Bauhaus played a key role in the modernist movement and brought about some of the most revolutionary and important cultural changes in recent history. It also made up a large part of my education at Rietveld Academy in Amsterdam. In fact, I was taught by one of the students of the Bauhaus. Even then, I was actually more fascinated by the many different cultural influences of the Bauhaus, from Johannes Itten's colour theories to Josef Albers's paper sculptures. I was also very interested in how much the Dutch artist Theo van Doesburg influenced Mies van de Rohe and I was enthralled by Oskar Schlemmer's costumes and how they abstracted the human form.

At the same time, I felt somewhat confined and stifled by this overarching focus within my education. I was young and had new ideas of my own. I wanted and needed to understand the past, but the world was changing. So of course I eventually became more interested in trying to understand the changes that were happening in my world at the time and what they could mean for the future.

But I also learned to understand the value of efficiency. In the years that followed, I discovered that the digital revolution opened up possibilities for new reductive approaches; new refined models of efficiency – almost hyper-efficiency – within architecture and design. It was no longer a case of paring things down to their bare minimum

through modernist geometric principles and their resulting forms, but instead looking at the balance between form and function in a new way. With computational design, it became possible to solve issues of multiple – and often conflicting – parameters in the most efficient ways possible, with the result that form and function could become interdependent.

The Bauhaus taught me that efficiency in design is essential, but parametric design and actual practice have enabled me to understand exactly why that is and how we can best achieve it – both with the tools that are currently available to us and a continued fascination with the fast-changing times in which we live.

Seemingly, I haven't changed too much.

Die vielen Gesichter des Bauhaus
Das Bauhaus spielt eine Schlüsselrolle in der Bewegung der Moderne und führte zu einigen der revolutionärsten und wichtigsten kulturellen Veränderungen der jüngsten Geschichte. Es dominierte auch den Großteil meiner Ausbildung an der Rietveld Academie in Amsterdam. Mein Lehrer war Student am Bauhaus gewesen, und mich faszinierten die unterschiedlichen, dort gelehrten Konzepte und Techniken, von Johannes Ittens Farbenlehre bis zu Josef Albers' Papierskulpturen. Ganz speziell interessierte mich der Einfluss des niederländischen Künstlers Theo van Doesburg auf Mies van der Rohe. Und von Oskar Schlemmers Kostümen und seiner Abstraktion der menschlichen Form war ich einfach nur begeistert. Zugleich jedoch fühlte ich

mich eingeengt und eingeschränkt durch den übergreifenden Raum, den dieser Schwerpunkt in meiner Ausbildung einnahm. Ich war jung und hatte eigene Ideen. Ich wollte und musste die Vergangenheit verstehen, doch die Welt war im Wandel. Und so beschäftigte ich mich letztlich mehr mit den Veränderungen in meinem aktuellen Umfeld und ihren möglichen Implikationen für die Zukunft. Den Stellenwert von Effizienz hatte ich allerdings sehr wohl begriffen.

In den folgenden Jahren entdeckte ich, dass die digitale Revolution neue Möglichkeiten für reduktive Ansätze in Architektur und Design eröffnete, ausgefeiltere Modelle der Effizienz – ja, fast schon Hyper-Effizienz. Es ging nicht mehr darum, alles mittels geometrischer Prinzipien und entsprechender Formen auf ein absolutes

Minimum zu reduzieren, sondern vielmehr um eine Neubewertung des Gleichgewichts zwischen Form und Funktion. Computational Design ermöglichte es, komplexe Probleme mit multiplen, häufig gegenläufigen Parametern auf höchst effiziente Weise zu lösen – mit dem Ergebnis, dass Form und Funktion sich optimal verschränkten.

Das Bauhaus hat mich gelehrt, dass Effizienz beim Entwerfen unerlässlich ist, doch parametrisches Design und die Erfahrungen aus der Praxis haben mir gezeigt, warum dem so ist und wie wir dies am besten erreichen können – nicht nur mit den uns derzeit zur Verfügung stehenden Mitteln, sondern auch mit einer anhaltenden Begeisterung für unsere schnelllebige Zeit.

So wie es aussieht, habe ich mich nicht wirklich allzu sehr verändert.

Ben van Berkel

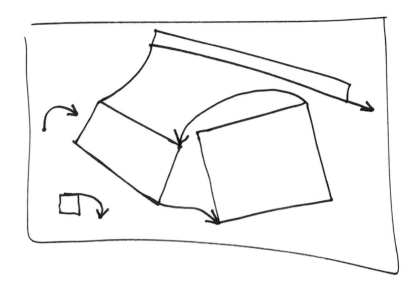

Aesthetics of austerity

For me, the Bauhaus is not only a historical event or movement, but a spirit. It was rooted in a time of social transformation and industrialiszation. It was an autonomous resistance raised by a group of young architects, designers and artists who challenged conventional class-consciousness as well as its ornamentation. As an outcome, Bauhaus represents a fresh interpretation of design aesthetics, a champion of austerity, honesty and straightforwardness, in which the transparency of form reflects function and craft.

Interestingly, after almost 100 years, China has entered a new stage of development boosted in recent decades by industrialization and economic growth. But commercialism and consumerism have become increasingly overwhelming, together with a polarization of wealth and the uneven distribution of social resources. As Chinese architects, what can we do in response?

Ästhetik der Askese

Für mich ist das Bauhaus nicht nur ein historisches Ereignis oder eine Bewegung, sondern eine Geisteshaltung mit Wurzeln in einer Zeit des sozialen Wandels und der Industrialisierung. Sie war Ausdruck des unabhängigen Widerstands einer Gruppe junger Architekten, Designer und Künstler, die das herkömmliche Klassenbewusstsein ebenso wie seine Ornamentik infrage stellten. Das Bauhaus repräsentiert daher eine Neuinterpretation der gestalterischen Ästhetik seiner Zeit. Es ist ein Verfechter asketischer Strenge, Ehrlichkeit und Geradlinigkeit, wobei sich in der Klarheit der Form Funktion und Handwerk widerspiegeln.

Interessanterweise ist China nach beinahe 100 Jahren in eine neue Entwicklungsphase eingetreten, die in den letzten Jahrzehnten von Industrialisierung und Wirtschaftswachstum angekurbelt wurde. Doch mit der wachsenden Schere zwischen Arm und Reich und der ungleichen Verteilung von sozialen Ressourcen sind auch Kommerzialisierung und Konsumorientierung immer erdrückender geworden. Wie können wir, die Architekten Chinas, darauf reagieren?

Gong Dong

Bauhaus all around us

The Bauhaus is a unique inspiration for me because it represents a rare example of radical ideas becoming truly transformative on a global scale. Everything that surrounds us, from the city to the ball pen, is Bauhaus. The designs of the Bauhaus marked a radical, avant-gardist departure from all prior architecture and design, and yet they conquered the totality of the built environment and the whole world of artefacts within the lifetime of the Bauhaus protagonists. The Bauhaus was a laboratory that rigorously worked through their concepts and artistic intuitions to make them compelling. The secret of its success lies in the congeniality of its design approach with the potentials of its historical era, an era it therefore helped to shape and advance, the era of democratic industrial mass society. This achievement was no accident but the result of a courageous and confident ideological programme based on a clear understanding of the challenges and opportunities of the epoch. This epoch is now a bygone era and the design disciplines are now, once more, faced with radically new challenges and opportunities that should lead us, once more, to the total makeover of the global built environment and the world of artefacts.

Wir sind vom Bauhaus umgeben

Das Bauhaus ist für mich eine einzigartige Inspiration, weil es ein seltenes Beispiel für radikale Ideen ist, die auf globaler Ebene zu wirklichen Transformationen geführt haben. Von der Stadt bis zum Kugelschreiber ist alles, was uns umgibt, Bauhaus. Seine Entwürfe stellten eine rigorose avantgardistische Abkehr von der gesamten vorhergehenden Architektur und Gestaltung dar und eroberten nichtsdestotrotz noch zu Lebzeiten der Bauhaus-Protagonisten die gesamte bebaute Umwelt und die gesamte Welt der Artefakte. Das Bauhaus war ein Labor, das seine Vorstellungen und künstlerischen Intuitionen konsequent durcharbeitete, um sie unwiderstehlich zu machen. Das Geheimnis seines Erfolges liegt in der Genialität seines gestalterischen Ansatzes und den Potenzialen jener Zeit – einer Ära, die es formte und vorantrieb und aus der die demokratisch-industrielle Massengesellschaft hervorging. Diese Leistung war kein Zufall, sondern das Ergebnis eines mutigen und selbstbewussten ideologischen Programms, dem ein klares Verständnis der Herausforderungen und Möglichkeiten der damaligen Zeit zugrunde lag. Das ist nun Geschichte, doch wieder ist ein Punkt erreicht, an dem wir Gestalter vor radikal neuen Herausforderungen und Möglichkeiten stehen. Und das sollte uns wie seinerzeit den Mut geben zur rigorosen Umgestaltung unserer globalen bebauten Umwelt und der Welt der Artefakte.

Patrik Schumacher

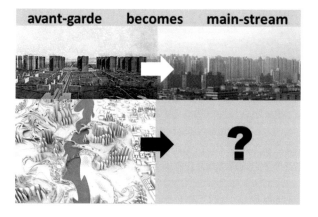

My house, my Bauhaus

"Bauhaus" was never a word with special meaning for me,
until I went to study at the Graduate School of Design at Harvard
in 1996. The school was considered to be the American reincarna-
tion of the Bauhaus, because Walter Gropius himself taught there
from 1938 to 1952. It was at GSD that I encountered the Bauhaus
legacy and began thinking about Gropius and Mies van der Rohe.

For me, the spirit of Bauhaus is the daring courage to envision
a new era in history, in which art, craft, design and architecture
could be radically different from how they were in the past. Is this
spirit of Bauhaus still valid today? Could it be possible that we are
confronting yet again a new period in history?

I see the spirit of Bauhaus in the new chair and table I am designing; I see Bauhaus in the new light I am envisioning; I see Bauhaus
in the phone and car I use every day; I see Bauhaus in the railway
stations and the airports I pass through; I see Bauhaus in the home
I will build one day – I hope it will be my own.

My Bauhaus will be my house.
My house will be my Bauhaus.

Mein Haus ist mein Bauhaus

Das Wort „Bauhaus" hatte nie eine besondere Bedeutung für
mich, bis ich 1996 an die Harvard Graduate School of Design kam.
Die Schule galt als seine amerikanische Reinkarnation, da Walter
Gropius von 1938 bis 1952 dort unterrichtete. Dort begann ich,
mich erstmals mit Gropius und Mies van der Rohe zu beschäftigen.

Der Geist des Bauhaus manifestiert sich für mich in der unglaublichen Kühnheit, sich eine ganze Ära der Geschichte auszumalen,
in der Kunst, Handwerk, Design und Architektur radikal anders
sein konnten als jemals zuvor. Ist dieser Spirit heute noch lebendig?
Könnte es denn möglich sein, dass wir erneut an der Schwelle zu
einem neuen Abschnitt der Geschichte stehen?

Ich sehe den Geist des Bauhaus in jedem neuen Tisch und
Stuhl, den ich entwerfe. Ich sehe das Bauhaus in jeder neuen
Leuchte, die ich mir vorstelle. Ich sehe das Bauhaus in meinem
Telefon und meinem Auto, die ich täglich benutze. Ich sehe das
Bauhaus in den Bahnhöfen und Flughäfen, durch die ich komme.
Ich sehe das Bauhaus in dem Zuhause, das ich eines Tages baue –
ich hoffe, es wird mein eigenes sein.

Mein Bauhaus wird mein Haus sein.
Mein Haus wird mein Bauhaus sein.

Zhang Ke

a house I
will build one
day.
could it be 2013.09.12.
for myself? . - - - -
ZHANG KE.

100 Biogra phies
100 Biogra fien

3XN Architects

Kim H. Nielsen (b. 1954) is the creative driving force behind 3XN Architects, which he founded in 1986. The Danish architect completed his studies in 1991 in Aarhus. His best-known projects include the new Sydney Fish Market, Quay Quarter Tower in Sydney, the International Olympic Committee's headquarters in Lausanne and the UN City headquarters in Copenhagen. He chaired the architecture committee of the Danish Arts Foundation from 2014 to 2018 and is a member of the Board of Trustees at the Van Alen Institute.

Kim H. Nielsen (geb. 1954) ist die treibende kreative Kraft hinter dem 1986 von ihm gegründeten Büro 3XN Architects. 1991 schloss der dänische Architekt sein Studium in Århus ab. Zu seinen bekanntesten Projekten zählen der neue Fischmarkt und der Quay Quarter Tower in Sydney, die Zentrale des Internationalen Olympischen Komitees in Lausanne und die Zentrale der UN City in Kopenhagen.

6a Architects

Tom Emerson (b. 1970) founded the London-based 6a architects with Stephanie Macdonald in 2001. The practice is known for its arts buildings, often in sensitive historic environments. Emerson studied architecture in Bath, London and Cambridge. He has taught at various institutions in England and has been a professor of Architecture at the ETH Zurich since 2010.

2001 gründete Tom Emerson (geb. 1970) zusammen mit Stephanie Macdonald 6a architects in London. Das Büro ist bekannt für seine Kulturbauten in oftmals höchst sensiblen historischen Umgebungen. Tom Emerson studierte Architektur in Bath, London und Cambridge. Er unterrichtete an verschiedenen Hochschulen in England und ist seit 2010 Professor an der ETH Zürich.

A L M project

Andrea Lenardin's work is informed by a sensitivity to the layers of time and meaning that accrue to places and objects. In addition to her architectural training at the University of Applied Arts Vienna and SCI-Arc in Los Angeles, she studied graphic, product and fashion design. Her multidisciplinary design studio in LA has earned numerous awards, including the James Beard Design Award.

Andrea Lenardins Arbeit ist von der Sensibilität vielschichtiger Bezüge zwischen Orten und Objekten im zeitlichen Kontext geprägt. Ihre Ausbildung an der Universität für Angewandte Kunst, Wien, und an der SCI-Arc, Los Angeles, hat Lenardin durch Studien in Grafik, Produktdesign und Mode erweitert. Ihr multidisziplinäres Design Studio in Los Angeles wurde mit zahlreichen Preisen ausgezeichnet, u.a. 2018 dem James Beard Design Award.

ACDF Architecture

After graduating from the University of Montreal School of Architecture in 2000, Maxime-Alexis Frappier co-founded ACDF in 2006, going on to gain international recognition for diverse projects in Canada and around the world. Awards include the Young Architect Award from the Royal Architectural Institute of Canada and a Governor General's Medal in Architecture. He has taught and lectured worldwide.

Maxime-Alexis Frappier studierte Architektur an der Université de Montréal. 2006 gründete er mit Kollegen das Büro ACDF, das für seine Projekte u.a. mit der Architekturmedaille des kanadischen Generalgouverneurs ausgezeichnet wurde. 2013 erhielt Frappier den Young Architect Award des Royal Architectural Institute of Canada. Er lehrt an verschiedenen Universitäten und hält weltweit Vorträge.

Agence Rudy Ricciotti

In addition to major museum buildings such as the Musée des Civilisation de l'Europe et de la Méditerranée in Marseille, the French architect Rudy Ricciotti (b. 1952 in Algeria) is known for his essays on architecture, such as "Architecture is a Combat Sport" and "Concrete in Custody". His many awards include the Grand Prix National d'Architecture and the Gold Medal of the Academy of Architecture in France.

Neben Museumsbauten wie dem Musée des Civilisation de l'Europe et de la Méditerranée in Marseille ist Rudy Ricciotti (geb. 1952 in Algerien) auch bekannt für seine Essays zur Architektur wie „L'architecture est un sport de combat" oder „Le béton en garde à vue". Er erhielt u.a. den Grand Prix national d'Architecture und die Médaille d'Or de la Fondation de l'Académie d'Architecture.

Alberto Campo Baeza

Spanish architect Alberto Campo Baeza (b. 1946) is known for the radical simplicity of his buildings. He has been professor of design at the School of Architecture of Madrid (ETSAM) since 1986, and has also taught in Zurich, Lausanne and Philadelphia, among others. His Madrid-based studio has completed numerous acclaimed works, particularly in Spain and more recently, Mexico.

Der spanische Architekt Alberto Campo Baeza (geb. 1946) ist für die radikale Schlichtheit seiner Bauten bekannt. Seine vielbeachteten Projekte sind vor allem in Spanien zu finden, in jüngster Zeit aber auch in Mexiko. Er hatte Lehraufträge u.a. in Zürich, Lausanne und Philadelphia. Seit 1986 unterrichtet Baeza als Professor für Entwurf an der ETSAM in Madrid.

Anna Heringer

Anna Heringer (b. 1977) became internationally known through her design of the Meti School in Bangladesh (2006, with Eike Roswag). She is currently Honorary Professor of the Unesco Chair of Earthen Architecture, Constructive Cultures and Sustainable Development in Germany. Her holistic projects are grounded in the use of local materials. Awards include the Aga Khan Award for Architecture.

International bekannt wurde Anna Heringer (geb. 1977) mit der Meti School in Bangladesch (2006, zusammen mit Eike Roswag). Heute ist sie Professorin des Unesco Chair of Earthen Architecture, Constructive Cultures and Sustainable Development in Deutschland. Ihre ganzheitlichen Projekte basieren auf der Idee, lokale Materialien zu verwenden. Erhielt u.a. den Aga Khan Award for Architecture.

Anupama Kundoo Architects

Launching her practice in 1990, Anupama Kundoo (b. 1967) focuses strongly on sustainable architecture appropriate to the socio-economic context. She completed her architecture studies at the Sir JJ College of Architecture in Mumbai in 1989 and received her PhD from the TU Berlin in 2008. Her internationally recognized work extends to urban design and planning and is included in MoMA's collection. A solo show on her work will be exhibited at Denmark's Louisiana Museum of Modern Art in 2020. She is currently a professor at the Fachhochschule Potsdam.

Anupama Kundoo (geb. 1967) studierte Architektur am Sir JJ College of Architecture in Mumbai. 1990 gründete sie ihr eigenes Büro mit Fokus auf nachhaltiger, dem sozioökonomischen Kontext angepasster Architektur. Ihre international anerkannten Arbeiten befassen sich auch mit Städtebau und Stadtplanung und sind Teil der Sammlung des MoMA. Derzeit lehrt sie an der Fachhochschule Potsdam.

Anzilutti/Mendiondo/Garrido/Cairoli Arquitectos

pabloanzilutti.com.ar

Anzilutti / Mendiondo / Garrido / Cairoli Arquitectos is a collective based in Santa Fe, Argentina, working for nearly 20 years in architecture, interior design and urbanism. It includes Pablo Anzilutti, Javier Mendiondo, Francisco Garrido and Federico Cairoli. The studio was selected to curate the Argentine Pavilion at the 2018 Venice Biennale with its proposal "Vertigo Horizontal", a multimedia installation recreating the Argentine pampa.

Das Kollektiv mit Sitz im argentinischen Santa Fe ist seit fast 20 Jahren in den Bereichen Architektur, Innenarchitektur und Städtebau tätig. Mit ihrer Multimedia-Installation „Vertigo Horizontal", einer „Nachbildung" der argentinische Pampa, bespielten Pablo Anzilutti, Javier Mendiondo, Francisco Garrido und Federico Cairoli den argentinischen Pavillon auf der Architekturbiennale 2018 in Venedig.

architecten de vylder vinck taillieu

architectendvvt.com

Jan de Vylder (b. 1968), Inge Vinck (b. 1973) and Jo Taillieu (b. 1971) founded architecten de vylder vinck taillieu (a dvvt) in Ghent in 2009. With their team of 12 collaborators today, they remain committed to practicing architecture critically and with a sense of social responsibility, understanding their "metier as the key to the future".

Das Büroa a dvvt wurde 2009 von Jan de Vylder (geb. 1968), Inge Vinck (geb. 1973) und Jo Taillieu (geb. 1971) in Gent gegründet. Mit einem Team von zwölf Mitarbeitern sind die Gründer noch immer einer kritischen Architekturpraxis und einem sozialen Verantwortungsbewusstsein verpflichtet. Sie verstehen ihr Metier als „Schlüssel für die Zukunft".

Architekt Krischanitz

krischanitz.at

Adolf Krischanitz (b. 1946) studied architecture in Vienna and founded the group Missing Link in 1970 with fellow architects Angela Hareiter and Otto Kapfinger. He co-founded UmBau – the journal of the Austrian Society for Architecture, was president of the Vienna Secession and taught at the University of the Arts Berlin. Since 1979, he has worked independently with studios in Vienna and Zurich.

Adolf Krischanitz (geb. 1946) studierte Architektur an der TU Wien. 1970 gründete er mit Angela Hareiter und Otto Kapfinger die Gruppe Missing Link. Er war Mitbegründer der Zeitschrift „UmBau" der Österreichischen Gesellschaft für Architektur, Präsident der Wiener Secession und lehrte an der Universität der Künste Berlin. Seit 1979 arbeitet er als freier Architekt mit Ateliers in Wien und Zürich.

Assemble Studio

assemblestudio.co.uk

James Binning is a founding member of Assemble, an award-winning, multi-disciplinary collective working across architecture, design and art. Founded in 2010, Assemble takes a democratic and cooperative approach that enables built, social and research-based work at various scales. James currently teaches a studio at the Cass Faculty of Art, Architecture and Design in London, focussing on responses to critical urban issues.

James Binning ist Gründungsmitglied von Assemble, einem interdisziplinär tätigen Kollektiv in den Bereichen Architektur, Design und Kunst. Das 2010 gegründete Büro verfolgt einen kooperativen Ansatz, der Architektur mit sozialen Anliegen verknüpft. James unterrichtet derzeit eine Studioeinheit an der Sir John Cass School of Art, die sich mit der aktuellen Städteproblematik auseinandersetzt.

Atelier Bow-Wow

Tokyo-based Atelier Bow-Wow was founded by Yoshiharu Tsukamoto and Momoyo Kaijima in 1992. Yoichi Tamai joined as a partner in 2015. Their interest ranges from from architectural design to urban research and the reconstruction of the commons, grounded in their theory of "Architectural Behaviorology". The practice has designed and built homes, public spaces, facilities and commercial buildings around the world.

Das in Tokio ansässige Atelier Bow-Wow wurde 1992 von Yoshiharu Tsukamoto (geb. 1965) und Momoyo Kaijima (geb. 1969) gegründet. 2015 kam Yoichi Tamai als weiterer Partner hinzu. Das weltweit tätige Büro orientiert sich stark an japanischen Bau- und Wohntraditionen und ist besonders spezialisiert auf die Bebauung kleiner, verschachtelter Grundstücke, wie sie die Städte Japans prägen.

Atelier Kempe Thill

André Kempe (b. 1968) and Oliver Thill (b. 1971) met while studying architecture at the Technical University of Dresden. After working together on urban planning studies in Paris and Tokyo, they launched their practice in Rotterdam in 2000. Both have lectured at the Delft University of Technology in Arnhem and the Academie van Bouwkunst in Rotterdam, and had visiting professorships in Lausanne, Dusseldorf and Berlin.

André Kempe (geb. 1968) und Oliver Thill (geb. 1971) lernten sich beim Architekturstudium an der TU Dresden kennen. Nach gemeinsamer Arbeit an städtebaulichen Studienprojekten in Paris und Tokio gründeten sie 2000 ihr Büro in Rotterdam. Beide hatten Lehraufträge an der TU Delft und an der Academie van Bouwkunst in Arnhem und in Rotterdam sowie Gastprofessuren in Lausanne, Düsseldorf und Berlin.

Atelier Mendini

Completing his studies in Milan in 1959, Alessandro Mendini (b. 1931) was a protagonist of the Radical Design movement. Based in Milan, he founded Studio Alchimia with Ettore Sottsass and Michele De Lucchi in 1979, and founded Studio Mendini with his brother Francesco in 1989. His multifaceted work has received numerous international awards. He was editor-in-chief of Casabella, Modus and Domus magazines.

Nach Abschluss seines Studiums 1959 in Mailand wurde Alessandro Mendini (geb. 1931) zu einem der Hauptvertreter des Radical Design. Mit Ettore Sottsass und Michele De Lucchi gründete er 1979 das Studio Alchimia in Mailand und mit seinem Bruder Francesco 1989 das Studio Mendini. Der vielfach ausgezeichnete Architekt und Designer war auch Chefredakteur der Magazine Casabella, Modus und Domus.

Atelier Paul Laurendeau

Paul Laurendeau established his practice in Montreal in 1995. Inspired by the clear spatial sequences of classical architecture, his work focuses on finding the right space and proportion to capture the building's essence. He has gained recognition with his recent theatre projects, such as the Cogeco Amphitheatre, which received a Governor General's Medal in 2016.

1995 gründete der Architekt sein Büro in Montreal. Inspiriert von den klaren Raumfolgen der klassischen Architektur, liegt der Schwerpunkt seiner Arbeit auf der Suche nach der idealen Proportion. In jüngster Zeit sorgte Paul Laurendeau mit Theaterprojekten für Aufsehen wie dem Cogeco Amphitheatre, für das er 2016 die Governor General's Medal des kanadischen Generalgouverneurs erhielt.

Auböck + Kárász Landschaftsarchitekten   auboeck-karasz.at

Maria Auböck and Janos Kárász have worked together since 1987. After studying architecture at the Technical University of Vienna and landscape architecture in Munich, Auböck (b. 1951) founded her own firm in Vienna in 1985. Kárász studied architecture and social sciences in Vienna, going on to specialize in landscape architecture. Both have lectured at various universities in Munich, Budapest and Rome, among others.

Maria Auböck (geb. 1951) studierte Architektur an der TU Wien und Landschaftsarchitektur in München. 1985 gründete sie ihr eigenes Büro in Wien. Seit 1987 arbeitet sie im Team mit János Kárász. Nach einem Studium in Architektur und Sozialwissenschaften in Wien spezialisierte er sich auf Landschaftsarchitektur. Beide lehrten an verschiedenen Universitäten, u.a. in München, Budapest und Rom.

Autoban Studio   autoban.com.tr

The multidisciplinary design studio was founded in 2003 by Seyhan Özdemir and Sefer Çağlar. The duo met and began collaborating at university, where Sarper studied architecture and Çağlar studied interior design. Autoban's work has redefined Istanbul's cityscape, including hospitality, retail, residential and public realm developments. Their work can also be found in Hong Kong, Maldives, Baku, Dubai, London, Zurich and Malta.

Das multidisziplinäre Designstudio wurde 2003 von Seyhan Özdemir und Sefer Çağlar gegründet. Die beiden begegneten sich an der Universität in Istanbul, wo Sarper Architektur und Çağlar Innenarchitektur studierte. Die Arbeiten des Büros haben das Stadtbild Istanbuls neu definiert. Mittlerweile hat Autoban Projekte in Hongkong, Baku, Dubai, London, Zürich, auf Malta und den Malediven realisiert.

Balkrishna Doshi, Vāstu Shilpā   sangath.org

Born in 1927 in Pune, the architect, urban planner and educator received the Pritzker Architecture Prize in 2018. He studied in Mumbai, London and Paris, was part of Le Corbusier's team in Chandigargh and Ahmedabad, and worked closely with Louis Kahn. Establishing his firm Vāstu Shilpā in 1959, he went on to complete over 100 projects. He was founding director of the School of Architecture in Ahmedabad.

Der indische Architekt, Stadtplaner und Lehrer (geb. 1927 in Pune) erhielt 2018 den Pritzker-Preis. Er studierte in Mumbai, London und Paris, gehörte zu Le Corbusiers Team in Chandigarh und Ahmedabad und war enger Mitarbeiter von Louis Kahn. Nach der Gründung seines Büros Vāstu Shilpā im Jahr 1959 realisierte er über 100 Projekte. Er war Gründungsdirektor der Architekturschule in Ahmedabad.

Barkow Leibinger   barkowleibinger.com

Barkow Leibinger is an American/German architectural practice, founded in 1993 by Frank Barkow and Regine Leibinger. Frank Barkow studied at Montana State University and the Harvard Graduate School of Design. He has held teaching posts at, among others, the Architectural Association in London, Cornell University, Harvard University and Princeton University School of Architecture.

Das amerikanisch-deutsche Architekturbüro wurde 1993 von Frank Barkow (geb. 1957) und Regine Leibinger (geb. 1963) gegründet. Frank Barkow studierte an der Montana State University und der Harvard Graduate School of Design. Er hat unter anderem an der Architectural Association in London, der Cornell University, der Harvard University und der Princeton University School of Architecture gelehrt.

Barthélémy Griño Architectes

barthelemygrinoarchitectes.eu

Over the past 30 years, Philippe Barthélémy from France and Sylvia Griño from Uruguay have worked on public and private buildings around the world. Philippe Barthélémy Philippe Barthélémy is head of the diploma unit at EAVT school of architecture in Paris and a member of the French Academy of architecture. The Paris-based firm is currently working on the French High School in Moscow and a distillery in Scotland, among others. Their many awards include the Trophée Bois 2017 for a grandstand in Fontainebleau and the Trophée Béton 2017 for a radar tower for Paris airports.

In den letzten 30 Jahren haben Philippe Barthélémy und Sylvia Griño öffentliche und private Bauten auf der ganzen Welt realisiert. Aktuell arbeitet das Pariser Büro u.a. am französischen Gymnasium in Moskau und an einer Brennerei in Schottland. Zu ihren zahlreichen Auszeichnungen zählen die Trophée Bois 2017 und die Trophée Béton 2017 für einen Radarturm der Pariser Flughäfen.

Behnisch Architekten

behnisch.com

Stefan Behnisch (b. 1957) studied philosophy, economics and architecture. In 1989, he launched his firm in Stuttgart, which has operated as Behnisch Architekten since 2005. Further offices were established in Los Angeles, Boston and Munich. Behnisch has taught at numerous universities in Germany and abroad. Among his most recent awards is the Global Award for Sustainable Architecture (2013).

Stefan Behnisch (geb. 1957) studierte Philosophie, Volkswirtschaft und Architektur. 1989 gründete er sein eigenes Büro in Stuttgart, das seit 2005 als Behnisch Architekten firmiert. Weitere Büros entstanden in Los Angeles, Boston und München. Behnisch lehrte an zahlreichen Universitäten im In- und Ausland. Zuletzt wurde er mit dem „Global Award for Sustainable Architecture" (2013) ausgezeichnet.

bogevischs büro

bogevisch.de

H.P. Ritz Ritzer (b. 1963) is co-founder of bogevischs buero in Munich, and Professor for Design and Urban Development at Beuth University of Applied Sciences Berlin. After training as a carpenter, he studied architecture at the Technical University of Munich and the Polytechnic University of Catalonia in Barcelona. From 2007 to 2016, he was chairman of Deutscher Werkbund Bayern.

H. P. Ritz Ritzer (geb. 1963) ist Mitgründer des Münchner Architekturstudios bogevischs büro und Professor für Entwerfen & Städtebau an der Beuth-Hochschule Berlin. Nach einer Zimmererlehre absolvierte er sein Architekturstudium an der Technischen Universität München und der Universität Politècnica de Catalunya in Barcelona. Von 2007–2016 war Ritz Ritzer Vorstand des Deutschen Werkbunds Bayern.

Boltshauser Architekten

boltshauser.info

After studying at the Swiss Federal Institute of Technology Zurich (ETHZ), Roger Boltshauser and his brother Markus founded Boltshauser Architekten. He has lectured at various institutions in Switzerland and Germany. Since 2018 he has been a guest lecturer at ETH Zurich and a member of the Building Commission of the City of Zurich.

Nach seinem Studium an der Eidgenössischen Technischen Hochschule Zürich (ETH) gründete Roger Boltshauser mit seinem Bruder Markus das Büro Boltshauser Architekten. Er war Dozent an verschiedenen Universitäten und Hochschulen in der Schweiz und Deutschland. Seit 2018 ist er Gastdozent an der ETH Zürich und Mitglied des Baukollegiums der Stadt Zürich.

Bruno Fioretti Marquez Architekten

bfm.berlin

Piero Bruno, Donatella Fioretti and José Gutierrez Marquez founded their firm in 1995, which has locations in Berlin and Lugano. Their work focuses on cultural, residential and educational buildings. BFM implemented their winning design for the Masters' Houses in Dessau in 2014.

1995 gründeten Piero Bruno, Donatella Fioretti und José Gutierrez Marquez ihr gemeinsames Büro mit Standorten in Berlin und Lugano. Schwerpunkte sind Kultur-, Wohnungs- und Bildungsbauten. Nach einem erfolgreichen Wettbewerb realisierten BFM 2014 ihren Entwurf für die Meisterhäuser in Dessau.

Büro Ole Scheeren

buro-os.com

Ole Scheeren (b. 1971 in Karlsruhe) founded his firm in 2010, which today has offices in Beijing, Hong Kong, Berlin and Bangkok. Before that, he was a partner at OMA, where he was responsible for the firm's activities in Asia. Among his most notable buildings are the award-winning CCTV headquarters for China Central Television in Beijing and The Interlace residential complex in Singapore.

Als Ole Scheeren (geb. 1971 in Karlsruhe) 2010 sein eigenes Büro gründete, mit Niederlassungen in Beijing, Hongkong, Berlin und Bangkok, hatte er schon als Partner von OMA in Rotterdam das Asiengeschäft verantwortet. Seine bis dato bekanntesten Bauwerke: die Zentrale des chinesischen TV-Senders CCTV in Beijing und The Interlace in Singapur – wofür er zahlreiche Awards erhielt.

Cebra

cebraarchitecture.dk

Mikkel Frost (b. 1971) co-founded Cebra in 2001 with Carsten Primdahl and Kolja Nielsen. The architectural studio is based in Århus, Denmark and Masdar City, Abu Dhabi. Frost graduated from the Århus School of Architecture in 1996 and is a member of the Danish Architect's Association and the Royal Institute of British Architects. He has lectured for many years in Denmark, Germany and Spain. Frost is also an acknowledged illustrator; two of his water-colours are part of the collection of the Museum for Architectural Drawing in Berlin.

Mikkel Frost (geb. 1971) ist Mitgründer des dänischen Architekturbüros Cebra in Århus und Masdar City, Abu Dhabi. 1996 machte er seinen Architekturabschluss an der Universität Århus. Er lehrt seit vielen Jahren in Dänemark, Deutschland und Spanien. Daneben arbeitet er erfolgreich als Illustrator. Zwei seiner Aquarelle befinden sich in der Sammlung des Museums für Architekturzeichnungen Berlin.

Coop Himmelb(l)au

coop-himmelblau.at

After studying architecture in Vienna, London and Los Angeles, Wolf D. Prix (b. 1942) co-founded Coop Himmelb(l)au in 1968. Today, he heads the renowned architectural practice as design principal and CEO. The group made its international breakthrough in 1988 with the exhibition "Deconstructivist Architecture" at MoMA in New York, and went on to receive numerous awards.

Nach dem Architekturstudium in Wien, London und Los Angeles wurde Wolf D. Prix (geb. 1942) Mit-gründer der Architektengruppe Coop Himmelb(l)au (1968). Heute leitet er das inzwischen international anerkannte Architekturbüro als Design Principal und CEO. 1988 gelang der Durchbruch mit der Aus-stellung „Deconstructivist Architecture" am MoMA New York. Das Büro erhielt zahlreiche Auszeichnungen.

Delugan Meissl Associated Architects

dmaa.at

Roman Delugan is co-founder and partner of DMAA. Born in South Tyrol, he studied architecture in Vienna and has lectured at various universities in Austria and Germany. In 2015, he and Elke Delugan Meissl were awarded the Grand Austrian State Prize.

Roman Delugan ist Mitgründer und Partner von DMAA. Der gebürtige Südtiroler studierte Architektur in Wien und war Dozent an verschiedenen Hochschulen in Österreich und Deutschland. 2015 wurde er gemeinsam mit Elke Delugan Meissl mit dem Großen Österreichischen Staatspreis ausgezeichnet.

Diener & Diener Architekten

dienerdiener.ch

Roger Diener (b. 1950) studied at the Swiss Federal Institute of Technology in Zurich (ETH) and the Federal Polytechnic Lausanne (EPFL). In 1980, he took over the practice of his father, Marcus Diener, in Basel. He has taught at various institutions such as the ETH Studio Basel, with Marcel Meili, Jacques Herzog and Pierre de Meuron, from 1999 to 2015. He is the recipient of the Prix Meret Oppenheim, among others.

Roger Diener (geb. 1950) studierte an der Eidgenössisch Technischen Hochschule in Zürich (ETH) und der École Polytechnique Fédérale de Lausanne (EPFL). 1980 übernahm er das Büro seines Vaters, Marcus Diener in Basel. Nach einer Professur in Lausanne an der École Polytechnique Fédérale (EPFL) und zahlreichen Gastprofessuren lehrte er 1999–2015 am ETH Studio Basel mit Marcel Meili, Jacques Herzog und Pierre de Meuron. U.a. ist er Träger des Prix Meret Oppenheim.

Dietrich Untertrifaller Architekten

dietrich.untertrifaller.com

Founded in 1994 by Helmut Dietrich and Much Untertrifaller, the firm is considered a representative of the Vorarlberg school of architecture. Together with Dominik Philipp and Patrick Stremler, they lead an international team of 70 architects in Austria, Switzerland, France and Germany. Their strongly context-oriented projects are often developed together with regional offices and partners.

1994 von Helmut Dietrich und Much Untertrifaller gegründet, gilt das Büro als typischer Vertreter der Vorarlberger Schule. Gemeinsam mit Dominik Philipp und Patrick Stremler leiten sie heute ein internationales Team von 70 Architekten in Österreich, der Schweiz, Frankreich und Deutschland. Die stark kontextorientierten Projekte werden oft gemeinsam mit regionalen Büros und Partnern entwickelt.

Dominique Coulon & Associés

coulon-architecte.fr

For 25 years, Dominique Coulon Associés in Strasbourg have worked to advance the quality of public buildings such as libraries, schools, sports facilities, performance halls and housing. Coulon and partners Steve Lethos Duclos, Olivier Nicollas and Benjamin Rocchi seek to combine contrast and complexity in their projects, giving particular importance to spatial quality, precise geometry and natural light.

Seit 25 Jahren arbeiten Dominique Coulon Associés in Straßburg an der Qualität von öffentlichen Gebäuden wie Mediatheken, Auditorien und Musikhochschulen. Für Coulon und seine Partner Steve Lethos Duclos, Olivier Nicollas und Benjamin Rocchi ist die Kombination aus Kontrast und Komplexität besonders wichtig, mit ihr entwickeln sie Räume, die durch eine präzise Geometrie geprägt sind.

Dominique Perrault Architecture

perraultarchitecture.com

Dominique Perrault, a leading figure in French architecture, gained international recognition for winning the competition for the French National Library in 1989 at the age of 36. He is professor and director of the Underground Architecture Laboratory (SUB) in Lausanne, Switzerland. Current projects include the Olympic Village – Paris 2024 and a transit centre in Gangnam.

Seinen internationalen Durchbruch erlebte Dominique Perrault (geb. 1953), als er 1989 im Alter von 36 Jahren den Wettbewerb für die französische Nationalbibliothek gewann. Heute ist er Professor und Leiter des Labors für unterirdische Architektur (SUB) im schweizerischen Lausanne. Aktuelle Projekte sind u.a. das Olympische Dorf in Paris für die Spiele von 2024 und ein Transitzentrum in Seoul.

Dorte Mandrup

dortemandrup.dk

Danish architect Dorte Mandrup (b. 1961) has 25 years of professional experience and several internationally recognized iconic buildings to her name. Mandrup runs an office in Copenhagen, is a professor and is renowned for her artistic talent and expertise in solving complex problems – offering solutions that are playful, innovative and poetic.

In ihrer 25-jährigen Arbeit als Architektin hat Dorte Mandrup (geb. 1961) international anerkannte, richtungsweisende Bauten geschaffen. Sie leitet ihr eigenes Büro in Kopenhagen und unterrichtet als Professorin. Die Arbeiten ihres Büros sind stark konzeptuell und analytisch ausgerichtet, aber zugleich auch geprägt von ausgesprochen spielerischen, innovativen und künstlerischen Lösungen.

Eva Jiřičná

Born in the Czech Republic in 1939, Eva Jiřičná studied engineering and architecture in Prague. She moved to London after the Soviet Invasion in 1968. She launched her own practice there in 1982, becoming well known for her design of retail interiors and private homes. In 1998, she opened a second firm in Prague. Jiřičná has received numerous awards for projects completed by both offices.

Eva Jiřičná (geb. 1939) erhielt ihre Architektur- und Kunstausbildung in Prag. Nach dem sowjetischen Einmarsch von 1968 zog sie nach London und gründete dort 1982 ihr eigenes Büro. 1998 folgte eine Dependance in Prag. Sie machte sich vor allem mit Interieurs für Ladenlokale und Wohnhäuser einen Namen. Eva Jiřičná erhielt zahlreiche Preise und lehrte lange Jahre als Professorin.

FAR frohn&rojas

f-a-r.net

FAR frohn&rojas was founded as a networked architectural practice between Berlin, Santiago de Chile and Los Angeles by Marc Frohn (b. 1976) and Mario Rojas (b. 1973). Their work has been shown at the Guggenheim in New York and the Venice Biennale, among others. Awards include the RIBA National Award, the Architectural League Prize for Young Architects and the DETAIL Prize. Frohn is a professor at Karlsruhe Institute of Technology.

FAR frohn&rojas wurde von Marc Frohn (geb. 1976) und Mario Rojas (geb. 1973) als Architekturbüro zwischen Berlin, Santiago de Chile und Los Angeles gegründet. Ihre Arbeiten waren u.a. im New Yorker Guggenheim Museum sowie auf der Biennale in Venedig zu sehen. Das Büro erhielt Auszeichnungen wie den RIBA National Award und den DETAIL-Preis. Frohn ist Professor am Karlsruhe Institute of Technology.

Feichtinger Architectes

feichtingerarchitectes.com

Dietmar Feichtinger (b. 1961) studied architecture in Graz. In 1993 he founded Dietmar Feichtinger Architectes in Paris, where he previously worked for four years as an architect for Chaix & Morel et Associées. He has lectured at various universities in Austria, Germany and France and received numerous international awards for his designs.

Dietmar Feichtinger (geb. 1961) studierte Architektur in Graz. 1993 gründete er sein Büro Dietmar Feichtinger Architectes in Paris, wo er zuvor vier Jahre lang als Architekt für das Studio Chaix & Morel et Associées tätig war. Er hatte Lehraufträge an verschiedenen Hochschulen in Österreich, Deutschland und Frankreich. Für seine Entwürfe erhielt er zahlreiche internationale Preise.

Flores & Prats Architectes

floresprats.com

The architectural office founded in 1998 by Ricardo Flores and Eva Prats (both b. 1975) is dedicated to confronting theory and academic practice with design and construction activity. They have received numerous international awards and exhibited at the last four consecutive architecture biennales in Venice. They are both professors in the Design Studio at the School of Architecture in Barcelona.

Das 1998 von Ricardo Flores (1965) und Eva Prats (geb. 1965) gegründete Architekturbüro verbindet Theorie und akademischen Anspruch mit praktischer Entwurfs- und Bautätigkeit. Flores & Prats erhielten zahlreiche internationale Auszeichnungen und waren auf den letzten vier Architekturbiennalen zu Gast. Beide lehren als Professoren für Entwurf an der Escola Tècnica Superior d'Arquitectura de Barcelona.

Florian Busch Architects

florianbusch.com

After graduating from Bauhaus University in Weimar and the Architectural Association in London, Munich native Florian Busch worked for Toyo Ito & Associates from 2004 until 2008. In 2009, he founded Florian Busch Architects (FBA). Based in Tokyo, FBA operates worldwide on architecture and urbanism projects and conducts research on new materials and building technologies.

Nach seinen Abschlüssen an der Bauhaus-Universität Weimar und der Architectural Association in London arbeitete der in München geborene Florian Busch 2004–2008 bei Toyo Ito & Associates. 2009 gründete er Florian Busch Architects (FBA). Das in Tokio ansässige Büro arbeitet weltweit an Architektur- und Stadtplanungsprojekten und forscht zu neuen Materialien und neuen Gebäudetechniken.

Foster + Partners

fosterandpartners.com

Born in 1935, Norman Foster is Founder and Executive Chairman of Foster + Partners. Over the past five decades, the practice has pioneered a sustainable approach to architecture and urbanism through a wide range of work. He has been awarded architecture's highest accolades, including the Pritzker Architecture Prize. In 1999, he was honoured with a Life Peerage, becoming Lord Foster of Thames Bank.

Norman Foster (geb. 1935) ist Gründer und Vorstandsvorsitzender von Foster + Partners. Seit fünf Jahrzehnten gilt das Büro als Wegbereiter eines nachhaltigen Ansatzes in Architektur und Städtebau. Foster erhielt die höchsten Auszeichnungen der Architektur, u.a. 1999 den Pritzker-Preis. Im gleichen Jahr wurde er in den Adelsstand erhoben und mit dem Titel Lord Foster of Thames Bank ausgezeichnet.

Goetz Castorph
Architekten und Stadtplaner

goetzcastorph.de

Together with partner Marco Goetz, Matthias Castorph (b. 1968) leads an office for architecture and urban planning in Munich. He studied architecture at the Technical University of Munich and currently teaches Urban Art and Design at the Technical University of Kaiserslautern. Castorph is also founding director of the Institut für Allgemeinarchitektur (Institute for General Architecture) in Munich, which opened in 2018.

Matthias Castorph (geb. 1968) leitet mit Marco Goetz ein Büro für Architektur und Städtebau in München. Er studierte Architektur an der TU München und lehrt heute Stadtbaukunst und Entwerfen an der TU Kaiserslautern. Darüber hinaus forscht er zu „Grundlagen des Normalstadtideals". Zugleich ist er Gründungsdirektor des 2018 eröffneten Instituts für Allgemeinarchitektur in München.

Gonzalez Haase
atelier architecture & scenographie

gonzalezhaase.com

Pierre Jorge Gonzalez, a native of Paris, together with Judith Haase, born in Bremen, launched their atelier for architecture and scenography in Berlin in 1999. The duo combine their backgrounds in the visual arts, scenography and architecture into an interdisciplinary approach. Their diverse portfolio includes retail, work and residential spaces, restaurant interiors and exhibition installations.

Der in Paris geborene Pierre Jorge Gonzalez und die aus Bremen stammende Judith Haase gründeten 1999 ihr Büro für Architektur und Szenografie in Berlin. Das Duo verbindet seine Kompetenzen in bildender Kunst, Szenografie und Architektur zu einem interdisziplinären Ansatz. Ihr breites Leistungsspektrum umfasst Ladenlokale, Wohn- und Arbeitsräume, Restaurants und Ausstellungsinstallationen.

Grafton Architects

graftonarchitects.ie

Yvonne Farrell (b. 1951) and Shelley McNamara (b. 1952) studied at University College Dublin and founded Grafton Architects in 1978. They have taught and lectured widely in European and American architecture schools. Notable projects include for Bocconi University in Milan and the University of Engineering and Technology in Lima, Peru. In 2018 they directed the Architecture Biennale in Venice focusing on the theme "Freespace".

Yvonne Farrell (geb. 1951) und Shelley McNamara (geb. 1952) studierten am University College Dublin und gründeten 1978 ihr Büro Grafton Architects. Sie lehren an zahlreichen europäischen und amerikanischen Hochschulen. Bekannte Projekte sind die Universität Bocconi in Mailand und die Universidad de Ingeniería y Tecnología in Lima. 2018 kuratierten sie die Architekturbiennale in Venedig.

Gregotti Associati

gregotti-associati.divisare.pro

One year after his participation at CIAM in England in 1951, Vittorio Gregotti (b. 1927 in Novara) began his career as an architect. In 1974, he founded Gregotti International in Milan, going on to design furniture and lighting as well. His projects are known for their formal rigor and have received several international awards.

Ein Jahr nach seiner Teilnahme am CIAM in England 1951 begann Vittorio Gregotti (geb. 1927 in Novara) seine Laufbahn als Architekt. 1974 gründete er das Büro Gregotti International in Mailand und entwirft seitdem auch Möbel und Leuchten. Seine Projekte stehen für die Strenge der Form und wurden mehrfach mit internationalen Preisen bedacht.

Henning Larsen

henninglarsen.com

Since 2003, Mette Kynne Frandsen (b. 1960) has been CEO of the Henning Larsen Group, which has subsidiaries in Hong Kong, Saudi Arabia, Germany, the United States, Norway, and the Faroe Islands. Starting with the firm as an architect in 1993, she joined its executive management in 1998. During her tenure as CEO, Henning Larsen received the Mies van der Rohe award for the Harpa Concert Hall and Conference Centre in Reykjavik.

Seit 1993 arbeitet Mette Kynne Frandsen (geb. 1960) für Henning Larsen, seit 1998 als Teil der Geschäftsführung. 2003 wurde sie zum CEO der Henning Larsen Group und ihrer Dependancen in Hongkong, Saudi-Arabien, Deutschland, den USA, Norwegen und den Färöer Inseln ernannt. In ihrer Zeit als CEO erhielt das Büro den Mies-van-der-Rohe-Preis für das Konzert- und Konferenzzentrum Harpa in Reykjavik.

Hermann Czech Architekt

hermann-czech.at

Architect in Vienna and author of numerous theoretical publications on architecture. He was a visiting professor at Harvard University, the Swiss Federal Institute of Technology Zurich (ETHZ) and the Academy of Fine Arts Vienna (Roland Rainer Chair). His architectural work includes urban planning, residential, school and hotel buildings as well as restaurants and exhibition design.

Architekt in Wien und Autor zahlreicher theoretischer Publikationen zur Architektur. Dabei spielen die Begriffe „Umbau" und „Manierismus" eine zentrale Rolle. Er war Gastprofessor an der Harvard University, der Eidgenössischen Technischen Hochschule Zürich und der Akademie der bildenden Künste Wien (Roland Rainer Chair). Sein architektonisches Werk umfasst Stadtplanung, Wohn-, Schul- und Hotelbauten ebenso wie Gastlokale und Ausstellungsgestaltungen.

Hild und K Architekten

hildundk.de

Founded in 1992 as Hild und Kaltwasser, the firm has been managed by Andreas Hild and Dionys Ottl since 1998. Matthias Haber joined the management team as partner in 2011. In 2012, a Berlin office was opened in addition to the headquarters in Munich. Respectful and creative handling of architectural heritage plays an essential role in the firm's creative approach.

Das 1992 als Hild und Kaltwasser gegründete Büro wird seit 1998 von Andreas Hild gemeinsam mit Dionys Ottl geführt. Seit 2011 verstärkt Matthias Haber als Partner das Führungsteam. 2012 wurde neben dem Münchner Stammsitz eine Berliner Niederlassung des Büros eröffnet. Der respektvolle und kreative Umgang mit dem baukulturellen Erbe spielt für alle Gestaltungansätze eine wesentliche Rolle.

Ingenhoven Architects

ingenhovenarchitects.com

After studying at RWTH Aachen University and Dusseldorf Art Academy, Christoph Ingenhoven (b. 1960) founded his architecture firm in 1985. In 1997, his RWE Tower in Essen became one of the world's first ecologically oriented skyscrapers. He is the designer of the Stuttgart 21 main railway station. Based in Dusseldorf, his firm has branches in St. Moritz, Sydney, Singapore and Santa Clara, California.

Christoph Ingenhoven (geb. 1960) studierte Architektur und Kunstgeschichte an der RWTH Aachen und der Kunstakademie Düsseldorf bei Hans Hollein. 1985 Gründung des Büros ingenhoven architects. Bau eines der ersten Öko-Hochhäuser weltweit (RWE Turm Essen, 1997). Planung des Bahnhofs Stuttgart 21. Hauptsitz ist Düsseldorf, mit Dependancen in St. Moritz, Sydney, Singapur und Santa Clara, Kalifornien.

Ippolito Fleitz Group

ifgroup.org

While studying architecture in Stuttgart and Chicago, Peter Ippolito also worked at Studio Libeskind in Berlin. In 2002 he founded the Ippolito Fleitz Group together with Gunter Fleitz. The multidisciplinary design studio became internationally known through their interior design, product design and communications projects. Peter Ippolito is a member of the German Designer Club. In 2015 his studio was inducted into the Interior Design Hall of Fame.

Während seines Architekturstudiums in Stuttgart und Chicago sammelte Peter Ippolito praktische Erfahrungen im Studio Libeskind in Berlin. 2002 gründete er gemeinsam mit Gunter Fleitz die Ippolito Fleitz Group. International bekannt wurde das multidisziplinäre Designstudio mit Innenarchitektur-, Kommunikations- und Produktdesignprojekten. Peter Ippolito ist Mitglied im Deutschen Designer Club. 2015 wurde die Ippolito Fleitz Group in die ›Interior Design Hall of Fame‹ aufgenommen.

John Pawson

johnpawson.com

John Pawson has spent over 30 years making rigorously simple architecture that speaks of the fundamentals but is modest in character. His work spans a range of scales and typologies, from private homes and museums to ballet sets, yacht interiors and a bridge across a lake. He approaches buildings and design commissions in the same manner: on the basis that "it's all architecture".

Seit über 30 Jahren propagiert John Pawson (geb. 1949) eine Architektur der Einfachheit, die diese radikal auf ihre Grundlagen reduziert. Sein Werk umfasst die unterschiedlichsten Typologien, von Privathäusern und Museen, Bühnenbildern fürs Ballett bis hin zur Ausstattung von Jachten und den Bau von Brücken. Ob Bauwerk oder Design – Pawsons Maxime lautet: „Alles ist Architektur."

KAAN Architecten

kaanarchitecten.com

Together with his partners Vincent Panhuysen and Dikkie Scipio, Kees Kaan founded Kaan Architecten in 2014. He graduated in architecture at Delft University of Technology, where he is currently Chair of the department of Complex Projects at the faculty of Architecture. Kaan is an international lecturer and sits on various juries and boards, both in the Netherlands and abroad. Numerous books and exhibitions have been dedicated to his body of work.

2014 gründete Kees Kaan (geb. 1961) mit Vincent Panhuysen und Dikkie Scipio das Büro Kaan Architecten in Rotterdam. Zu seinem internationalen Team gehören auch Landschaftsarchitekten, Stadtplaner, Ingenieure und Grafikdesigner. Kaan selbst studierte an der TU Delft, wo er derzeit den Fachbereich Komplexe Projekte leitet. Seinem Werk sind zahlreiche Bücher und Ausstellungen gewidmet.

kadawittfeldarchitektur

kadawittfeldarchitektur.de

Kilian Kada (b. 1975) studied architecture in Vienna and New York. He is a managing partner of kadawittfeldarchitektur. Founded in 1999 in Aachen, the architectural firm and its team of 150 architects stand for an interdisciplinary approach that combines architecture and interior architecture, design and urban development projects.

Kilian Kada (geb. 1975) studierte Architektur in Wien und New York. Er ist geschäftsführendes Mitglied der kadawittfeldarchitektur. Das 1999 in Aachen gegründete Architekturbüro steht mit einem Team von 150 Architekten für einen interdisziplinären Ansatz, der Architektur mit Innenarchitektur, Design und städtebaulichen Projekten verbindet.

Kimmel Eshkolot Architects

kimmel.co.il

Etan Kimmel and Michal Kimmel Eshkolot founded their firm in Tel Aviv in 1986. They enjoy working on a broad scale and quantity of projects from urban planning and public buildings to interior design. Teamwork and genuine discourse between site, context, client and project consultants are critical values cultivated in their work ethic. The architects aspire for each project to be true to its essence, rich in complexity yet simple in design while fundamentally integrating sustainability ideals.

1986 gründeten Etan Kimmel und Michal Kimmel Eshkolot ihr Büro in Tel Aviv. Sein Portfolio bietet ein breites Spektrum unterschiedlicher Projekte, von der Stadtplanung und öffentlichen Bauten bis hin zur Inneneinrichtung. Ein echter Diskurs zwischen Standort, Kontext und Bauherr ist Teil ihres Arbeitsethos. Ihre Projekte sind komplex und einfach zugleich und setzen voll auf Nachhaltigkeit.

Landau Kindelbacher

landaukindelbacher.de

After studying architecture in Munich, Gerhard Landau (b. 1965) worked for Michael Hopkins + Partners in London. In 1994 he and Ludwig Kindelbacher founded Landau + Kindelbacher focusing on architecture and interior design.. Today, Gerhard Landau is the firm's managing partner and in addition to concrete planning is also actively involved in academic discourse.

Nach seinem Architekturstudium in München war Gerhard Landau (geb. 1965) bei Michael Hopkins + Partners in London beschäftigt. 1994 gründete er gemeinsam mit Ludwig Kindelbacher das Büro Landau + Kindelbacher Architekten – Innenarchitekten. Heute ist Gerhard Landau geschäftsführender Gesellschafter des Studios und neben der konkreten Planungsarbeit auch in den akademischen Diskurs eingebunden.

Lissoni Associati

lissoniassociati.com

In 1986 together with Nicoletta Canesi, the architect, designer and art director Piero Lissoni (b. 1956) founded the interdisciplinary studio Lissoni Associati in Milan. Graph.x, which focuses on branding and corporate identity, followed in 1996. With Lissoni Architettura since 2013 and Lissoni Inc. in New York since 2015, Lissoni has positioned himself as a leading architect on the international market.

1986 gründet der Architekt, Designer und Art Director Piero Lissoni (geb. 1956) zusammen mit Nicoletta Canesi das interdisziplinäre Studio Lissoni Associati in Mailand. 1996 folgt das Grafikbüro Graph.x mit den Schwerpunkten Markenentwicklung und Corporate Identity. Mit Lissoni Architettura (seit 2013) und Lissoni Inc. in New York (seit 2015) positioniert sich Piero Lissoni als führender Architekt auf dem internationalen Markt.

LRO Lederer Ragnarsdóttir Oei

archlro.de

Arno Lederer (b. 1947) studied architecture in Stuttgart and Vienna. In 1979 he founded his office in Stuttgart. Today he manages LRO together with Jórunn Ragnarsdóttir (b. 1957) and Marc Oei (b. 1962). The office is known for its distinctive formal and material language. The most recent example is the Historical Museum in Frankfurt. Arno Lederer has taught at various German universities.

Arno Lederer (geb. 1947) studierte Architektur in Stuttgart und Wien. 1979 gründete er sein Büro in Stuttgart. Heute leitet er zusammen mit Jórunn Ragnarsdóttir (geb. 1957) und Marc Oei (geb. 1962) LRO. Das Büro ist bekannt für seine markante Formen- und Materialsprache. Jüngstes Beispiel ist das Historische Museum in Frankfurt. Arno Lederer lehrte an verschiedenen deutschen Hochschulen.

Marie-José Van Hee Architecten

mjvanhee.be

In her work, Marie-José Van Hee (b. 1950) renews the tradition of building into a timeless architecture, devoting particular attention to space, natural materials and light. Born in 1950 in Ghent, she founded her own practice in 1975. She has taught and lectured on architecture in Belgium, the Netherlands, Switzerland and the UK. In 2018, she participated for the third time in the Venice Architecture Biennale.

1975 gründete Marie-José Van Hee (geb. 1950) ihr eigenes Büro in Gent. Ihr Ziel ist eine Erneuerung der Tradition einer zeitlosen Architektur mit einem starken Fokus auf Raum, natürliche Materialien und Licht. Sie hatte Lehraufträge und hielt Vorträge in Belgien, den Niederlanden, der Schweiz und Großbritannien. 2018 nahm sie zum dritten Mal an der Architekturbiennale in Venedig teil.

Massimiliano Fuksas

fuksas.com

Massimiliano Fuksas (b. 1944 in Rome) graduated in Architecture from the University of Rome in 1969. Since the 1980s, he has worked in partnership with his wife, Doriana Mandrelli (b. 1955).. In addition to his many built projects, he has taught at numerous universities and written about architecture and design. As director of the 7th Venice Architecture Biennale (2000), he focused on the topic "Less Aesthetics, More Ethics".

1969 beendete Massimiliano Fuksas (geb. 1944) sein Architekturstudium an der Universität in Rom. Seit den 1980er-Jahren arbeitet er zusammen mit seiner Frau Doriana Mandrelli (geb. 1955). Er lehrt an verschiedenen Universitäten und publiziert über Architektur und Design. Die vom ihm geleitete 7. Architekturbiennale in Venedig stand unter dem Motto „Weniger Ästhetik, mehr Ethik".

Matteo Thun & Partners

matteothun.com

Matteo Thun (b. 1952 in Bolzano) studied at the Academy of Art in Salzburg under Oskar Kokoschka and at the University of Florence. He co-founded the Memphis movement in Milan and was a partner at Sottsass Associati from 1980 to 1984. His office in Milan specializes in interior architecture and design. Thun teaches at the University of Applied Arts in Vienna.

Matteo Thun (geb. 1952 in Bozen) studierte an der Akademie für Kunst in Salzburg unter Oskar Kokoschka und an der Universität von Florenz. Er war Mitbegründer der Memphis-Bewegung in Mailand und arbeitete von 1980 bis 1984 als Partner von Sottsass Associati. Sein Büro in Mailand ist auf Innenarchitektur und Design spezialisiert. Thun lehrt u.a. an der Hochschule für Angewandte Kunst in Wien.

meck architekten

meck-architekten.de

After studying architecture at the Technical University of Munich, Andreas Meck launched his practice in Munich in 1989. The architect has been a professor at the Munich University of Applied Sciences since 1998 and dean of its Architecture department since 2013. Axel Frühauf studied at the Munich University of Applied Sciences. He joined meck architekten in 2004 and has been a managing partner since 2011.

Nach dem Architekturstudium an der TU München gründete Andreas Meck sein Büro 1989 ebenfalls in München. Seit 1998 ist der Architekt Professor an der Hochschule für Angewandte Wissenschaften München und seit 2013 Dekan der dortigen Architekturfakultät. Axel Frühauf studierte an der Hochschule für Angewandte Wissenschaften in München. Seine Mitarbeit bei meck architekten begann 2004, seit 2011 ist er geschäftsführender Gesellschafter.

Michael Maltzan Architecture

mmaltzan.com

Michael Maltzan founded his studio in 1995. His work includes cultural, educational, commercial, housing and infrastructural projects that have been published and exhibited around the world. He is a fellow of the American Institute of Architects, a recipient of the American Academy of Arts and Letters Architecture Award, and an AIA Los Angeles Gold Medal Honoree.

1995 gründete Michael Maltzan (geb. 1959) sein Büro in Los Angeles. Seine Arbeiten umfassen Bauten für Kultur- und Bildungseinrichtungen, gewerbliche Zwecke sowie Wohn- und Infrastrukturprojekte, die weltweit in Zeitschriften vorgestellt und auf Ausstellungen gezeigt wurden. Er ist u.a. Preisträger des American Academy of Arts and Letters Architecture Award sowie der Goldmedaille des AIA Los Angeles.

Michele De Lucchi

amdl.it

Michele De Lucchi was part of the Memphis movement as well as its precursor, Studio Alchimia. He designed furniture for various Italian and other European companies and has realized architectural projects in Italy and abroad. He has been a professor of architecture in Venice and Milan, and since 2018 has been editor-in-chief of Domus magazine.

Der italienische Architekt und Designer Michele De Lucchi (geb. 1951) war Mitglied der Memphis-Bewegung wie auch ihres Vorläufers Studio Alchimia. Er entwarf Möbel für namhafte Hersteller und realisierte Architekturprojekte in Italien wie im Ausland. Daneben lehrte er Architektur an den Universitäten von Venedig und Mailand. Seit 2018 ist er Chefredakteur des Architekturmagazins Domus.

Miralles Tagliabue EMBT

mirallestagliabue.com

After studying architecture in Venice, Benedetta Tagliabue and Enric Miralles founded Miralles Tagliabue EMBT in Barcelona in 1994, and in Shanghai in 2010. Tagliabue's poetic architecture, always attentive to its context, has won international awards in the fields of public space and design. Tagliabue directs the Enric Miralles Foundation, named for her late husband, which promotes experimental architecture.

Nach ihrem Studium in Venedig gründete Benedetta Tagliabue gemeinsam mit Enric Miralles 1994 das Büro Miralles Tagliabue EMBT in Barcelona. Die Architekten realisierten Parlamentsgebäude, Markthallen, Universitätsgebäude und öffentliche Plätze. Derzeit arbeitet EMBT unter anderem an Bürotürmen in Xiamen und Taichung. Die Entwürfe von EMBT wurden in vielen Ländern mit internationalen Preisen ausgezeichnet. Heute ist Benedetta Tagliabue auch Direktorin der Enric Miralles Foundation.

Monica Armani

monica-armani.com

Monica Armani (b. 1964) divides her time between Trento and Milan, working in the fields of architecture, interior design and industrial design. In collaboration with her partner Luca Dallabetta, she has designed lighting, furniture and accessories for the likes of Tribù, Poliform, Moroso, Boffi, B&B Italia, Studio TK and Luceplan. Larger scale projects include private residences, retail interiors and temporary structures.

Monica Armani (geb. 1964) lebt und arbeitet als Architektin, Innenarchitektin und Industriedesignerin in Trient und Mailand. Mit ihrem Partner Luca Dallabetta entwirft sie Leuchten, Möbel und Accessoires für Labels wie Tribù, Poliform, Moroso, Boffi, B&B Italia, Studio TK und Luceplan. Architekturprojekte sind Privatwohnungen, Ladenlokale und temporäre Bauten. Ihr Credo: „Weniger ist mehr".

Morphosis

Thom Mayne (b. 1944) is founding principal of Morphosis, an award-winning global design firm engaged in architecture, urban planning and research since 1972. Mayne's honours include the Pritzker Prize (2005) and the American Institute of Architects Gold Medal (2013). He has held teaching positions throughout his career, including a tenured professorship at the University of California, Los Angeles, since 1993.

Thom Mayne (geb. 1944) ist Mitbegründer von Morphosis, einem preisgekrönten internationalen Büro, das seit 1972 in den Bereichen Architektur, Stadtplanung und -forschung tätig ist. Mayne wurde 2005 mit dem Pritzker-Preis ausgezeichnet und u.a. mit der Goldmedaille des American Institute of Architects geehrt (2013). Seit 1993 lehrt er als Professor an der University of California, Los Angeles.

Murman Arkitekter

After completing his degree in architecture in 1975, Hans Murman (b. 1947) founded his practice in Stockholm in 1985, which today has a team of 27 architects, interior architects and civil engineers. The firm works within a wide range of scale and complexity, including public buildings, offices (refurbishment, new buildings, interior organization and design), housing and private homes as well as master plans.

Hans Murman (geb. 1947) studierte Architektur in Stockholm. 1985 eröffnete er hier sein eigenes Büro, das heute aus 27 Architekten, Innenarchitekten und Bauingenieuren besteht. Murman Architects erstellen Masterpläne und realisieren Projekte in jeder Größenordnung, darunter öffentliche Bauten, Büros (inkl. Sanierung, Modernisierung, Innenausstattung und Design) sowie Wohngebäude.

Nagler Architekten

After interrupted studies in art history and Bavarian history in Munich, Florian Nagler (b. 1967) trained as a carpenter. In 1994, he completed his degree in Architecture in Kaiserslautern. In 1996, he launched his practice in Munich, which he has managed together with Barbara Nagler since 2001. Since 2010, he has been Chair of Design and Construction at the Technical University of Munich.

Nach einem unvollendeten Studium der Kunstgeschichte und Bayerischen Geschichte in München machte Florian Nagler (geb. 1967) zunächst eine Zimmermannslehre. 1994 folgte sein Architektur-Abschluss in Kaiserslautern. 1996 eröffnete er sein eigenes Büro in München, das er seit 2001 zusammen mit Barbara Nagler führt. Seit 2010 leitet er den Lehrstuhl für Entwerfen und Konstruieren an der TU München.

Neri & Hu Design and Research Office

Lyndon Neri and Rossana Hu both studied architecture at the University of California at Berkeley, and then Harvard and Princeton University, respectively. After working for Michael Graves, they launched their own studio in 2004. Today, the highly acclaimed interdisciplinary studio is based in Shanghai and London. The duo is actively involved in teaching and using research as a design tool.

Lyndon Neri und Rossana Hu studierten Architektur an der University of California in Berkeley sowie an der Harvard bzw. der Princeton University. Nach ihrer Tätigkeit für Michael Graves machten sie sich 2004 selbständig. Heute verfügt ihr hochangesehenes Büro über Niederlassungen in Shanghai und London. Neri und Hu lehren an verschiedenen Universitäten und nutzen ihre Forschung als Design-instrument.

Níall McLaughlin Architects

niallmclaughlin.com

Educated in Dublin, Níall McLaughlin (b. 1962 in Geneva) founded his practice in London in 1990. He designs buildings for education, culture, health, religious worship and housing. Awards include Young British Architect of the Year (1998) and the RIBA Charles Jencks Award for Simultaneous Contribution to Theory and Practice (2016). He is a professor at the Bartlett School of Architecture, University College London.

Níall McLaughlin (geb. 1962) studierte Architektur in Dublin. 1990 gründete er sein eigenes Büro in London. Seine Arbeit umfasst Projekte im Bildungs-, Kultur- und Gesundheitsbereich sowie Kirchen und Wohngebäude. 1998 wurde er zum Young British Architect of the Year gewählt. 2016 erhielt er den Charles Jencks Award des RIBA. McLaughlin lehrt an der Bartlett School of Architecture in London.

Nieto Sobejano Arquitectos

nietosobejano.com

Fuensanta Nieto and Enrique Sobejano (both b. 1957) founded their practice in 1985 in Madrid, and later Berlin. Their work has been widely exhibited, such as at the Venice Biennale, and awarded prizes including the Aga Khan Award for Architecture and the Alvar Aalto Medal. They both currently teach at the University of the Arts in Berlin (Sobejano) and European University of Madrid (Nieto).

Fuensanta Nieto und Enrique Sobejano (beide geb. 1957) gründeten 1985 ihr Büro in Madrid und eröffneten später eine Dependance in Berlin. Sie erhielten u.a. den Aga Khan Award for Architecture und die Alvar-Aalto-Medaille und waren auch auf der Biennale in Venedig vertreten. Fuensanta Nieto lehrt an der Universidad Europea de Madrid, Enrique Sobejano an der Universität der Künste in Berlin.

OMA

OMA.eu

Reinier de Graaf (b. 1964) is a Dutch architect, architectural theorist, urbanist, writer and a partner at the Office for Metropolitan Architecture (OMA). He co-founded OMA's think tank, AMO, in 2002, and co-founded and developed the Strelka Institute for Media, Architecture and Design in Moscow from 2010 to 2013. His book "Four Walls and a Roof: The Complex Nature of a Simple Profession" was published in 2017.

Der niederländische Architekt, Architekturtheoretiker, Stadtplaner und Autor Reinier de Graaf (geb. 1964) ist Partner von OMA, dem Büro von Rem Koolhaas. 2002 war er Mitbegründer der OMA-Denkfabrik AMO. 2010–2013 entwickelte er als einer der Initiatoren das Strelka Institute for Media, Architecture and Design in Moskau. 2017 erschien sein Buch „Four Walls and a Roof: The Complex Nature of a Simple Profession".

Ofis arhitekti

ofis-a.si

Ofis arhitekti was established in 1996 by Rok Oman (b. 1970) and Špela Videčnik (b. 1971). Both graduated from the Ljubljana School of Architecture and the Architectural Association in London. The international team firm based in Ljubljana and Paris collaborates with other studios in London and Moscow, and works with clients from the private and commercial sectors as well as with state institutions.

Ofis arhitekti wurde 1996 von Rok Oman (geb. 1970) und Špela Videčnik (geb. 1971) gegründet. Beide studierten an der Universität Ljubljana und der Architectural Association in London. Hauptsitze von Ofis arhitekti sind Ljubljana und Paris mit Partnerbüros in London und Moskau. Sie entwickeln Projekte für private wie gewerbliche Auftraggeber, aber auch für staatliche Institutionen.

Palais Mai

Peter Scheller (b. 1968), Ina-Maria Schmidbauer (b. 1967) and Patrick von Ridder (b. 1969) founded Palais Mai in Munich in 2005, two years after co-founding the PAM architectural group. Scheller himself completed an apprenticeship as a carpenter before studying architecture at the Technical University of Munich. In 2017, Palais Mai received the Fritz Höger Prize for its housing development with integrated daycare centre in Munich.

Bevor Peter Scheller (geb. 1968), Ina-Maria Schmidbauer (geb. 1967) und Patrick von Ridder (geb. 1969) ihr Büro Palais Mai 2005 in München eröffneten, waren sie 2002 Mitgründer der Architekten-gruppe PAM. Scheller selbst absolvierte vor seinem Architekturstudium an der TU München eine Zimmermannslehre. 2017 erhielt das Büro den Fritz-Höger-Preis für eine Wohnbebauung mit Kinder-haus in München.

Peter Haimerl Architektur

Born in the Bavarian Forest, Peter Haimerl founded his firm in Munich in 1991. He went on to develop holistic concepts combining architecture with computer programming, sociology, economics, politics and conceptual art. In 2000, he founded Zoom Town, an open research platform to optimize and reorganize the urban environment.

1991 gründete der gebürtige Bayerwälder sein Büro in München. Seither entwickelt er ganzheitliche Konzepte, die Architektur mit Computer-Programmierung, Soziologie, Wirtschaft, Politik und konzep-tioneller Kunst verbinden. 2000 gründete Peter Haimerl die offene Forschungsplattform „Zoom Town" zur Optimierung und Reorganisation städtischer Umwelt.

Pezo von Ellrichshausen

Mauricio Pezo (b. 1973) and Sofia von Ellrichshausen (b. 1976) founded their art and architec-ture studio in 2002. They live and work in the southern Chilean city of Concepción and are visiting professors at the Harvard Graduate School of Design. Their work has been featured in several monographs and in the essay books "Spatial Structure" and "Naïve Intention", and been exhibited in museums around the world.

2002 gründeten Mauricio Pezo (geb. 1973) und Sofia von Ellrichshausen (geb. 1976) ihr Kunst- und Architekturbüro in der chilenischen Stadt Concepción. Beide sind Gastprofessoren an der Harvard Graduate School of Design in Massachusetts. Ihre Arbeiten wurden in verschiedenen Monografien sowie dem Essayband „Spatial Structure and Naïve Intention" publiziert und weltweit in Museen aus-gestellt.

Plasma Studio

Holger Kehne, Eva Castro, Ulla Hell and Chuan Wang have collaborated as Plasma Studio since 1999, with offices in Beijing, Hong Kong and Sexten, Italy. German native Holger Kehne is a founding partner and based in Hong Kong. Replacing specificities of scale and type with those of context and affect, Plasma fuses objects, surfaces, architecture and landscape to link global, regional, urban and environmental systems.

1999 gründeten Holger Kehne (geb. 1970) und Eva Castro (geb. 1969) Plasma Studio. Ulla Hell (geb. 1973) und Chuan Wang kamen als Partner dazu. Das internationale Team hat Büros in London, Beijing und Bozen. Sein stark kontextbezogener Fokus liegt auf der Verschmelzung von Architektur und Land-schaft, um das Globale mit dem Regionalen und das Urbane mit dem Ökologischen zu verbinden.

querkraft architekten

querkraft.at

Frankfurt native Jakob Dunkl studied architecture in Vienna, where he founded querkraft architekten in 1998 together with Gerd Erhartt, Peter Sapp and Michael Zinner. Dunkl was a visiting professor at Roger Williams University in Rhode Island (US) and at Vienna University of Technology. From 2013 to 2016 he hosted the TV documentary "Meine Stadt / ("My City") for the television station Arte.

Nach seinem Studium in Wien gründete der gebürtige Frankfurter Jakob Dunkl 1998 gemeinsam mit Gerd Erhartt, Peter Sapp und Michael Zinner das Wiener Büro querkraft architekten. Dunkl war Gastprofessor an der Roger Williams University (US) und an der TU Wien. Von 2013–2016 moderierte er die TV-Dokumentation „Meine Stadt / Ma ville" für den Fernsehsender Arte.

RCR Arquitectes

rcrarquitectes.es

In 1988, Rafael Aranda (b. 1961), Carmen Pigem (b. 1961) and Ramon Vilalta (b. 1960) founded the architectural firm RCR Arquitectes in Olot, Spain. In 2013, they established the RCR Bunka Foundation, and in 2017, RCR Lab A. Their works include the Soulages Museum in France, an athletics facility for Tossols Basil in Olot, and the Waalse Krook media centre in Belgium. They received the Pritzker Prize in 2017.

1988 eröffneten Rafael Aranda (geb. 1961), Carmen Pigem (geb. 1961) und Ramon Vilalta (geb. 1960) das Architekturbüro RCR Arquitectes in Olot, Spanien. 2013 gründeten sie die RCR Bunka Stiftung, 2017 das RCR Lab·A. Sie entwarfen u.a. das Soulages Museum in Frankreich, die Leichtathletikanlage von Tossols Basil in Olot und die Waalse Krook Mediathek in Belgien. 2017 erhielten sie den Pritzker-Preis.

Realarchitektur

realarchitektur.de

After studying in Lund, Sweden and at the Mackintosh School of Architecture in Glasgow, where she received her diploma in Architecture in 1991, Petra Petersson worked in various architectural firms in Glasgow, Auckland, Stockholm and Berlin. The Swedish architect founded Realarchitektur in Berlin in 2003. She has been a professor at the Graz University of Technology since 2013.

Nach ihrem Studium im schwedischen Lund und an der Mackintosh School of Architecture in Glasgow, wo sie 1991 ihr Architekturdiplom erhielt, war Petra Petersson in verschiedenen Architekturbüros in Glasgow, Auckland, Stockholm und Berlin tätig. 2003 gründete die Schwedin ihr Büro Realarchitektur in Berlin. Seit 2013 ist sie Professorin an der TU Graz.

Sauerbruch Hutton

sauerbruchhutton.de

Matthias Sauerbruch and Louisa Hutton founded their practice in London in 1989 and relocated their headquarters to Berlin shortly afterwards. The Federal Environment Agency (UBA) in Dessau, planned by Sauerbruch Hutton, was completed in 2005. The building is regarded as a model for innovative building. Sauerbruch Hutton's projects have been awarded numerous international prizes.

Matthias Sauerbruch und Louisa Hutton gründeten ihr Büro 1989 in London und verlegten den Hauptsitz wenig später nach Berlin. 2005 wurde das von Sauerbruch Hutton geplante Umweltbundesamt (UBA) in Dessau fertiggestellt. Das Gebäude gilt als Modell für innovatives Bauen. Die Projekte von Sauerbruch Hutton wurden mit zahlreichen internationalen Preisen ausgezeichnet.

Schulz und Schulz

schulz-und-schulz.com

Brothers Ansgar and Benedikt Schulz (b. 1966 and 1968) studied in Aachen, Madrid and Asunción (Paraguay) and founded their practice in 1992 in Leipzig. Their award-winning projects include the Church of St. Trinity in Leipzig. From 2010 to 2018, they taught Building Design at the Technical University of Dortmund, and Design and Construction at the Technical University of Dresden as of 2018.

Die Brüder Ansgar und Benedikt Schulz (geb. 1966 und 1968) studierten Architektur in Aachen, Madrid und Asunción (Paraguay). 1992 gründeten sie ihr Büro in Leipzig, das vielfach ausgezeichnete Projekte wie die Kirche St. Trinitatis in Leipzig realisierte. 2010 bis 2018 lehrten sie als Professoren am Lehrstuhl Baukonstruktion der TU Dortmund. Seit 2018 sind sie Professoren für Entwerfen und Konstruieren an der TU Dresden.

Sean Godsell Architects

seangodsell.com

Sean Godsell was born in Melbourne, Australia in 1960 where he founded Sean Godsell Architects in 1994. His work has been published in the world's leading architectural journals and he has lectured and exhibited in the USA, UK, China, Japan, India, France, Finland, Germany, Italy and New Zealand as well as across Australia.

Sean Godsell (geb. 1960) gründete sein Büro Sean Godsell Architects 1994 in Melbourne. Seine Arbeiten sind in den weltweit führenden Architekturzeitschriften erschienen. Godsell war auf Vortragsreisen unterwegs in den USA, Großbritannien, China, Japan, Indien, Frankreich, Finnland, Deutschland, Italien, Neuseeland und natürlich Australien und hat an zahlreichen Ausstellungen teilgenommen.

Skälsö Arkitekter

skalso.se

Skälsö Arkitekter was founded in Visby, Sweden in 2010, with a studio in Stockholm added in 2016. The firm includes Erik Gardell (partner and founder), Joel Phersson (partner and founder), Lisa Ekström, Mats Håkansson, Kristin Karlsson and Axel Wolgers. Their master plan to revive Bungenäs, a former quarry and military grounds on the island of Gotland, has received widespread praise, and was featured at the Venice Biennale in 2018.

Das Büro wurde 2010 von Erik Gardell und Joel Phersson im schwedischen Visby gegründet. Seit 2016 gibt es auch eine Niederlassung in Stockholm. Der Masterplan von Skälsö Arkitekter zur vielbeachteten Wiederbelebung von Bungenäs, einem ehemaligen Militärgelände und Steinbruch auf Gotland, war auf der Architekturbiennale 2018 in Venedig zu sehen.

Snøhetta

snohetta.com

Norwegian architect Kjetil Trædal Thorsen (b. 1958) is a partner at Snøhetta, which he co-founded in 1989 in Oslo with Craig Dykers (b. 1961). The collaborative studio works internationally across the fields of architecture, landscapes, interiors, product design and graphic design. They have designed renowned structures such as the Norwegian National Opera and Ballet and the Bibliotheca Alexandrina in Egypt.

1989 gründete der norwegische Architekt Kjetil Trædal Thorsen (geb. 1958) zusammen mit Craig Dykers (geb. 1961) Snøhetta in Oslo. Das in interdisziplinären Teams zusammengesetzte Büro arbeitet weltweit auf den Gebieten Architektur, Landschafts- und Innenarchitektur, Produkt- und Grafikdesign. Es hat so renommierte Bauten entworfen wie das Opernhaus in Oslo und die Bibliotheca Alexandrina in Ägypten.

Solid Objectives – Idenburg Liu SO-IL so-il.org

Florian Idenburg (b. 1975) founded SO – IL in 2008 together with Jing Liu (b. 1980) in New York. Idenburg's practice is collaborative. With a strong background in cultural spaces, he has overseen projects such as "Pole Dance", a temporary installation in the courtyard of the Museum of Modern Art PS1, and the recently completed Manetti Shrem Museum of Art at University of California, Davis. He is currently Associate Professor of Practice at Harvard University.

2008 gründete Florian Idenburg (geb. 1975) mit Jing Liu (geb. 1980) das Architektur- und Designbüro SO – IL in New York. Alle Projekte sind Gemeinschaftsarbeiten. Bekannt wurden SO – IL mit (temporären) Installationen wie „Pole Dance" im Innenhof des Museum of Modern Art PS1, aber auch mit Bauten wie dem jüngst fertiggestellten Manetti Shrem Museum of Art an der University of California in Davis.

Sou Fujimoto Architects sou-fujimoto.net

Sou Fujimoto (b. 1971), earned a degree in architecture at Tokyo University in 1994 and launched his own practice in 2000. Today based in Tokyo and Paris, his award-winning firm has a multifaceted portfolio including housing, cultural buildings, exhibition installations, product design and urban master plans. In 2013, he became the youngest architect to design the Serpentine Gallery Pavilion in London.

1994 machte Sou Fujimoto (geb. 1971) seinen Abschluss in Architektur an der Universität Tokio. 2000 eröffnete er sein eigenes Büro mit Niederlassungen in Tokio und Paris. Sein Portefeuille umfasst Wohnbauten ebenso wie kulturelle Einrichtungen, Ausstellungsinstallationen, Produktdesign und Stadtplanung. 2013 entwarf er den jährlich wechselnden Pavillon der Serpentine Gallery in London.

Staab Architekten staab-architekten.com

Volker Staab launched his practice in Berlin in 1991; Alfred Nieuwenhuizen joined as a partner in 1996. Staab has taught at universities in Berlin, Münster and Stuttgart, and has been Professor for Design at Braunschweig University of Technology since 2012. He received the German Order of Merit in 2008 and the Grand Award of the Association of German Architects (BDA) in 2011. He is a member of the Berlin Academy of the Arts.

1991 gründete Volker Staab sein Büro in Berlin. Seit 1996 arbeitet er mit Alfred Nieuwenhuizen als Partner zusammen. Nach Gastprofessuren an der TU Berlin, der FH Münster und der Kunstakademie in Stuttgart übernahm er 2012 einen Lehrstuhl für Entwurf an der TU Braunschweig. 2008 erhielt er das Bundesverdienstkreuz am Bande und 2011 erhielt er den großen BDA-Preis. Er ist Mitglied der Akademie der Künste Berlin.

Studio Gang studiogang.com

Jeanne Gang (b. 1964) is founding principal of Studio Gang, an architecture and urbanism practice with offices in Chicago, New York and San Francisco. She received the Louis I. Kahn Memorial Award and the Marcus Prize for Architecture, and teaches at Harvard Graduate School of Design. Current projects include the expansion of the American Museum of Natural History in New York and the new US Embassy in Brasilia.

Jeanne Gang (geb. 1964) ist Gründerin und Leiterin von Studio Gang, einem Büro für Architektur- und Städtebau mit Dependancen in Chicago, New York und San Francisco. Sie erhielt u. a. den Louis I. Kahn Memorial Award und lehrt an der Harvard Graduate School of Design. Aktuelle Projekte sind die Erweiterung des American Museum of Natural History in New York und die US-Botschaft in Brasilia.

Studio Libeskind

libeskind.com

Together with his partner Nina Libeskind, the architect established his studio in Berlin in 1989 after winning the competition to build the Jewish Museum Berlin. Studio Libeskind relocated its headquarters to New York City in 2003 after being selected as the master planner for the World Trade Center redevelopment. Today, Studio Libeskind is involved in the design and implementation of urban, cultural and commercial projects around the globe.

Nachdem er den internationalen Wettbewerb für das jüdische Museum Berlin gewonnen hatte, gründeten Daniel Libeskind (geb. 1946) und seine Frau Nina 1989 das Studio Libeskind in Berlin. 2003 zog das Büro nach New York um, wo es mit dem Masterplan zum Wiederaufbau des World Trade Center beauftragt wurde. Studio Libeskind arbeitet weltweit an öffentlichen Projekten und in der Stadtplanung.

Studio MK27

studiomk27.com.br

After studying architecture, Marcio Kogan (b. 1952) divided his work between filmmaking and architecture. In 2001, he renamed his practice in São Paulo as studio mk27. He has gained international acclaim for his work; in 2012, studio mk27 represented Brazil at the Venice Architecture Biennale. Today, Kogan and his team are working on projects in Brazil and beyond.

Nach dem Architekturstudium arbeitete Marcio Kogan (geb. 1952) teils als Filmemacher, teils als Architekt. 2001 nannte er sein Büro in São Paulo in studio mk27 um. Seine Arbeiten fanden schnell internationale Beachtung. 2012 vertrat er Brasilien auf der Architekturbiennale in Venedig. Heute arbeiten Kogan und sein Team an Projekten in Brasilien und weltweit.

Studio Odile Decq

odiledecq.com

Odile Decq (b. 1955) is a French architect, urban planner and academic. She has received numerous awards for her work, from the Golden Lion at the Venice Biennale in 1996 to Architizer's Lifetime Achievement Award in 2017. In 2014 she founded the Confluence Institute for Innovation and Creative Strategies in Architecture in Lyon, which moved into its permanent building that she designed in 2016.

Die Französin Odile Decq (geb. 1955) ist Architektin, Stadtplanerin und Professorin. Sie erhielt zahlreiche Auszeichnungen, u.a. den Goldenen Löwen der Architekturbiennale Venedig von 1996 und 2017 den Architizer A+ Lifetime Achievement Award. 2014 gründete sie das Confluence Institute for Innovation and Creative Strategies in Architecture in Lyon, das 2016 das von ihr gebaute Gebäude bezog.

Tezuka Architects

tezuka-arch.com

Tezuka Architects is a Tokyo-based practice led by husband and wife Takaharu (b. 1964) and Yui (b. 1969) Tezuka. Since its founding in 1994, the studio has received widespread international acclaim, especially for its residences and community buildings, which prioritize the human experience and harmonize with the outside environment. Examples include their Roof House, the Echigo-Matsunoyama Museum of Natural Science and Fuji Kindergarten.

Das in Tokio ansässige Büro wird von dem Ehepaar Takaharu (geb. 1964) und Yui Tezuka (geb. 1969) geleitet. Seit seiner Gründung 1994 hat es breite internationale Beachtung gefunden. Bekannt sind Tezuka Architects für ihre Wohn- und Gemeinschaftsbauten, die perfekt mit ihrer Umgebung harmonieren wie das Roof House, das Echigo-Matsunoyama Naturkundemuseum und der Fuji Kindergarten.

Tham & Videgård Arkitekter

Bolle Tham (b. 1970) and Martin Videgård (b. 1968) founded Tham & Videgård in Stockholm
in 1999. They have since completed a large number of projects ranging from private homes
to large-scale public buildings for museums and universities. They have received numerous
awards and continuously participate in exhibitions worldwide, most recently at the Chicago
Biennial and several times at the Venice Architecture Biennale. Both teach and lecture on
architecture internationally.

Bolle Tham (geb. 1970) und Martin Videgård (geb. 1968) gründeten ihr Büro 1999 in Stockholm.
Die Bandbreite ihrer Projekte reicht von Privathäusern bis hin zu großen öffentlichen Gebäuden wie
Museen und Universitäten. Tham & Videgård wurden mit zahlreichen Preisen bedacht und beteiligen
sich an Ausstellungen weltweit, darunter bereits mehrfach an der Architekturbiennale in Venedig.

Titus Bernhard Architekten

After completing his studies of architecture in Braunschweig in 1991, Titus Bernhard (b. 1963)
worked in the New York office of Richard Meier, among others. He founded his own firm in
1994. His credo is reduction to the essential, combined with the highest quality in craftsmanship and aesthetics. The firm's work has won several awards and was featured twice at the
Architecture Biennale in Venice.

Nach dem Architekturstudium in Braunschweig 1991 arbeitete Titus Bernhard (geb. 1963) u.a. im Büro
Richard Meier, New York. 1994 gründete er sein eigenes Büro. Sein Credo ist die Reduktion auf das
Wesentliche, verbunden mit höchsten Ansprüchen an handwerkliche und ästhetische Qualitäten.
Die Arbeiten des Büros wurden mehrfach prämiert und zweimal auf der Architekturbiennale in Venedig
gezeigt.

Topotek 1

After studying art history and landscape architecture in Hanover and Karlsruhe, Martin
Rein-Cano (b. 1967 in Buenos Aires) founded Topotek 1. The firm has worked on a wide range
of projects that have received several awards, including the Aga Khan Award for Architecture
in 2016. Rein-Cano has been a visiting professor in Europe and North America, and currently
teaches at the Dessau Institute for Architecture.

Nach dem Studium der Kunstgeschichte und Landschaftsarchitektur in Hannover und Karlsruhe
gründete Martin Rein-Cano (geb. 1967 in Buenos Aires) das Büro Topotek 1. Seither arbeitet es an
einer großen Bandbreite von Projekten, die mehrfach ausgezeichnet wurden, unter anderem mit dem
Aga Khan Award for Architecture 2016. Rein-Cano lehrt als Gastprofessor in Europa und Nordamerika.
Zur Zeit unterrichtet er am Dessau Institute for Architecture.

UNStudio

Ben van Berkel (b. 1957) and Caroline Bos (b. 1959) set up their practice in 1988 in Amsterdam,
renaming it UNStudio in 1998. UNStudio specializes in urban development, infrastructure
and master plan projects. Current projects by the award-winning firm include the design for
Doha's Integrated Metro Network in Qatar, the large-scale mixed-use project Four Frankfurt
in Germany and the Wasl Tower in Dubai.

1988 gründeten Ben van Berkel (geb. 1957) und Caroline Bos (geb. 1959) ihr Büro in Amsterdam und
nannten es 1998 in UNStudio um. Das preisgekrönte Büro ist spezialisiert auf Stadtentwicklung, Infra-
strukturen und Masterpläne. Aktuelle Projekte sind u.a. der Entwurf für das integrierte Metrosystem
in Doha, Katar, das gemischt genutzte Hochhausprojekt FOUR Frankfurt und der Wasl Tower in Dubai.

Vector Architects

vectorarchitects.com

Gong Dong is the Design Principal of Vector Architects in Beijing, China, which he founded in 2008. He studied architecture at Tsinghua University and the University of Illinois. He previously worked at Solomon, Cordwell, Buenz & Associates in Chicago, then Richard Meier & Partners and Steven Holl Architects in New York. He has been a visiting studio professor at Tsinghua University since 2014.

2008 gründete Gong Dong das Büro Vector Architects im Beijing, wo er als Design Principal fungiert. Er studierte Architektur an der Tsinghua University und der University of Illinois und arbeitete im Büro Solomon, Cordwell, Buenz & Associates in Chicago sowie bei Richard Meier & Partners und Steven Holl Architects in New York. Seit 2014 ist er Gastprofessor an der Tsinghua University.

Zaha Hadid Architects

zaha-hadid.com

Patrik Schumacher (b. 1961) is an architect, architectural theorist and principal of the architecture practice Zaha Hadid Architects (ZHA), based in London. He joined the practice in 1988 while still a student and has served as its director since the late 1990s. ZHA was founded by the late Zaha Mohammad Hadid (d. 2016), an Iraqi-British architect and the first woman to receive the Pritzker Architecture Prize, in 2004.

Patrik Schumacher (geb. 1961) ist Architekt, Architekturtheoretiker und (seit Ende der 1990er-Jahre) Leiter des in London ansässigen Architekturbüros Zaha Hadid Architects. Noch als Student schloss er sich 1988 dem Büro an. Gegründet wurde ZHA von der 2016 verstorbenen Zaha Hadid, einer irakisch-britischen Architektin und Designerin – der ersten Frau, die 2004 den Pritzker-Preis erhielt.

ZAO / standardarchitecture

standardarchitecture.cn / z-a-o.cn

Born in 1970, Zhang Ke founded ZAO/standardarchitecture (标准营造) in 2001. With a wide range of realized works, his studio has emerged as one of the most important protagonists among the new generation of Chinese architects. The studio's works have been exhibited and published to international acclaim. Zhang Ke won the Aga Khan Award for Architecture in 2016, and a year later, was awarded the Alvar Aalto Medal. He has been teaching Option Studios at Harvard Graduate School of Design since 2016.

2001 gründete Zhang Ke (geb. 1970) sein Büro ZAO/standardarchitecture (标准营造) in Beijing. Er avancierte damit zu einem der wichtigsten Protagonisten der neuen Generation chinesischer Architekten. 2016 erhielt er den Aga Khan Award for Architecture, 2017 die Alvar-Aalto-Medaille. Seit 2016 betreut Zhang Ke die Unterrichtsreihe OptionStudios an der Harvard Graduate School of Design.

Gmund Paper, based at Lake Tegernsee in the Bavarian Alps of Southern Germany, is the most modern paper mill for exquisite paper design in Europe. Its production and environmental technologies operate at the highest level. Artisanal paper is now being produced for a broad market, thanks to the facility's modern and efficient techniques. This enables custom solutions for sustainable brand identities.

The Gmund Paper range comprises more than 100,000 different types of paper. Gmund develops and produces paper that is manufactured in extremely precise work processes in order to emphasize the intrinsic value of the paper.

The paper collection "Gmund Bauhaus Dessau", on which this book is printed, is based on a deep understanding of the material and its exploration shared by the Bauhaus Dessau Foundation and Gmund Paper.

It highlights the synthesis of material, craftsmanship and standardized production with the special importance of paper as a material of universal communication. "Gmund Bauhaus Dessau" paper stands out with its pure materiality and quality. In its radical modernity and minimalist, black-and-white colour palette, it upholds the principles of the Bauhaus.

Gmund Papier, mit Sitz am Tegernsee, ist die modernste Design-papierfabrik in Europa. Produktions- und Umwelttechnologien arbeiten auf dem höchsten Niveau. Das handwerkliche Produkt Papier wird dank moderner und effizienter Technologien heute für einen breiten Markt produziert. Es entstehen maßgeschneiderte Lösungen für nachhaltige Markenauftritte.

Das Sortiment von Gmund Papier umfasst insgesamt über 100 000 verschiedene Papiervarianten. In Gmund werden Papiere entwickelt und produziert, die in sehr präzisen Arbeitsprozessen gefertigt werden, um den Eigenwert des Papiers herauszuarbeiten. Grundlage der Papierkollektion „Gmund Bauhaus Dessau", auf der dieses Buch gedruckt ist, ist das übereinstimmende Grundverständnis der Stiftung Bauhaus Dessau und Gmund Papier zu Materialgerechtigkeit und Materialerkundung.

Die Verbindung von Material, Handwerk und standardisiertem Produktionsprozess mit der besonderen Bedeutung des Papiers als Material der universellen Kommunikation wird hervorgehoben. Das „Gmund Bauhaus Dessau" Papier besticht durch reine Materialität und Qualität. In seiner radikalen Modernität mit der Reduzierung auf Weiß und Schwarz folgt es den Bauhaus-Prinzipien.

Imprint / Impressum

Editor /
Herausgeberin:
Sandra Hofmeister

Project management /
Projektleitung:
Eva Herrmann

Copy editing /
Lektorat DE:
Hannes Schmidt

Proofreading /
Schlusskorrektur DE:
Karin Pollems-Braunfels

Copy editing / Lektorat /
Proofreading /
Schlusskorrektur EN:
Alisa Kotmair

Übersetzung ins Deutsche /
Translation into german:
Claudia Kotte

Übersetzung ins Englische /
Translation into English:
Alisa Kotmair

Design /
Gestaltung:
strobo B M
(Matthias Friederich,
Julian von Klier,
Samuel Hinterholzer)

Reproduction /
Reproduktion:
ludwig:media, Zell am See

Printing and binding /
Druck und Bindung:
Grafisches Centrum Cuno
GmbH & Co. KG, Calbe

Paper /
Papier:
Gmund Bauhaus Dessau

The FSC-certified paper used
for this book is manufactured
from fibres originating from
environmentally and socially
compatible sources. /
Die für dieses Buch verwendeten
FSC-zertifizierten Papiere
werden aus Fasern hergestellt,
die nachweislich aus umwelt-
und sozialverträglicher Herkunft
stammen.

© 2018, first edition /
erste Auflage

DETAIL – Detail Business
Information GmbH,
Munich/München
detail.de
detail-online.com
ISBN 978-3-95553-451-6 (Print)
ISBN 978-3-95553-452-3
(E-Book)
ISBN 978-3-95553-453-0
(Bundle)